# WATERCOLOR
## *Portraits*

NELLI ANDREJEW

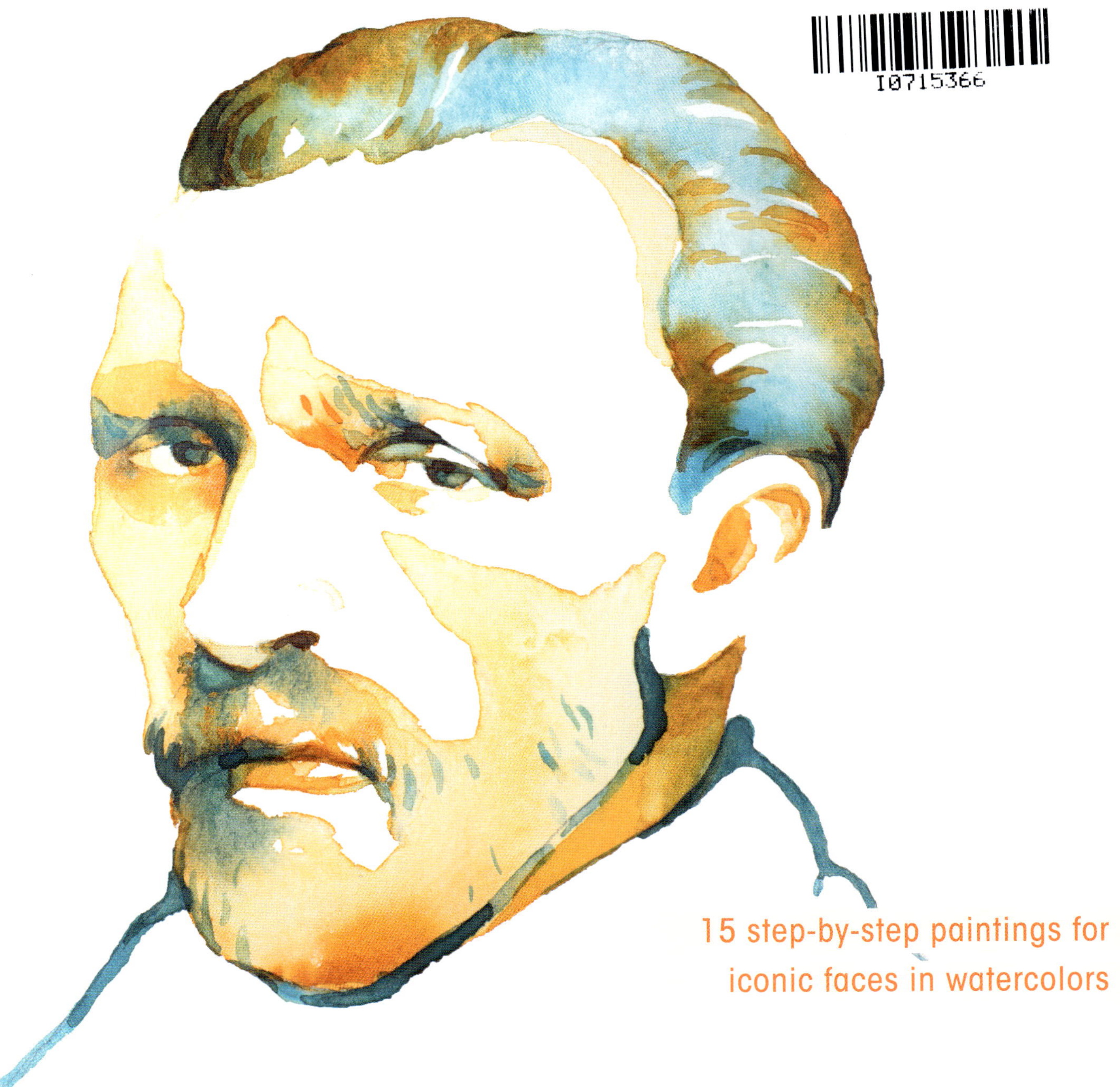

15 step-by-step paintings for
iconic faces in watercolors

# DAVID & CHARLES

www.davidandcharles.com

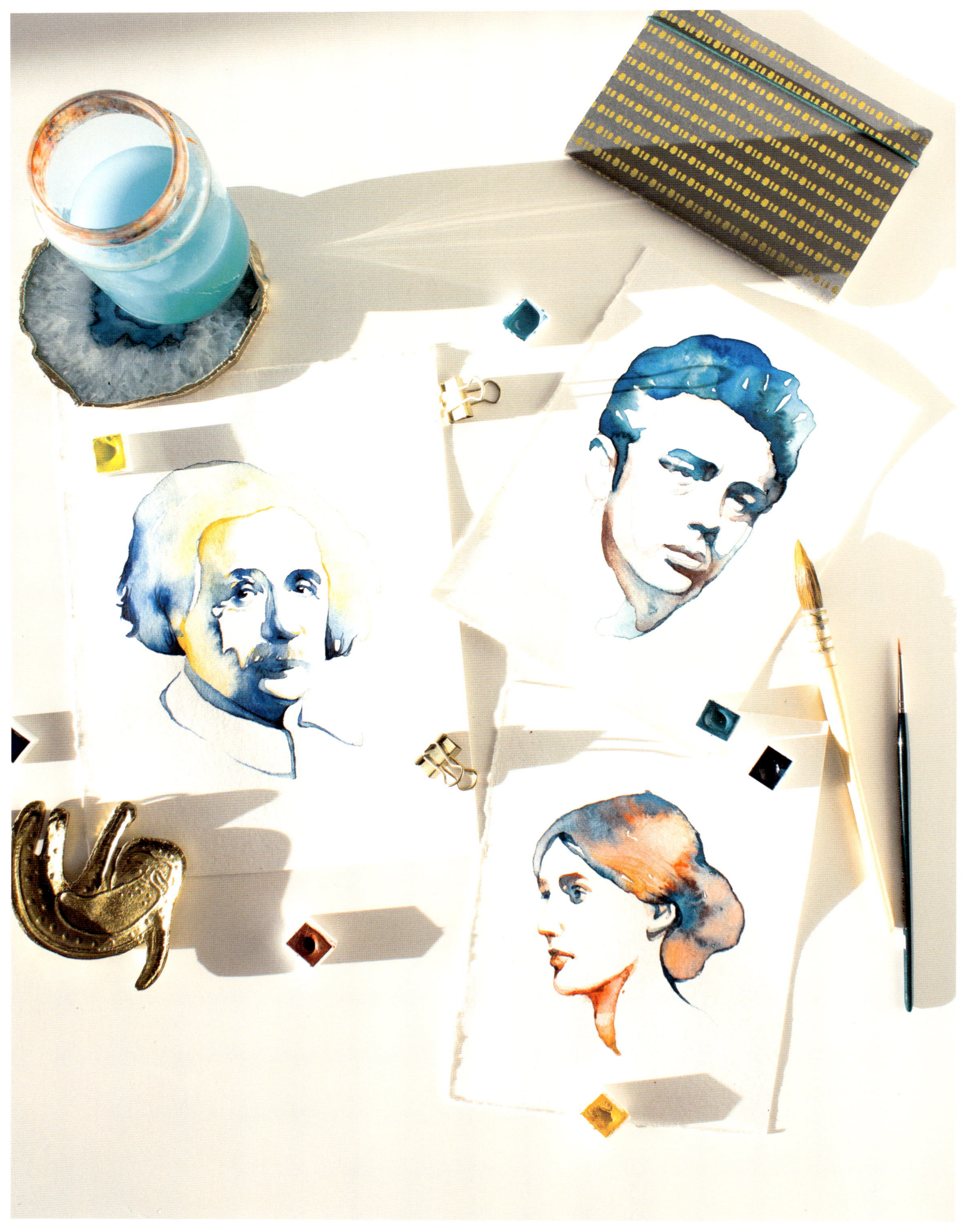

# Contents

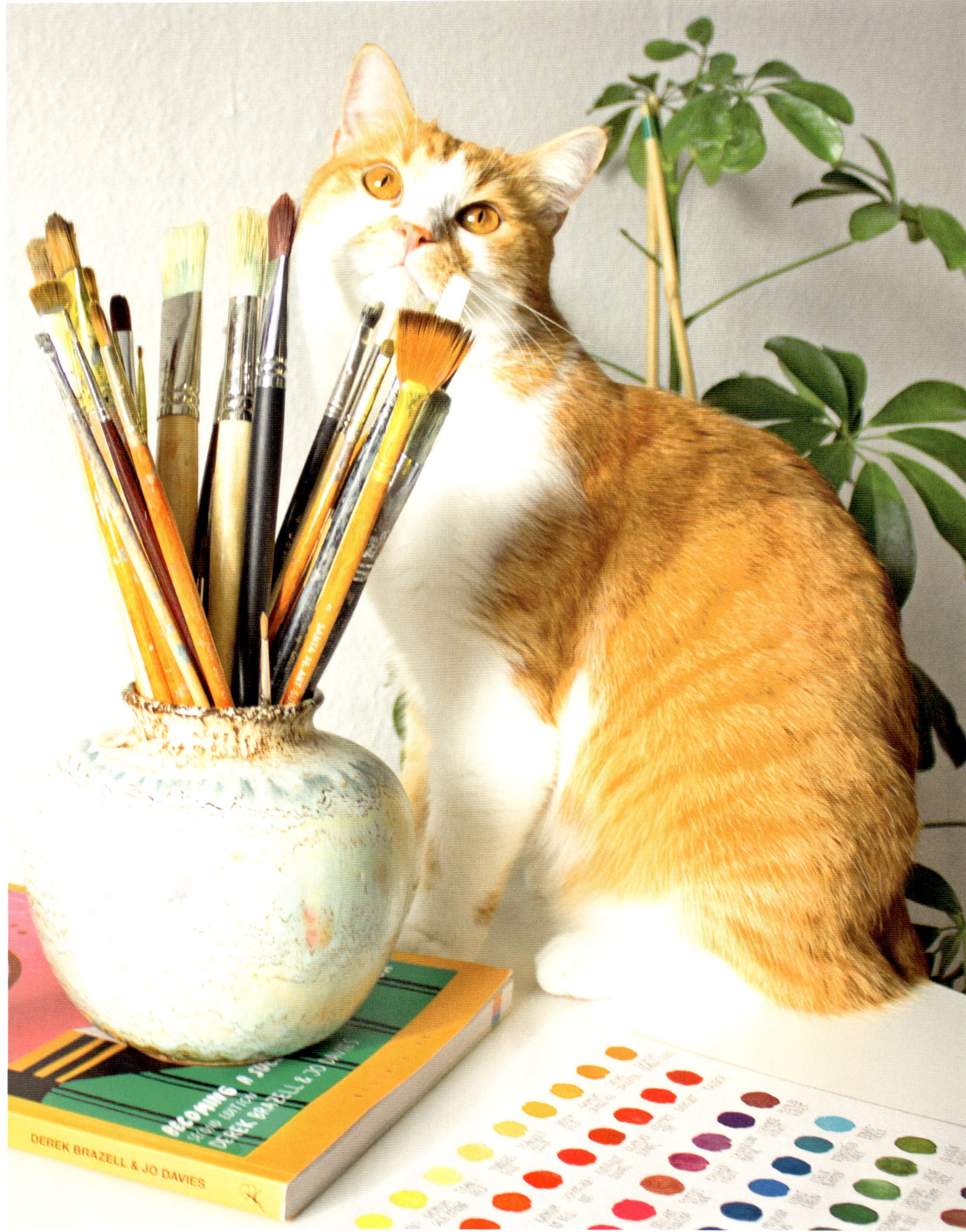

BECOMING A SUCCESSFUL ILLUSTRATOR
SECOND EDITION
DEREK BRAZELL & JO DAVIES

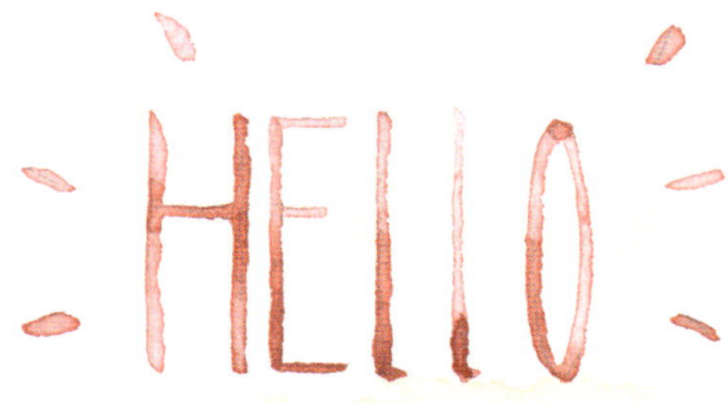


I'm glad you have decided to dive into the wonderful world of watercolor painting with this book. An exciting, perhaps even completely new painting experience awaits you!

Watercolor paints are constantly in flux, seeking out their path on the paper, and in so doing they are sometimes unpredictable. While painting, you'll never be able to completely influence the end result – and that's pretty much what this medium is all about. The biggest appeal is in relinquishing control over the color gradations and leaving things open to chance. So, keep at it, enjoy the painting experience, and play with the colors. Accept compromises, and don't be afraid to discard paintings, because even though it may be hard, that's as much a part of the process as the sense of accomplishment. Basically, it comes down to how enjoyable you make your painting. If you have fun with it, then ultimately this will keep you motivated.

We start with the basics, including materials and the essential techniques. Then we explore colors and discover how to conjure up a wide variety of textural effects using only water and pigment. Short exercises will help you to estimate the right proportions of water and pigment, to practice the basic techniques, and to mix your desired hues. Before beginning on the actual projects, I will show you again, step-by-step, what to look out for when painting the portraits, and with a few final tips and a pep talk on the role a flexible approach plays in watercolor painting, you will be ready to get started.

From representational to abstract, from subtle to expressive colors, you will find a cast of 15 famous personalities: People who have achieved extraordinary things with their abilities and who have made our world a much better place as a result. Although they are all very different, they all share these characteristics: An unconditional passion and the courage to change.

The watercolor portraits featured come to life through both clear white spaces as well as two-dimensional, abstract, wet-on-wet shadows, but at the same time we are never in any doubt about who is being portrayed. The hardest part of painting a portrait is capturing the personality with just a few brushstrokes. Making the persona easily recognizable and combining liveliness with expression – that's what this is all about!

Feel free to share your portraits on Instagram under the hashtag #watercolormitnelliadee. We (my little animal helper and I ) would be incredibly happy to see them and to connect with you!

Now, get ready for lots of surprises and exciting watercolor effects as you explore the fun of watercolor portraiture. I wish you a wonderful time.

Yours, Nelli ♡

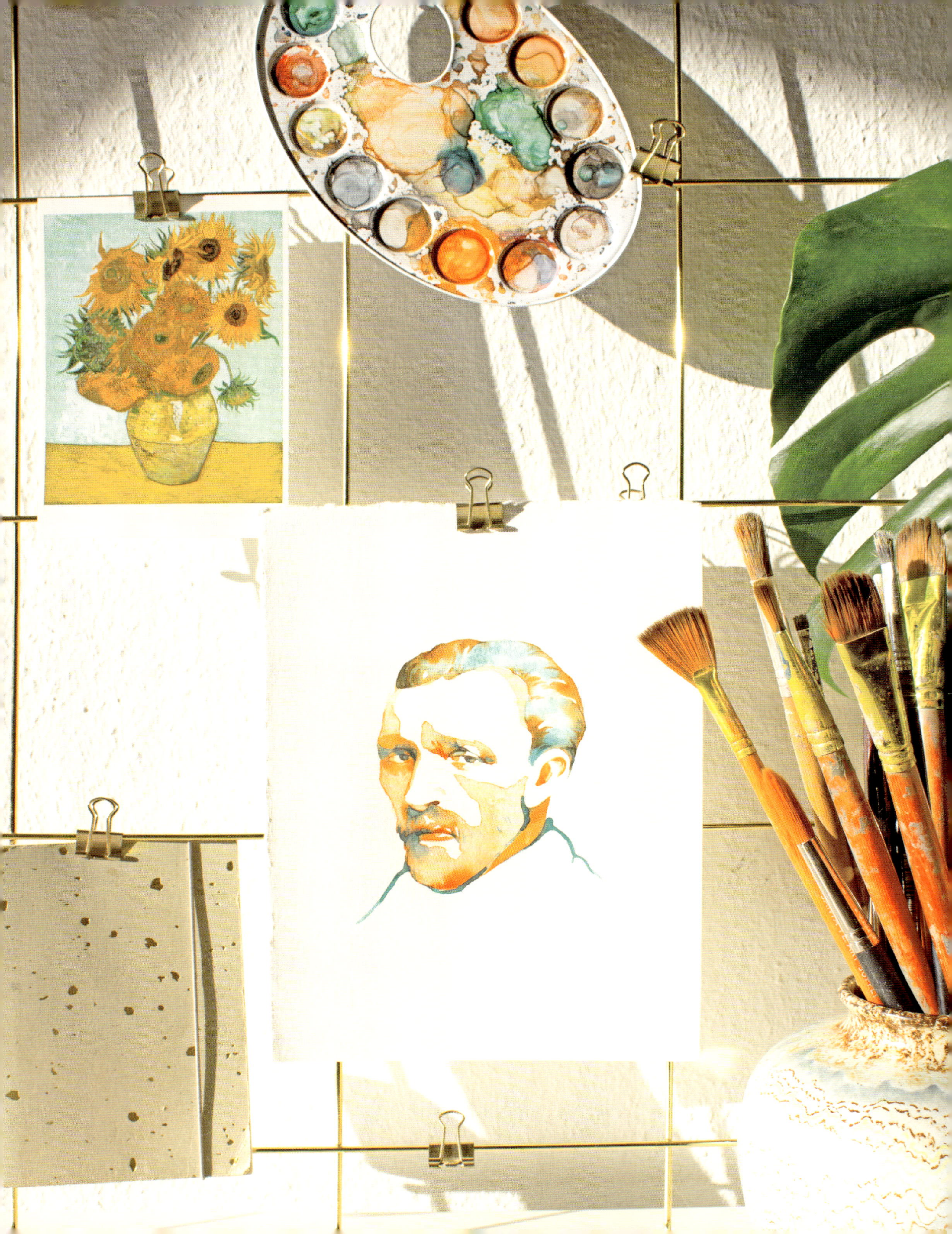

# Basics

# Watercolor and Portraits

As you begin your creative journey into watercolor portraiture, I would like to briefly share with you how I got into watercolor painting. Once I discovered the expressive possibilities of the medium, there was no turning back.

So, what are its special features and challenges? And what is important to consider when painting watercolor portraits?

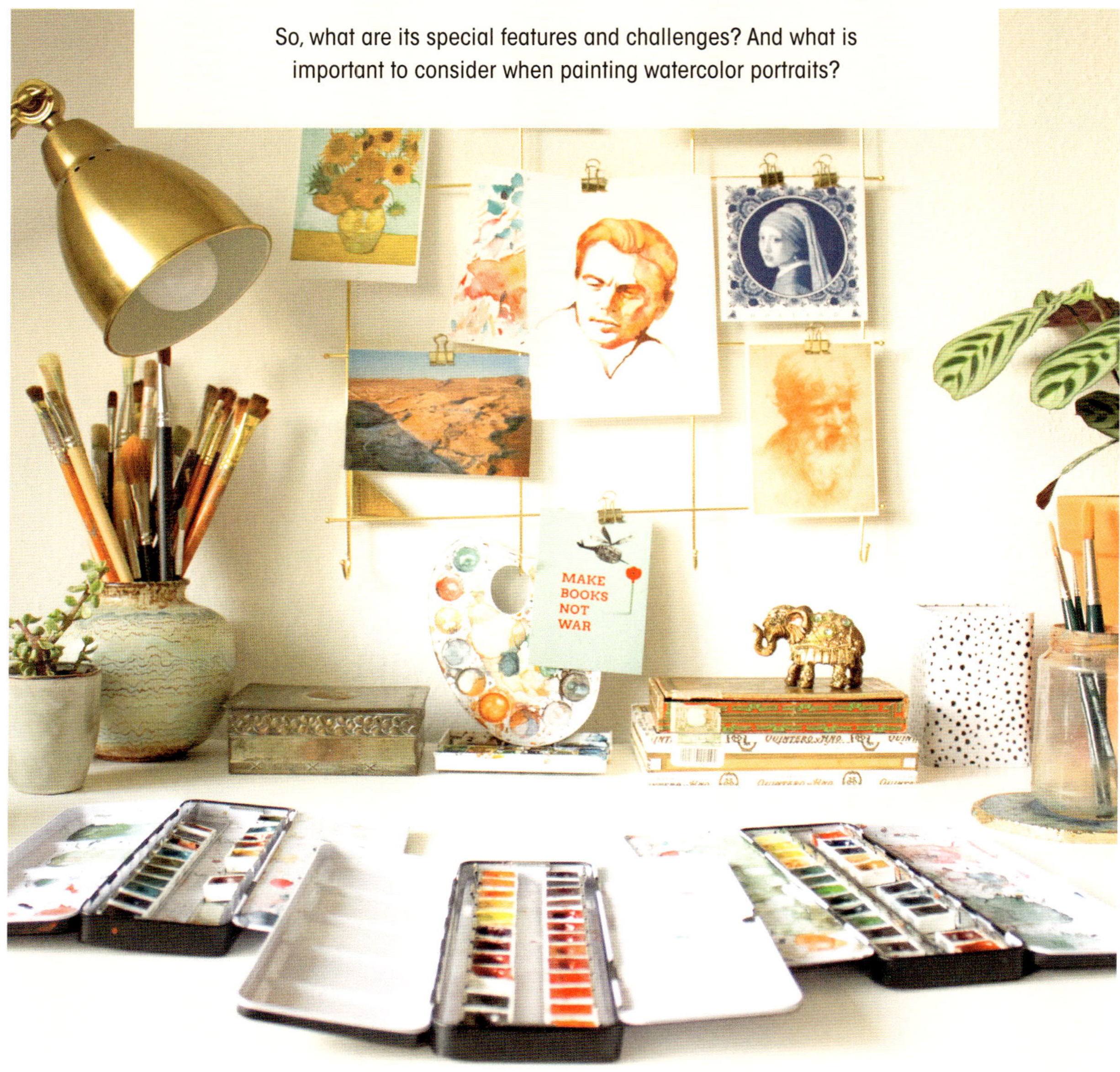

## MY PATH TO WATERCOLOR PAINTING

When I started my studies, for quite a long time I wanted to depict my surroundings in as detailed and realistic way as possible, whichever drawing or painting medium I tried. It was only towards the end, when I discovered the experimental side of watercolor painting, that I began to break away from this idea, and to look for new ways of expression to bring more liveliness to my work.

Suddenly, a huge spectrum of visualization options opened up. I could try out the most diverse range of interesting textural effects, and in doing so, I realized how expressively one can paint with the medium. My attitude changed because from here on I was more interested in the **painting process**, experiencing spontaneity by constantly attuning to new effects and painting quite intuitively because of how fast the paint dries.

I began to accept that no two watercolors are alike, no matter how hard one tries. This made for a more relaxed approach to my painting. Paintings that didn't turn out well were no longer taken too seriously and were unceremoniously recycled into scrap paper. In fact, I think such a strategy is extremely important in watercolor painting! You will notice that there is a big difference in the way you work, especially if up until now you have mostly been drawing. Working with a brush is completely different from working with a pencil, because firstly, when you paint, you mainly think in terms of spaces instead of lines; and secondly, you automatically work faster and more intuitively because of the short drying time.

In the beginning I was mainly painting plants, but later I tried my hand at other subjects. I played with different effects until I created my first **watercolor portrait**. In retrospect, it was precisely this **experimental approach** that made me fall in love with watercolor painting. It triggered something in me that had a lasting effect, a desire to discover things with curiosity, to grow with it, a feeling I still have to this day.

With this book I want to offer you an opportunity, above all, to experiment. Short exercises will help you test out different techniques, which you can later apply in the portrait projects, one chapter at a time!

## PORTRAIT AND STYLE

Probably the most important job of a portrait is to provide an image of the person that is instantly recognizable, while at the same time reflecting a bit about their personality. Even if we can recognize the person who is being depicted (and the featured portraits are representational in that sense), with their colorful, textural spaces they have something of the abstract about them.

If you look at the light and shade areas, you will notice that both are clearly defined. Strong, sometimes very dark spaces clash with the brilliant white of the paper. In order for these to produce the most harmonious picture possible, they should be tied together and synchronized. The most essential part of the portrait, the **facial expression**, should always be in the foreground. Precision and patience are required here. Observe the facial features carefully beforehand, and be patient with each layer of paint as it gradually brings the personality of your subject to life.

# Materials

Watercolor is a painting medium that offers limitless possibilities for textural effects with just a few tools and not much effort. This makes bright colors, absorbent paper and quality brushes all the more important – it all starts with the right materials!

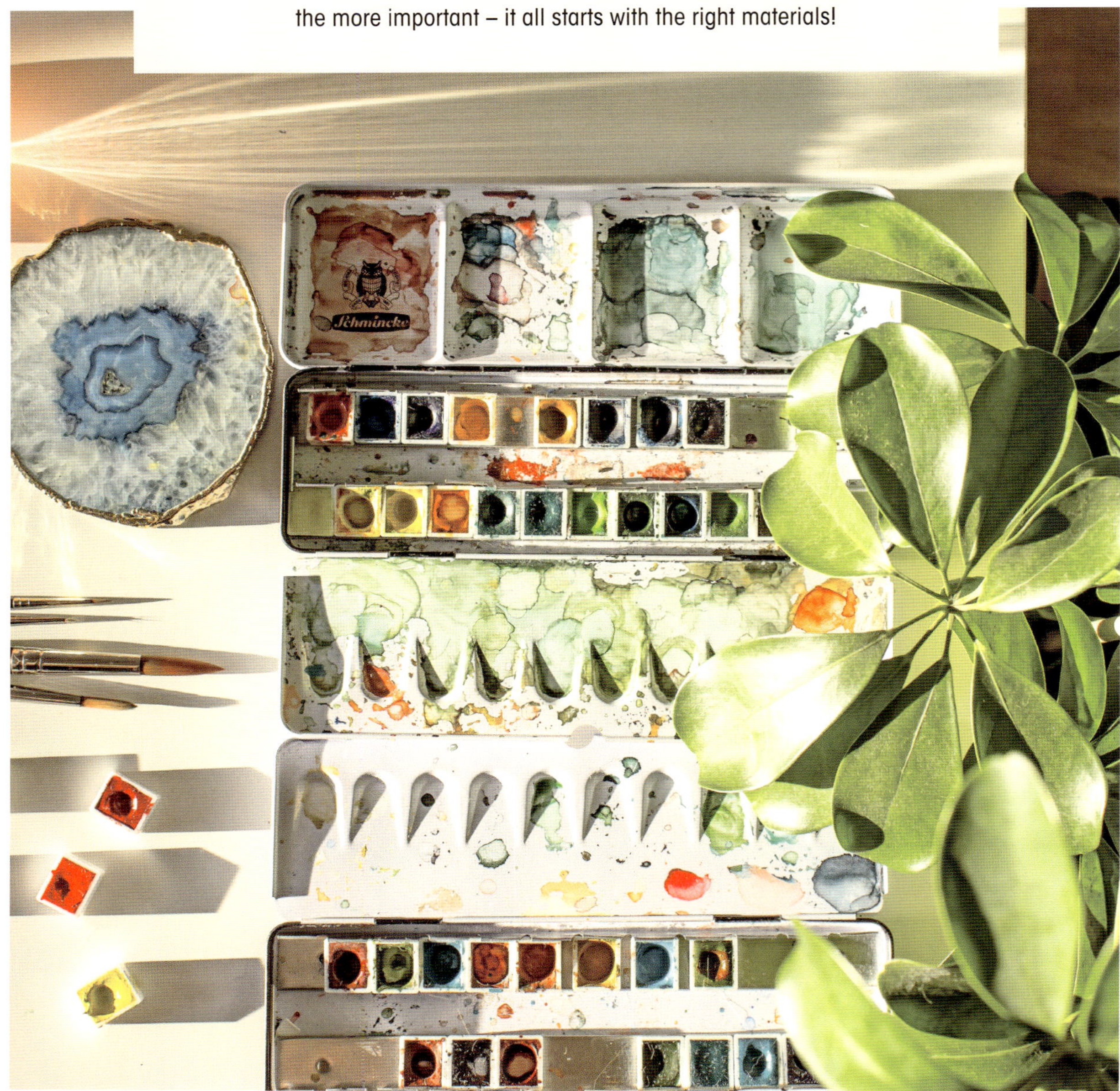

## PAPER

Watercolor paper has the capability to hold a lot of water on its surface and to eventually absorb it without any problems. Its density is higher than that of normal drawing paper, which usually makes it heavier and also somewhat more expensive.

The range extends from very coarse to fine, through satin and matte to pure white and natural white. Therefore, the decision of which to buy – especially if you are choosing watercolor paper for the first time – will not necessarily be easy. However, since pretty much all papers are acid-free and age-resistant, it's essentially the grammage that matters; that is, how heavy and absorbent the paper is per square meter. If you are applying washes using a lot of water, I recommend **300 gsm paper or heavier**. This certainly applies to the portraits in this book, as generally you will be painting them using the wet-on-wet technique which requires plenty of water.

You can get watercolor paper either as individual sheets or in edge-glued pads at the artists' supply store of your choice. The glued edges of these blocks provide the necessary tautness to avoid unsightly rippling on the surface of the paper when water is applied. So normally, the sheets are not removed from the pad until they have dried. However, with larger paper sizes, it is advisable to do this before painting.

**Tip:** *Use a flat, sharp object to detach the sheets of paper.*

Detaching the paper before starting work has several advantages: The format can be adjusted to the design, you waste less paper, and it's just easier to paint in smaller formats!

**Tip:** *A quick and precise alternative to cutting is folding and tearing. Since watercolor paper is thicker than drawing paper, you will need to use more force. Fold the sheet over several times, and then very carefully tear along the fold line. As an added bonus, the frayed edges will give the impression of handmade paper!*

**Tip:** *You can also fix your sheet of paper to the work surface with masking tape – this has a similar effect to the glue used on the paper blocks.*

As far as color and texture are concerned, this is a matter of personal taste. Do you want the paper texture to show through? Then go for a coarse surface. Do you prefer an off-white color? Then choose a natural white paper instead of a pure white one.

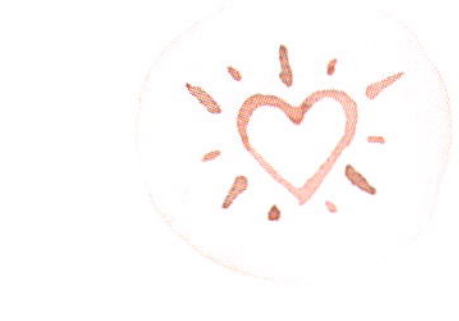

RECOMMENDATION

The projects in this book were painted on Canson Montval and Boesner Aquarelle 300 gsm paper.

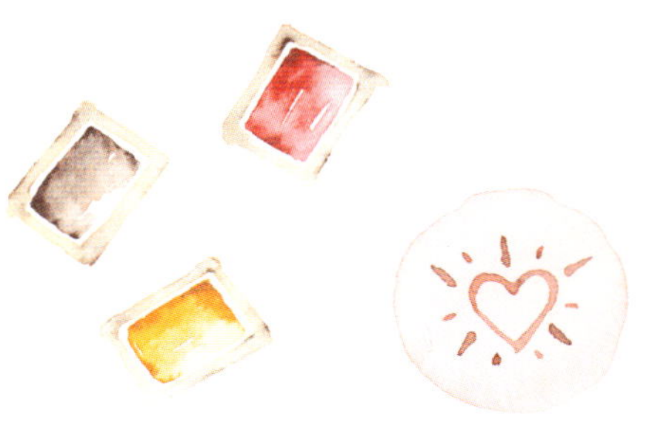



I have been using Horadam Aquarell watercolor paints from Schmincke for years and have never been disappointed!

## PAINTS

Compared with acrylic and oil paints, watercolor paints are very high-yielding. You often only need just a little bit of pigment because they are used in combination with a lot of water. The key here is a strong brightness, which makes the colors look rich and radiant despite the large amounts of water being used.

They are available in solid form in half or full pans or in liquid form in tubes, but the composition is the same. The advantage of a **watercolor pan tin**, however, is that you have a better overview and can use the colors more spontaneously. If you own one or are planning to buy one, you will often find that they are already equipped with several pigments and mixing surfaces.

Twelve pigments are all you need to start with. It makes sense to have a selection of primary colors (red, yellow, blue) in cold and warm gradations. You can also add exciting secondary colors and thus put your palette together as you wish!

**Tip:** *Be sure to create a color chart with the pigment names, because when you buy more, you will no longer be able to tell which pigment it is on the base of the pans!*

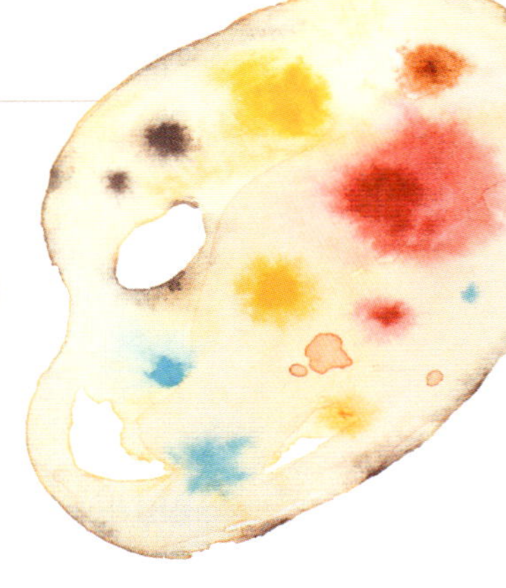

**Tip:** *Get yourself an additional mixing palette, as you can quickly run out of mixing space.*

## BRUSHES

These come in different shapes, grades and price ranges. In the end, however, it all comes down to whether your brush has the ability to hold a lot of water while retaining its shape! Out of all the brush shapes, round brushes are the most suitable for watercolor painting. A sharp point is important here to render the tiny details as well as the larger areas.

You can paint a great picture with just a few brushes and, basically, the size of the brush you should use is determined by the subject you are painting. For the portraits in this book, you will be fine with just **three to four round brushes** in different sizes, choosing a size 0 for the finest, and about a size 12 for the largest.

**Tip:** *To preserve the brush tip for as long as possible, bring it back into shape with your fingers each time you wash it out. Then let the brush air-dry. And very important: Never leave brushes bristles down in the water glass!*

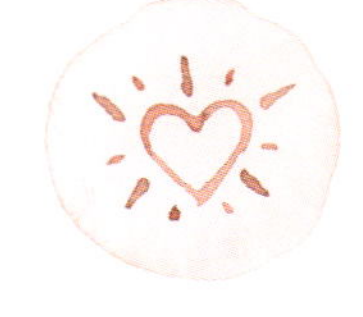



I really like to use Nova synthetic hair brushes from the Da Vinci watercolor range. I used sizes 0, 3, 6 and 12 for the portraits.

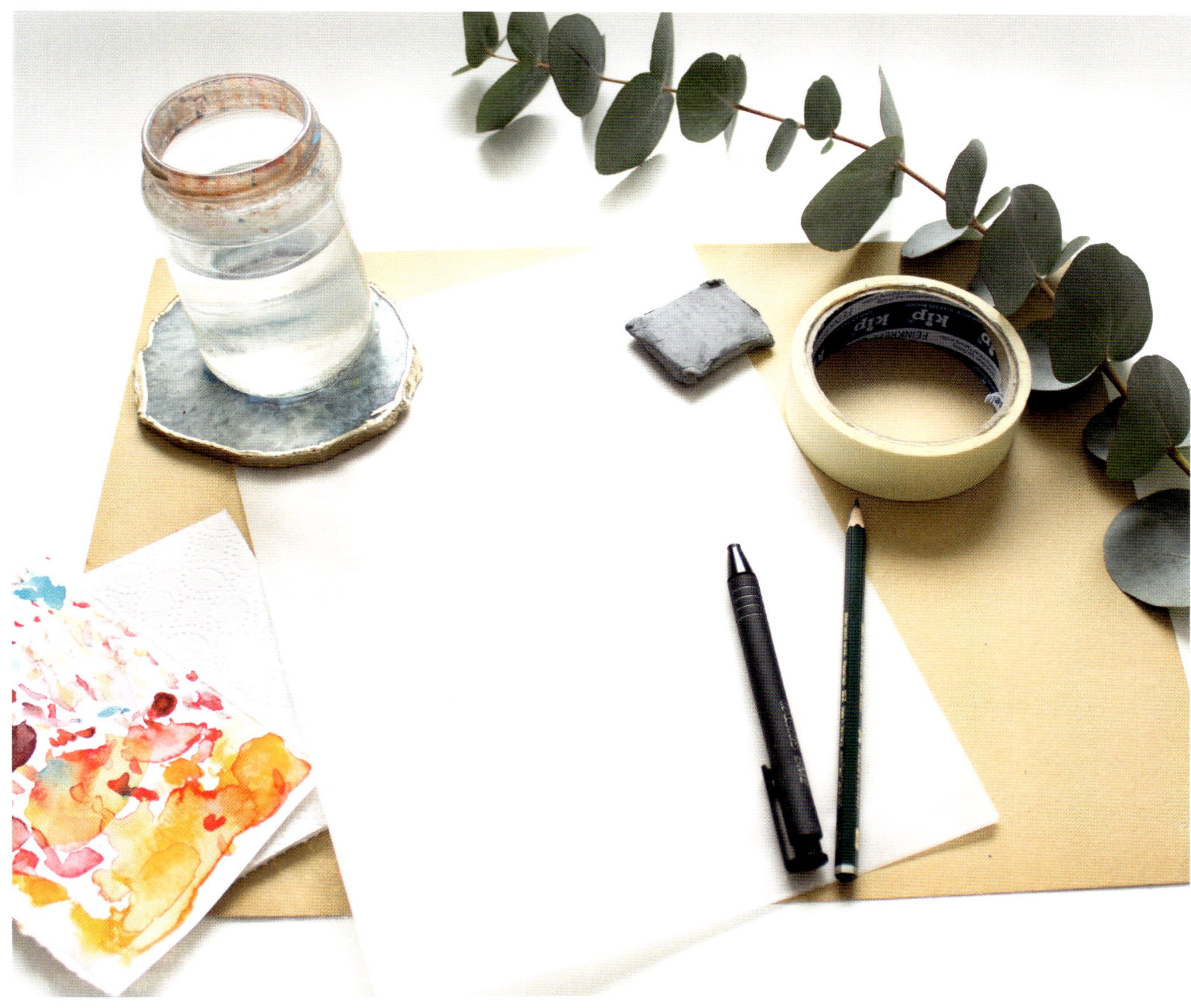

## ADDITIONAL SUPPLIES

You will also need a **water glass** and a piece of absorbent **paper towel** or tissue, to clean your brushes in between or to correct areas where too much water has been applied. Also very important is to have a piece of **scratch (scrap) paper** to hand, to test your colors and to wipe your brush.

**Tip:** *Pictures that don't turn out well can be usefully recycled as scratch paper!*

For the preliminary drawing, you also need a **soft pencil** in grade 5B or higher. Some **tracing paper** and **masking tape** are also must-haves when tracing.

I recommend that you use a **kneaded eraser** if this proves necessary while making the preliminary drawing, as this will ensure that the paper surface doesn't get too roughed up. However, for erasing the pencil lines after your painted portrait has dried, an **eraser pencil** is more suitable.

# Basic Techniques

In watercolor painting, paint can be applied to a wet or dry paper surface. In this section, we'll look in detail at the **wet-on-wet technique**, where paints are applied on a **wet** background, and the **glazing technique**, where paints are applied on a **dry** background.

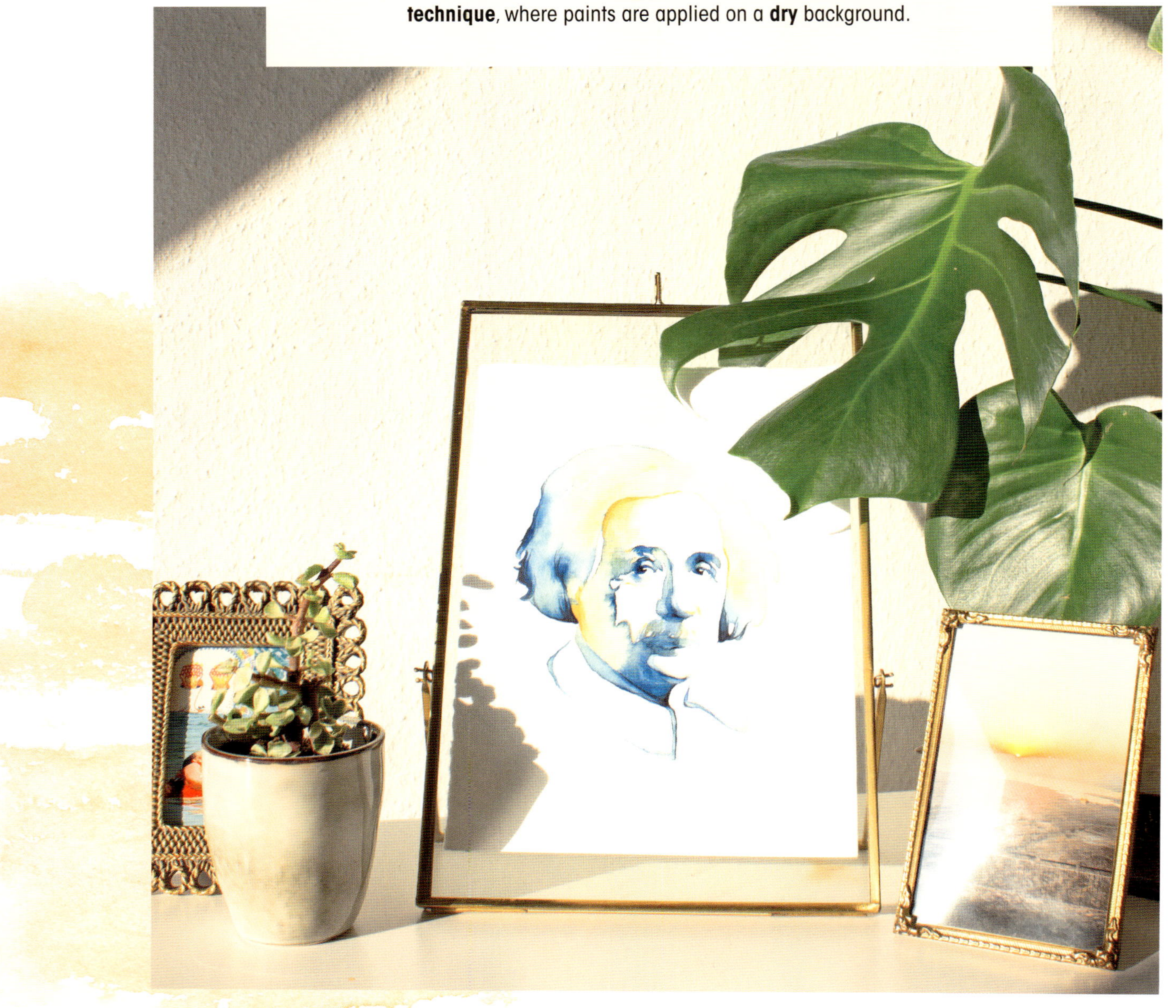

## WET-ON-WET TECHNIQUE

In wet-on-wet painting, you use a lot of water with your paints. The surface should be kept constantly wet so that you can paint into it with more colors.

The water carries the pigments, distributes them and creates wonderfully soft color gradations. Depending on the concentration of your paint – that is, how much or little water you add to the pigment – and which brushstroke you choose, the results can vary greatly as we will explore later (see Textures).

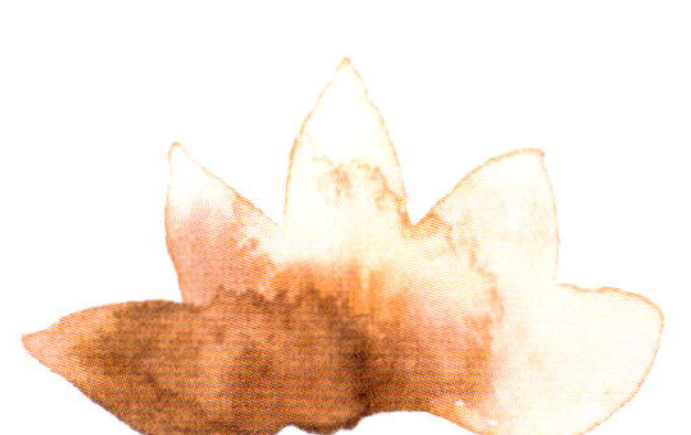

**Tip:** *The wet-on-wet technique, with its two-dimensional way of painting, forms the basis of your portraits. You will use it during the first and sometimes also the final steps, for facial shadows and hair.*

The amount of water used makes painting a bit of a challenge. Estimating where the pigments will be carried by the water and how they will ultimately dry requires practice, but if you have the courage to experiment, you will be rewarded with exciting gradations and textures.

With this technique, the color flow changes during the entire drying time, so give the colors enough space and time to develop. You can see the change quite clearly here on the leaf painting: The first image shows the design directly after painting, and the second after it has completely dried.

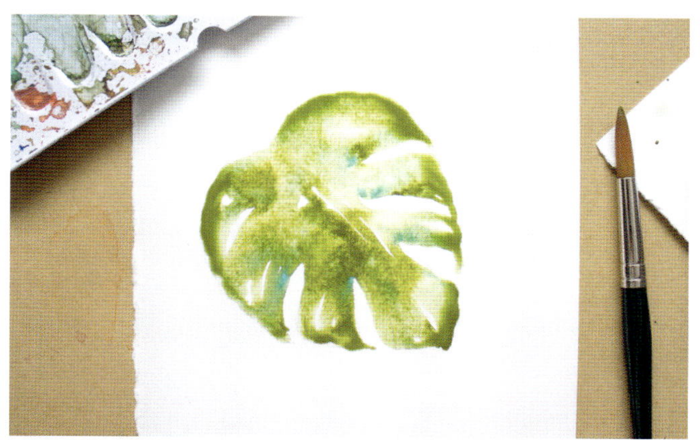

*Before drying*

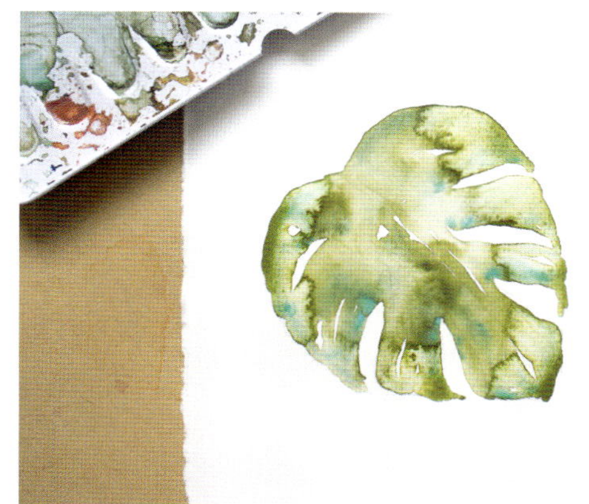

*After drying*

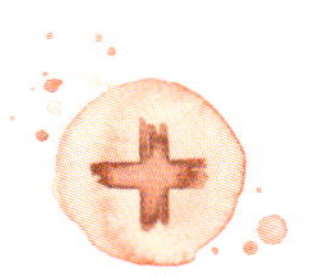

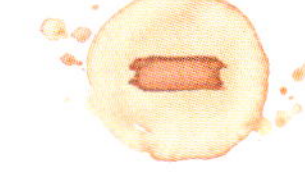

→ Free and expressive way of working

→ Soft color gradations

→ Watercolor effects

→ Not entirely controllable

→ Timing and water amounts require practice

→ Limited painting time

## GLAZING TECHNIQUE

When diluted paint is applied in layers to a dry painting surface, it is called a glaze. This application of paint often leaves the layer underneath visible, as it is painted transparently.

It is essential that you wait until the paint layer underneath is dry before applying each subsequent layer. These drying periods ensure that, unlike the wet-on-wet technique, the colors do not blend with each other.

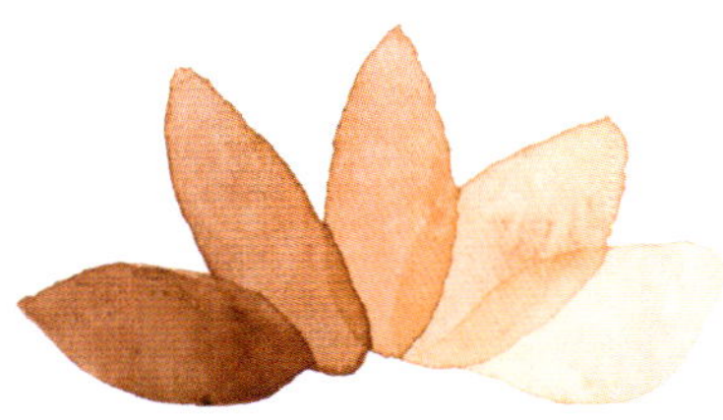

**Tip:** *The glazing technique gives your portraits the final sharpness and darkness. You will mainly use it during the intermediate and last steps.*

Precise spaces and sharp lines can be effortlessly created, and the layering process gives your image clarity and depth. The best way to do this is to start with a light, well-diluted shade. With each layer, you add more and more pigment. It is most interesting when you layer different colors on top of each other, because the overlaps create new mixed color values.

**Tip:** *In the portrait project steps, where the first layer of pigment is applied to the un-painted dry surface of your paper, I have referred to this as wet-on-dry to distinguish it from glazing, where you'll be working over previously applied paint layers.*

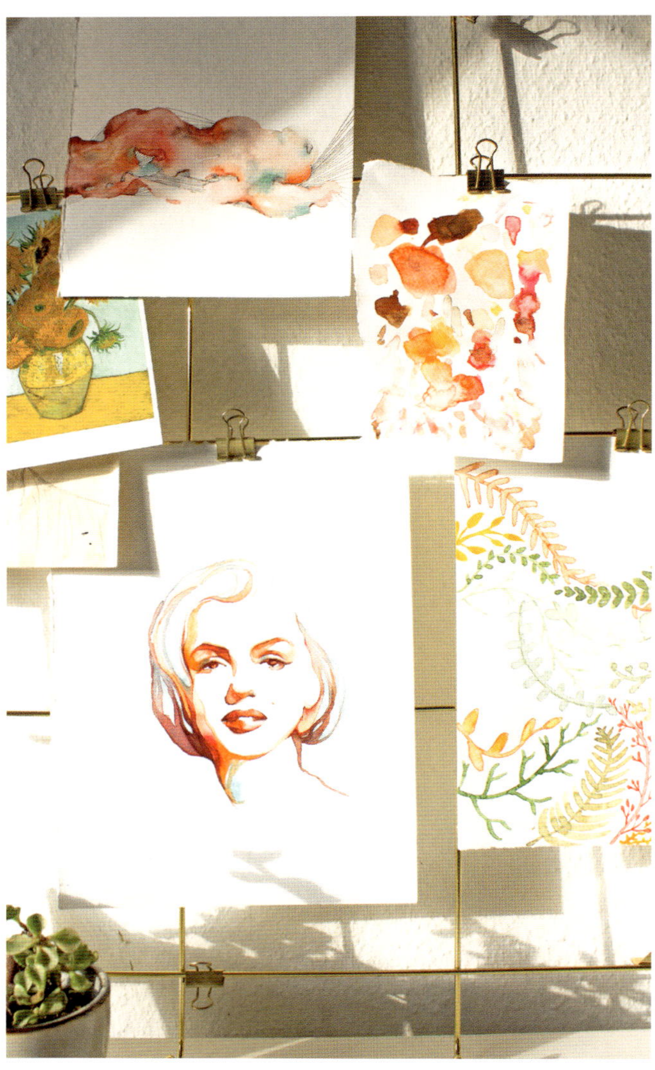

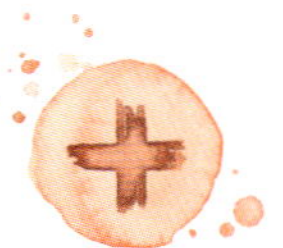

→ Clear, slower way of working

→ Easily controllable

→ Transitions are harder to paint

→ Hardly any watercolor effects

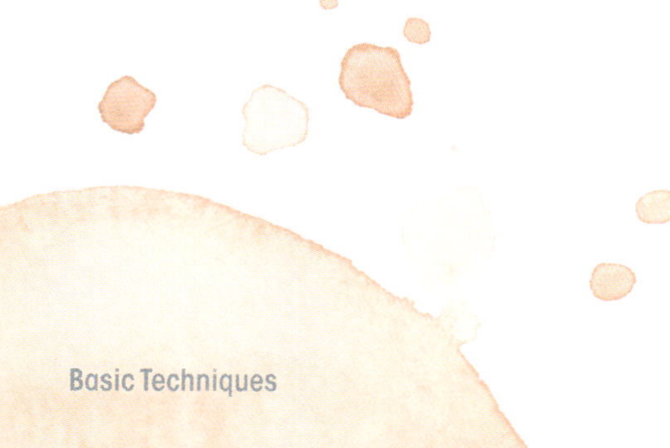

## THE RIGHT TIMING – WATER AND PIGMENT QUANTITIES

As we have seen, the appearance of your painting will be affected by whether you paint the colors **on top of each other** with drying periods in between (glazing) or **into each other**, without drying periods (wet-on-wet). We'll take a closer look at the latter, because the biggest challenge in watercolor painting is to maintain a certain control over the paint flow. This depends on the proportions of water and pigment. Determining **at what point** the colors should be applied to the surface in order to achieve the desired effect is what we're going to look at first, i.e., how wet should the paper be.

## CONDITION OF THE SURFACE

### Too soon

If the background is too wet, the water will remain on the surface and collect to form paint puddles. When you apply more paint, you will notice that it too remains on the surface and as a result, unfortunately, no soft gradations will be created. When this happens, you can either wait a moment until some of the liquid has been absorbed by the paper, or use a brush or paper towel to remove the excess paint (see Final Tips).

**Tip:** *Look at your image from the side so that you can better see how wet the surface is.*

### Just right

You have the maximum control when applying paint when some of the water has soaked in and the surface is only just slightly shimmering, as can be seen in this picture. The paints applied to the damp surface will only run into each other to a certain extent. So, it's just right when the paper itself is still damp, but there are no more paint puddles on the surface, as seen here.

### Too late

If you apply the paint too late, the painting surface is already dry, and the colors will not run into each other at all. When this happens, dampen the dry areas with a thin layer of water, and continue as before.

**Tip:** *Make sure you apply the water with only very little pressure so that the layer underneath is not activated.*

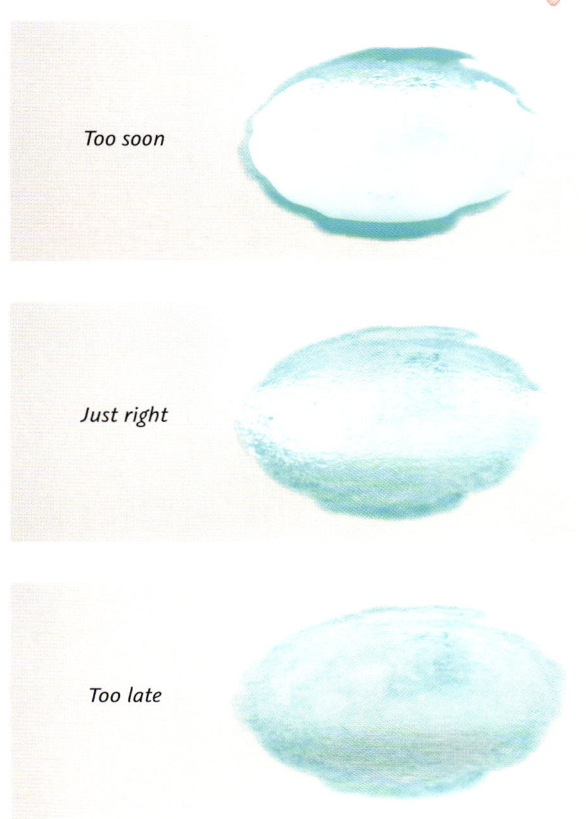

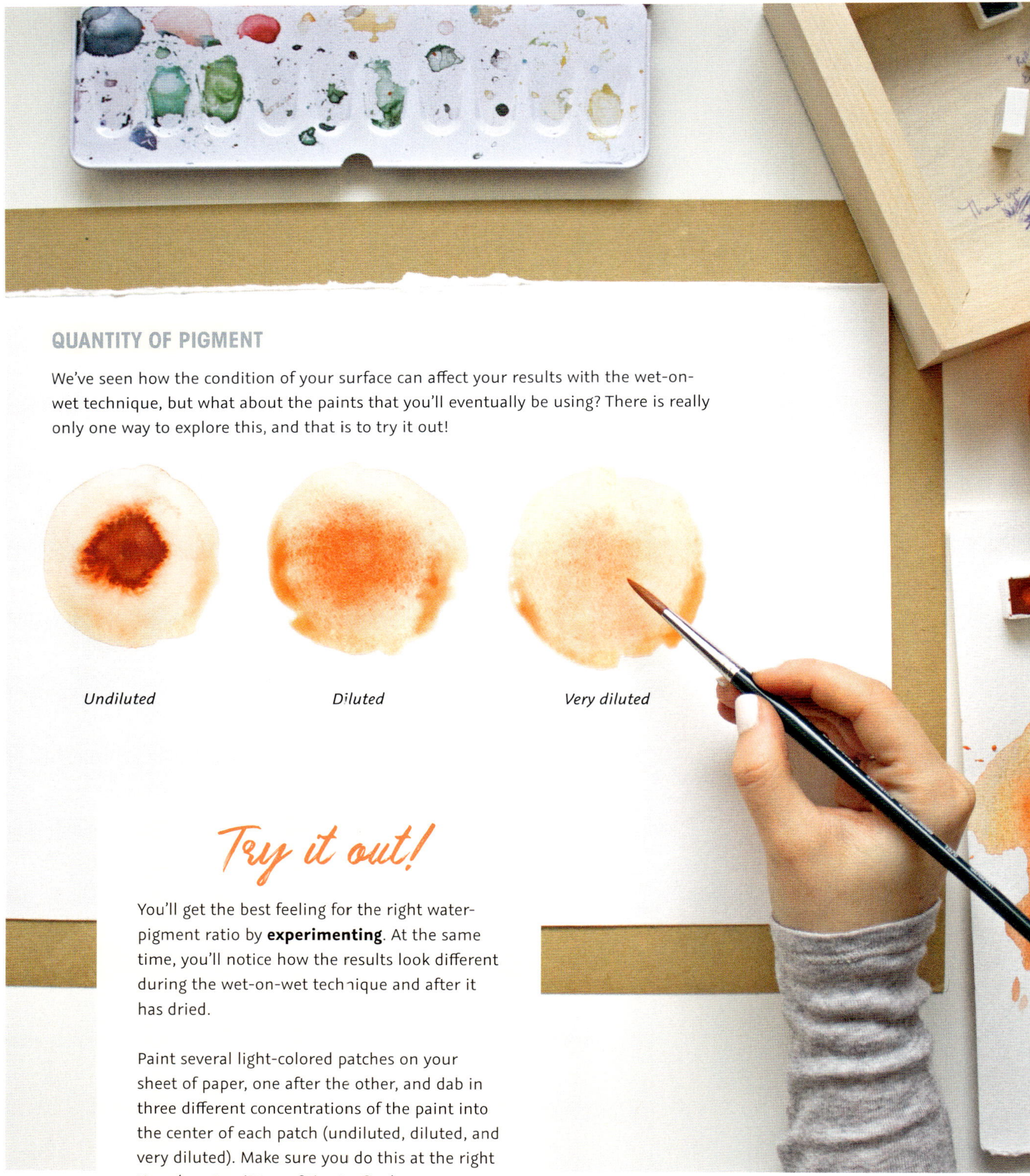



## QUANTITY OF PIGMENT

We've seen how the condition of your surface can affect your results with the wet-on-wet technique, but what about the paints that you'll eventually be using? There is really only one way to explore this, and that is to try it out!

## Try it out!

You'll get the best feeling for the right water-pigment ratio by **experimenting**. At the same time, you'll notice how the results look different during the wet-on-wet technique and after it has dried.

Paint several light-colored patches on your sheet of paper, one after the other, and dab in three different concentrations of the paint into the center of each patch (undiluted, diluted, and very diluted). Make sure you do this at the right time (see Condition of the Surface).

# Colors

Colors surround us, no matter where we go. Whether consciously or unconsciously, they can have an effect on how we feel; they carry meanings and revive our emotions and memories at the mere sight of them.

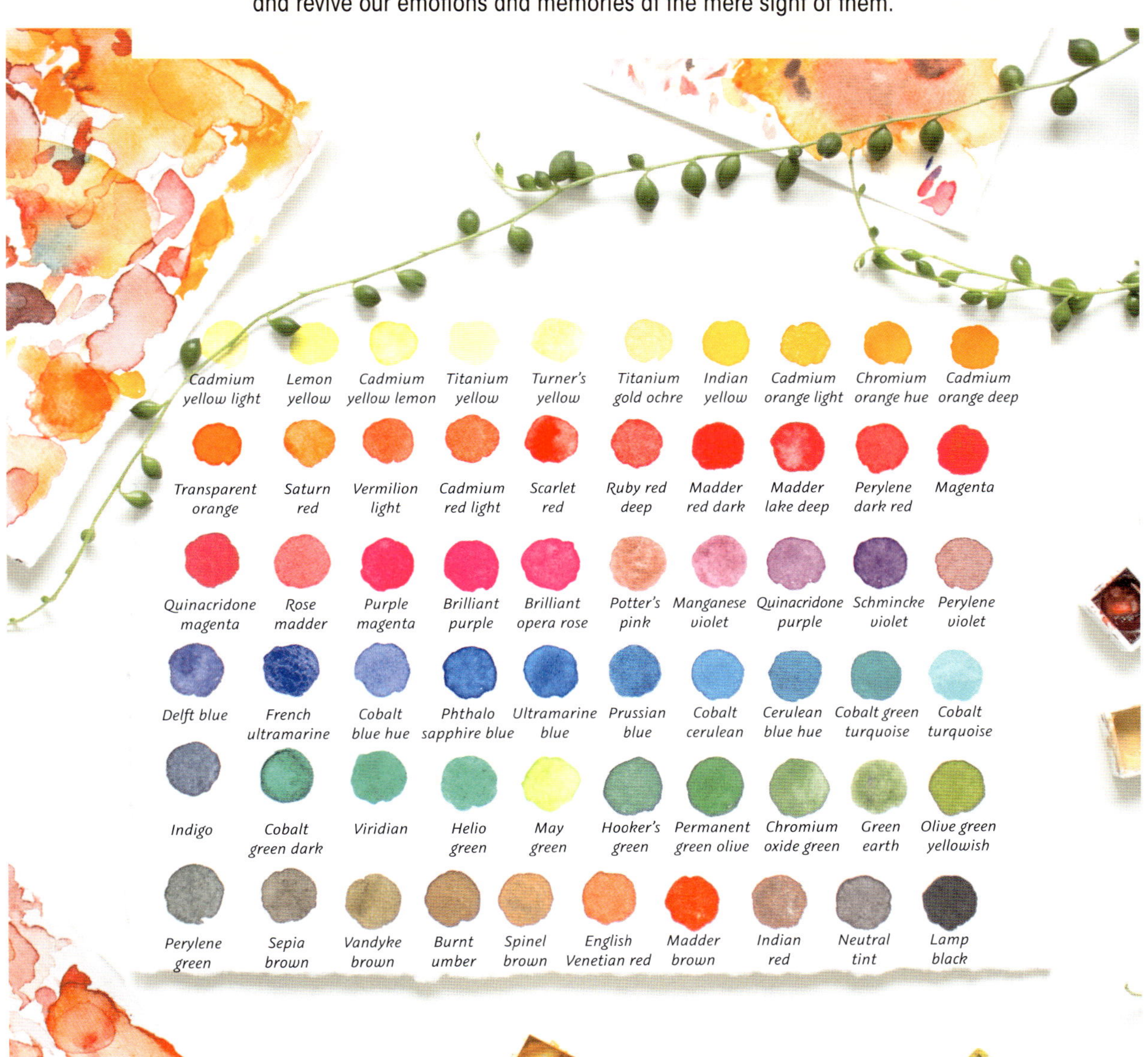

When it comes to our pictures, we have absolute freedom, especially when we paint non-representationally. The portraits in this book are abstract in their choice of colors, meaning that they do not reflect, for example, actual skin and hair colors. When painting, I chose colors that I spontaneously associated with that person, yet the colors you associate may be cuite different, so by all means make your own color choices to express your personal point of view!

## PRIMARY AND SECONDARY COLORS

As I'm sure you know, you can mix pretty much any other color with the primary colors (red, yellow, blue) and the neutral colors black and white – provided you have warm and cool shades at hand. With watercolor, however, it is best to paint with "ready-made" color pigments. They are more radiant if you use them pure, i.e., unmixed from the pans, but that doesn't mean you don't need to mix them at all. On the contrary, by using **mixed and unmixed, primary and secondary colors**, you can cover a much broader color spectrum.

## COLOR FAMILIES AND CONTRASTS

Your image will be especially coherent and atmospheric if you combine analogous colors. For example, by choosing warm colors like red, pink and orange. Related tones mix very harmoniously on paper and these sit next to each other on the color wheel.

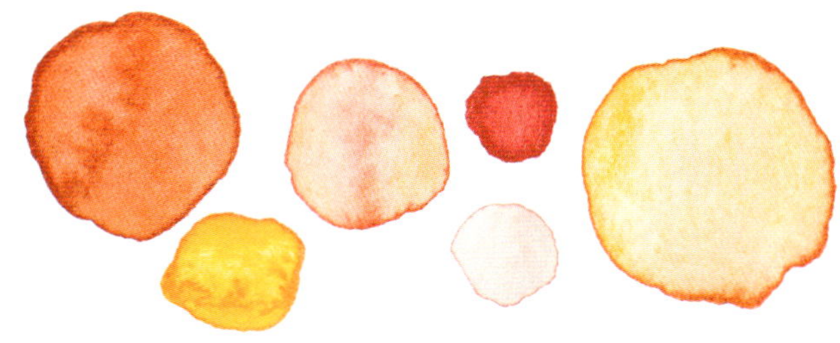

*Analogous colors*

However, it gets really exciting when you integrate a complementary color. This creates a contrast that brings the picture to life. Although, with the risk of mixing them to gray, less is more. A few splashes of color or streaks of glaze are usually enough. Complementary colors are opposite each other on the color wheel.

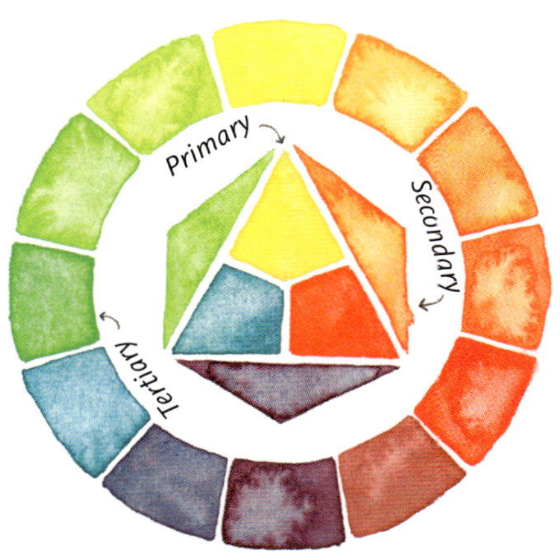


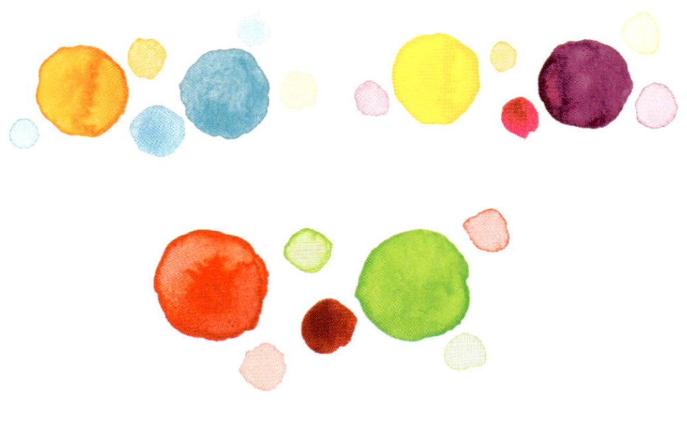

*Complementary colors*

## TEST

Over time, you'll get to know your pigments and learn exactly how they behave on the paper: Whether they are opaque, granulating, or how much lighter they are when they dry. The appearance of the colors also differs in the pan, on the palette and on the paper. For this reason, it makes sense to always **test the colors** on a piece of scratch paper beforehand.

**Tip:** *I often mix paint on my scratch paper instead of on the palette. This is quite practical because you can both test and mix directly on one surface. The only disadvantage: At some point, the mixed colors will inevitably soak into the paper.*

I would also recommend that you create a color chart on paper with the respective pigment names before starting your painting, as shown in the photograph at the beginning of the Colors chapter. This way you always know the name of the color you want to buy again. Also, it helps a lot to see the pigments on paper because it's especially hard to tell the darker shades apart in the tray. Different tonal values will naturally occur depending on how much water you add to your pigment.

## ALL ABOUT MIXING

Mixing paint is a minor art in itself. As colors are painted on with a lot of water, it is often unclear at which point they are ready to be used, and then, how to mix the two together correctly.

### Mixing process

Activate the pigment with water and soak it up with your brush, then wipe the paint off on your palette. Wash out your brush and repeat with a second pigment. Now, mix both colors, and gradually add water or more of one pigment or the other until you have achieved your desired shade.

**Tip:** *Always wash out your brush briefly before using another pigment from another pan, or choose different brushes for different colors.*

### Mixing desired shades

Does this sound familiar? You have a certain idea of a color very clearly in your head, but you just can't get it mixed. If so, it can help to reflect on the following questions while color mixing:

**Should the color be lighter or darker?**

*Lighten*

Generally, mix from light to dark because you can always darken anyway. Lightening with a white pigment on the other hand, takes the saturation out of your color and leaves you with a pastel color that no longer looks vibrant. Therefore, to lighten the color, it is best to gradually add water.

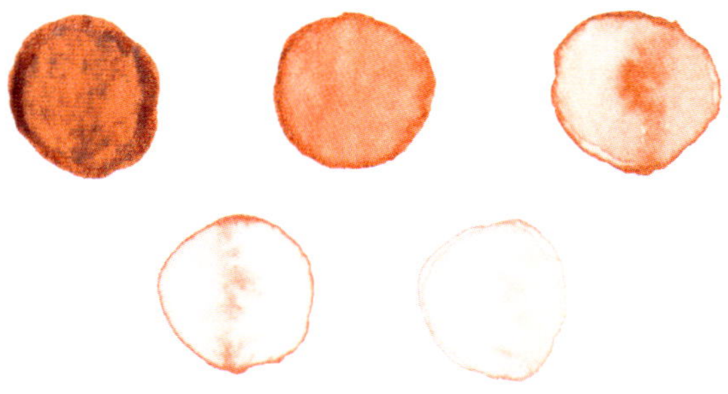

*Tonal values*

### Darken

For darkening, you can use a little black or another dark color. Caution: A little is already enough here because black is a dominant color! Otherwise, you have the option right from the start of diluting your shade with as little water as possible.

**Tip:** *Keep the used pans clean by giving them a quick wipe with a piece of paper towel at the end of your painting session.*

**Should the color be warmer or colder?**

### Complementary colors

If you have a brown shade that is a bit too reddish, for example, and therefore too warm, add some green, and the brown shade will become cooler. It also works the other way around, of course, and this is a trick that works on any color. The secret lies in complementary colors, which cancel each other out in saturation.

I often mention **strong** shades in the book. By strong, I mean that your mixed shade consists of a lot of pigment and little water. This makes the color look richer and darker when applied. A diluted shade, on the other hand, contains a lot of water and is therefore lighter and less vibrant.

The pigments I have used are listed at the start of each portrait as a guide for your reference. Each is a Horadam Aquarell paint from Schmincke. You can, of course, use similar pigments, or completely different ones if you prefer.

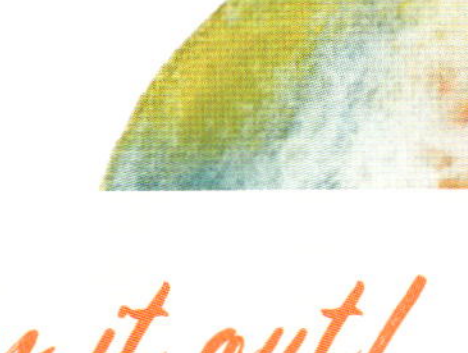

## Try it out!

The following two exercises are good for observing how colors mix with each other and what color values can be created in this way:

### Wet-on-wet

Dip your brush into clear water, paint a circular space on the paper and wait briefly until the dampness of the paper is ideal. Now dab the shades of your choice into the wet space and watch how the colors mix. Tilt your sheet so that the colors run into each other better. By painting them sometimes on top of each other and sometimes next to each other, you will develop a feel for how to handle different stages of dampness and amounts of water.

### Glazing

Paint circles in different tonal values and sizes. Wait until they are all dry and paint another layer, but in such a way that the circles on top partially overlap the ones underneath. Here, you are practicing using different water-pigment concentrations and at the same time learning about the mixed values that can be created between colors.

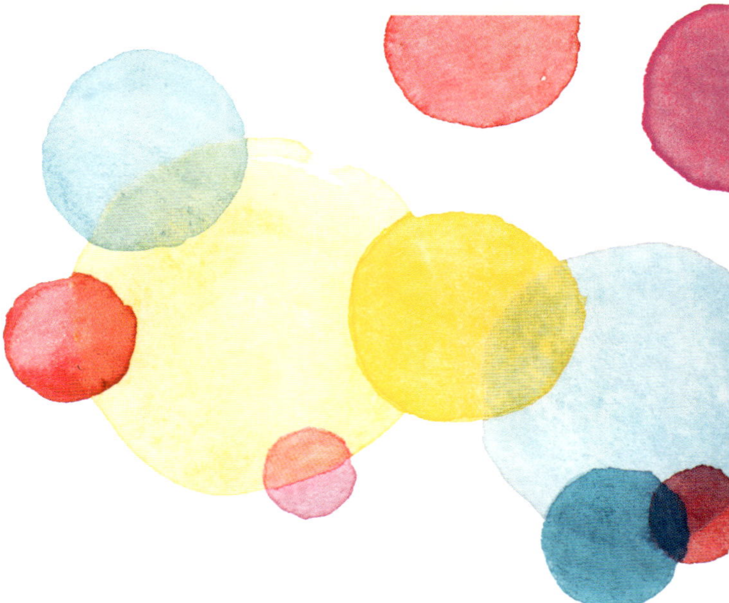

# Textures

Watercolor painting offers a lot of interesting effects, which you can use to
create a sense of substance in your pictures, or which you can simply
experiment with in a playful abstract way. In this chapter, I will introduce you to
a small collection of textures that you will use in the painting of the portraits.

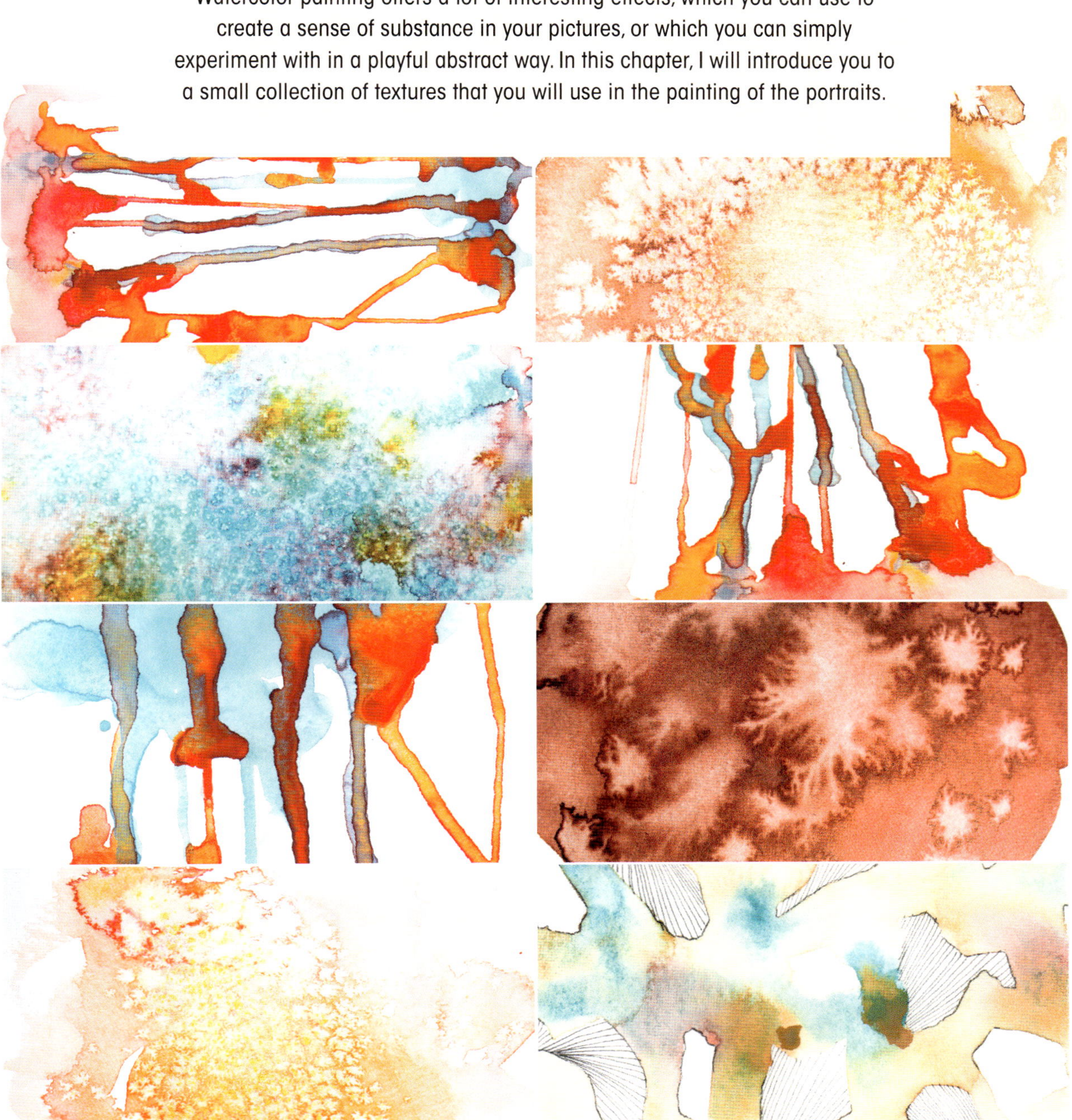

**Tip:** *Textural effects are suitable for larger spaces. In the case of portraits, you can enjoy yourself with the hair and decide for yourself whether you want to swap one technique for another. The more interesting, the better!*

# Try it out!

This exercise will help you get an idea of what kinds of textures can be created with a little water and pigment. At the same time, you'll learn to appreciate the ratio between the two.

The procedure is always the same: Paint a rough shape on your paper using a light color (I've chosen a circle), and then, wet-on-wet, paint into it in different ways. As always, make sure you get the timing right.

## DABBING

Dab in several spots with the undiluted paint and watch how the blobs develop. Basically, the drier the background, the clearer the dabs of color. Play with this knowledge and create interesting, gradated textures. Go one step further and add another color. You can also change the brush size.

**Tip:** *Applying paint by dabbing is the perfect choice if you want to create almost unmixed and above all, radiant color gradations.*

**Tip:** *Remember, if you use short and dabbing brushstrokes, you will create texture. Conversely, painting over a large area will result in a uniform space.*

## WASHING

For the next space, take up two more colors, one after the other, and move your brush back and forth over a large area. Compared to just dabbing in, you can control the flow of color better when washing, because as you will see, the pigments can be pushed around wonderfully on the wet surface. Start with the darker shade on the left side and wash it in towards the center. Wash out your brush and work the opposite side with a lighter color.

**Tip:** *If you want subtle mixed color values, washing is the way to go.*

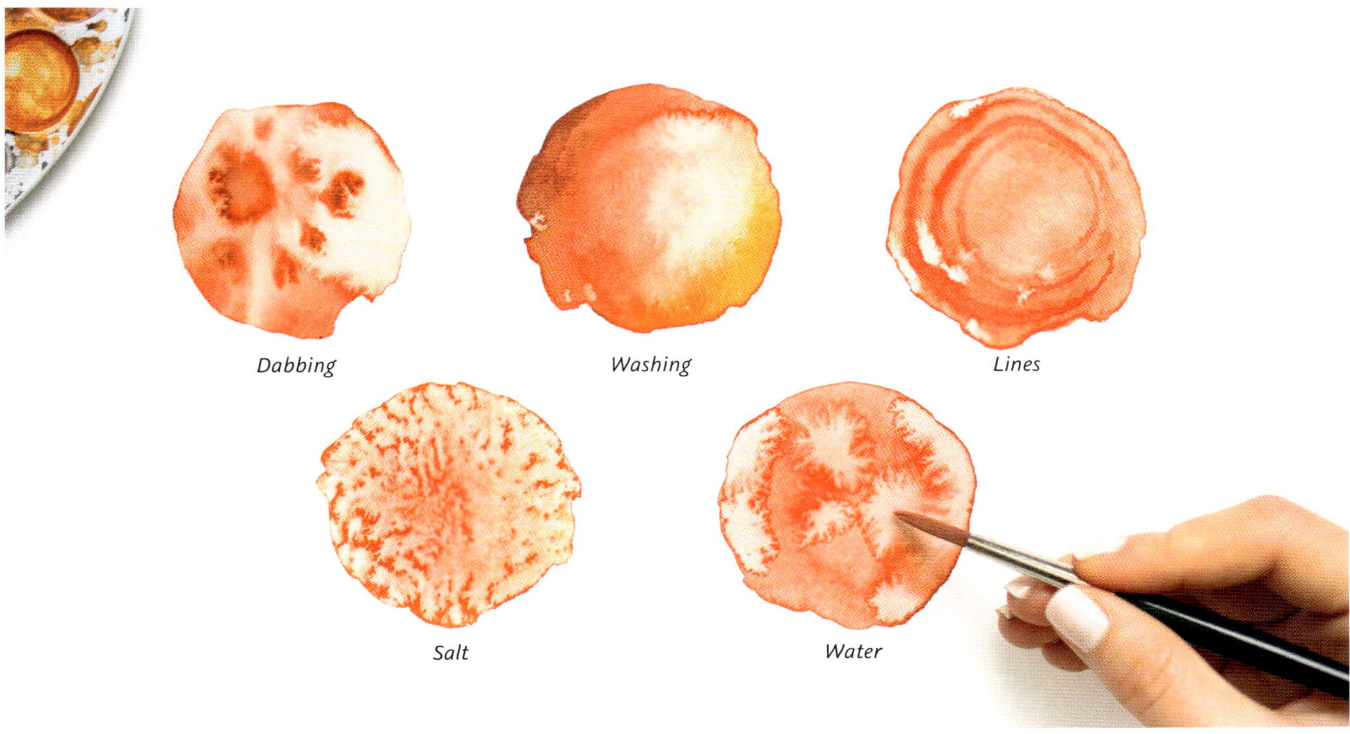

Dabbing    Washing    Lines

Salt    Water

## LINES

Use a thin brush to draw several lines in the damp color space. These will run to varying strengths depending on the dampness of the paper surface and the pigment concentration. In principle, the drier the layer underneath, the sharper the line will be. Therefore, always just wait a moment, otherwise the line will blur.

**Tip:** *The lines effect is ideal for creating soft strands of hair.*

## SALT

This time, apply a bold color layer, consisting of a lot of pigment and less water, and wait briefly until some of the paint has been absorbed by the paper. Now sprinkle a pinch of salt over the area and wait for everything to dry completely. The grains of salt will absorb the liquid. What remains on the surface is pigment residue. Finally, remove the salt using a hard-bristled brush.

**Tip:** *Try sprinkling varying amounts of salt onto the spaces, sometimes just a little, sometimes a lot.*

## WATER

Similar to the process for the salt effect, first undercoat your space with a bold color and wait for it to reach the right stage of dampness. Wash out your brush, take up some clear water, and drizzle some of it onto the surface. Feathered textures will emerge, but the results will vary from pigment to pigment.

**Tip:** *Supplement your texture chart with other materials, such as coffee, alcohol, rice or nail polish. Sprinkle or drizzle the material into the damp paint layer and observe what happens!*

# Step-by-Step

Before you start your first portrait project, you will find outlined here the general sequence of working, along with a few important tips.

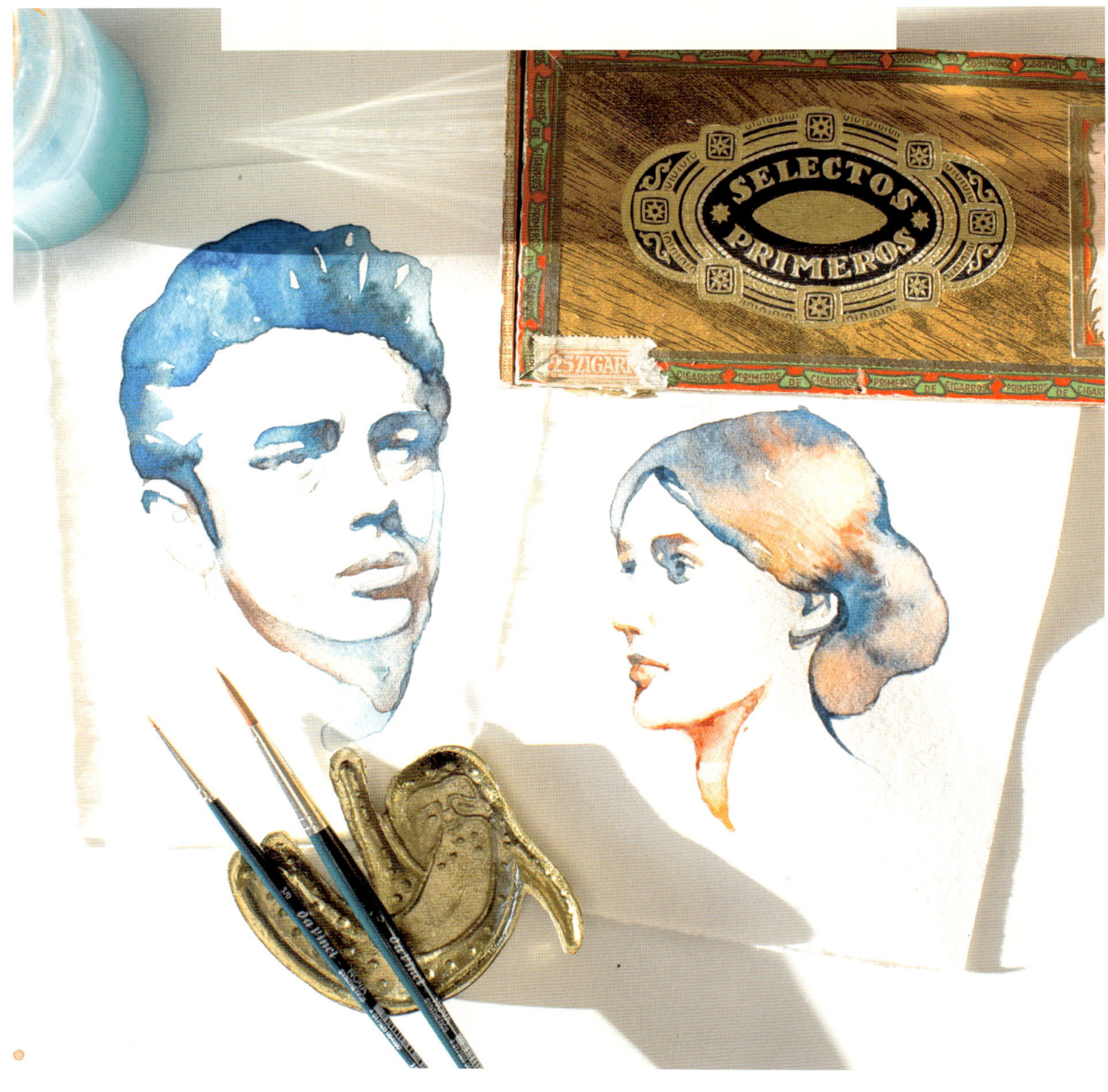

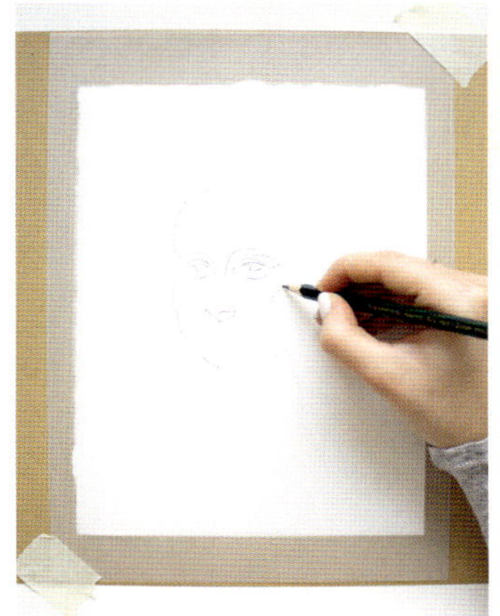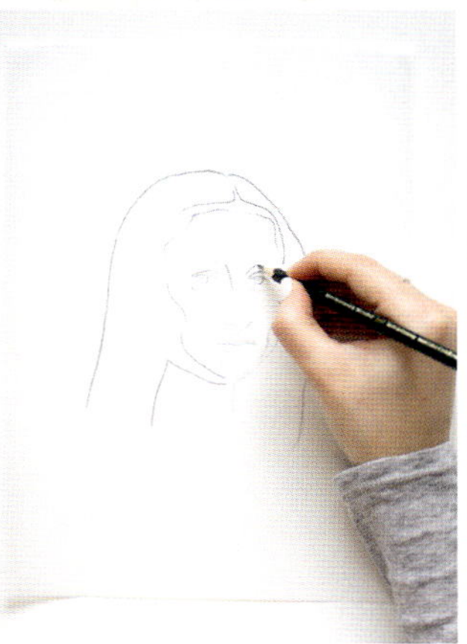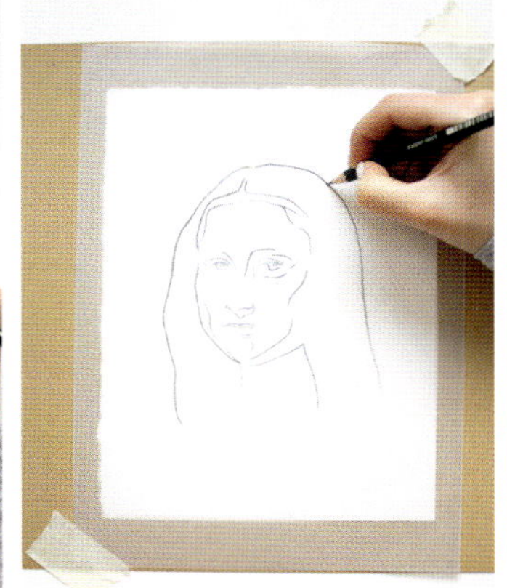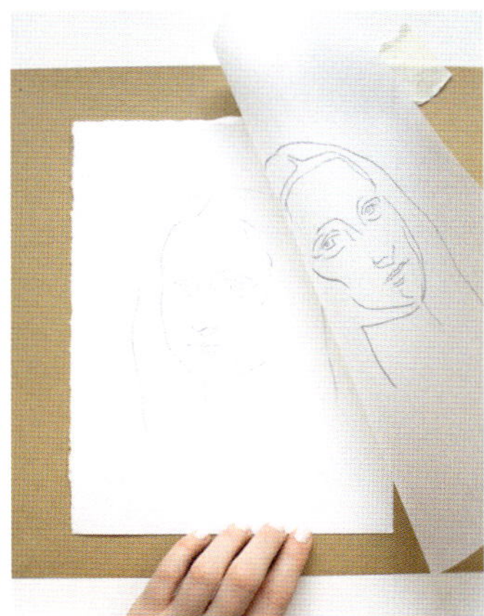

## THE PRELIMINARY SKETCH

The preliminary sketch is the first and perhaps the most important step, as it determines the recognizability of the person to a great extent. You can either draw the outlines freehand or use the illustration at the end of each chapter as a template for **tracing**.

### Step 1

Take your tracing paper and place it on the template. To prevent it from slipping, fix it at the edges with some masking tape. Use a sharp pencil to trace over all the lines. Work systematically from one side to the other to keep track.

### Step 2

Now loosen the tracing paper and turn it over. Place it on a light surface so that all the lines are clearly visible. Important: Now take a very soft pencil – preferably a 5B – and **firmly** go over the lines that you have already traced on the other side of the paper.

**Tip:** *Make a mental note of the traced lines so that you don't miss anything.*

### Steps 3 and 4

Position the tracing paper on the sheet of paper. Pay attention to the format and trim it if necessary. Turn the tracing paper with the original side facing up and fix it in place. Use a pencil to firmly go over all the lines. The graphite will be pressed through the tracing paper onto your sheet, leaving the outline of the portrait behind. Loosen one corner and check whether the lines underneath have actually been reproduced. If in doubt, go over it several times to get all the lines. When you are done, you can remove the tracing paper and start painting.

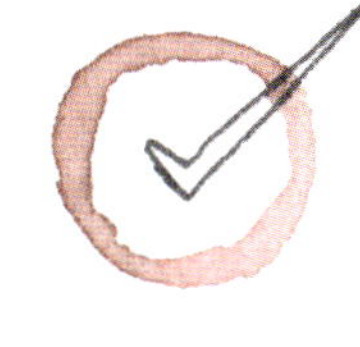

CHECKLIST

→ Clearly traced lines

→ Neither too dark nor too light

→ Correct proportions – or does something look funny? Now would be the moment to correct it

## PAINTING

### Wet-on-wet

The sequence varies depending on the portrait, but it is fair to say that after the preliminary sketch you will most often start by painting wet-on-wet. Sometimes the hair and sometimes the facial shadows are wetted with a lot of diluted paint, so that you can then paint in the damp layer with additional bold colors. As already explained in Textures, you will create different effects depending on the way you paint in.

Mix a lot of paint with a thick brush before the first application so that you don't run out while you are painting. This way you will prevent the layer from drying out too quickly while you are busy mixing paint; do use enough water as it will keep the surface damp to give you more time.

**Tip:** *If the paint dries in the meantime, it's not a problem. Apply a layer of water to these areas and then continue with the wet-on-wet technique.*

**Tip:** *Test your colors on your scratch paper before each application!*

Also, when painting in the facial shadows, make sure to paint **precisely** along the pencil lines, as these are what make the personality recognizable. A fraction of an inch here and there can change the face quite a bit.

The dampness of the surface is now quite crucial. The ideal time for painting in is when the surface is slightly shiny. Use **strong shades**, i.e., a lot of pigment to a little water, to create contrast. Use a finer brush, and don't hesitate to use more pigment sometimes, as the colors will look much brighter after drying.

**Tip:** *Frequently switch between brush sizes. Always use your thin brushes for the eyes. Conversely, large-area cheek shadows are, of course, easier to paint with a larger brush.*

Keep an overview of all parts of the face and switch spontaneously between them instead of just concentrating on a single one. For example, if you notice that the eyes are not dark enough, keep painting them in before the layer is dry.

**Tip:** *To make the colors spread better, tilt your page in the appropriate direction.*

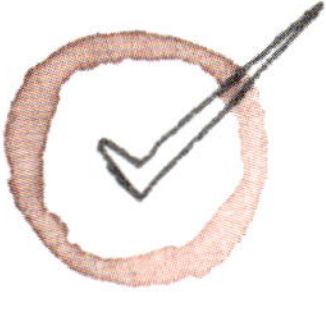

## CHECKLIST

→ Mixed enough paint for the first layer

→ Layer of paint stays constantly wet on the paper

→ Precisely painted along the pencil lines

→ Ideal dampness – time to paint in the second shade

→ Bold second shade

→ Harmonious color selection – do the color mixing exercises in the Colors chapter beforehand if necessary

→ Enough contrast between the lightest and darkest tone

## Glazing

Sometimes the wet-on-wet step is repeated on individual parts of the face, which are wetted in stages with water. The technique is also used at the very end for final color highlights.

However, it is the glazing that will undoubtedly bring your portrait to life. Sometimes you will supplement the mid-tones of the face with a light shade, sometimes you will layer dark areas in particularly shadowy places. Other times you'll just draw very sharp lines to accentuate areas such as the eyes.

**Tip:** *To paint fine lines, you should shape the tip of the brush, hold it perpendicular while painting, and press down as little as possible.*

It is particularly important to create a transition between the hard, sometimes very bold spaces and the gleaming white of the paper. You can blend these edges with the help of light mid-tones. Similarly, you can intensify hard, shadowy areas. For example, you will often darken expressive areas of the face, such as the eyes or lips, with a glaze to draw attention to them.

**Tip:** *Is your portrait balanced, or does it perhaps need a little bit more darkness? Anything obvious can be seen better from further away. Look at your picture perpendicular from several yards away and compare it with the original by quickly looking back and forth.*

You can also make certain areas look warmer and more vivid by glazing a layer of paint evenly over the corresponding areas.

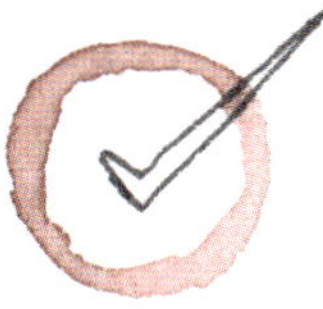

CHECKLIST

→ Soft edges – shaded and white spaces connected by mid-tone transitions

→ Enough detail

→ Balance between blurriness and sharpness

→ Balance between space and line

→ Balance between light and dark

→ Clear attention to specific parts of the face

→ Finished picture that has completely dried – now you can erase the pencil lines

**Tip:** *For a final comparison, turn your picture and the template upside down. This helps to trick your brain into perceiving the parts of the face differently, since you are no longer focused on the correct appearance of an eye or mouth. You just see the parts of the face as shapes, and in this way, you can see much easier which areas could still be improved.*

The very last step is always to erase the pencil lines. Before you do that, however, be patient, and only erase them when your picture is completely dry!

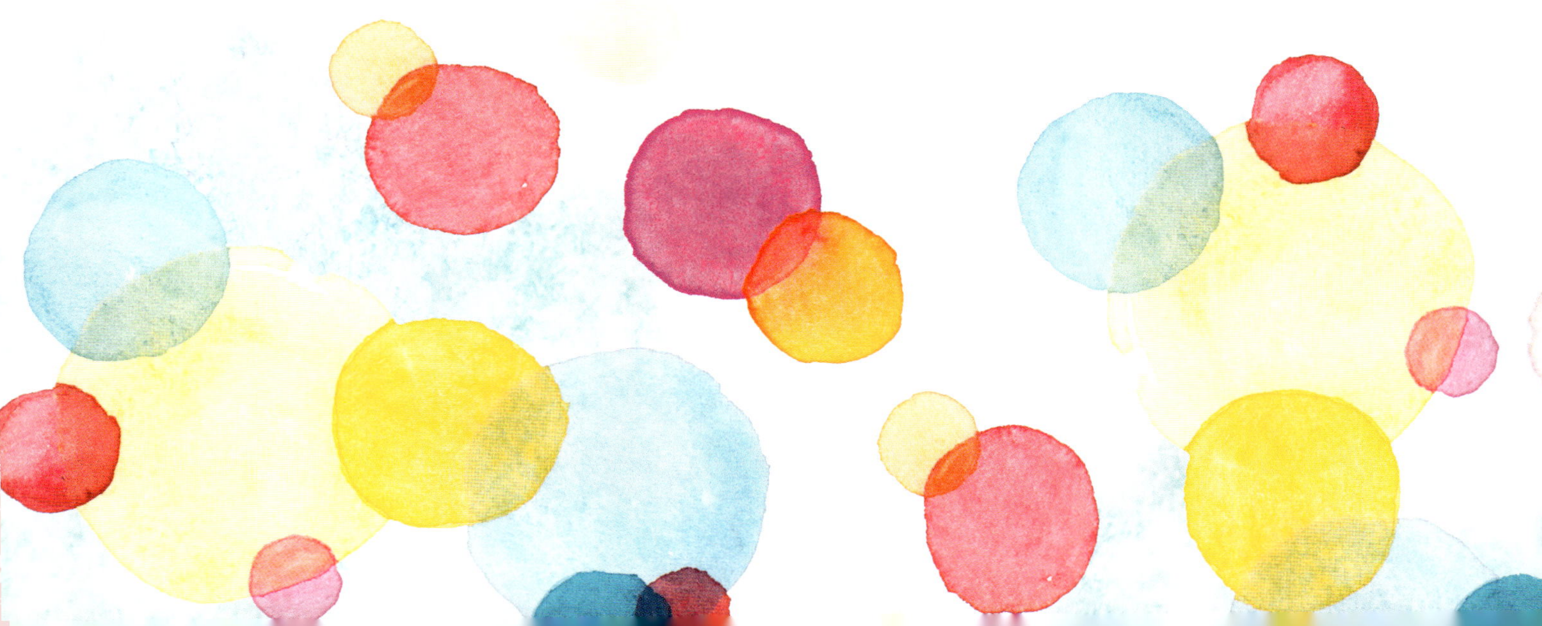

# Final Tips

What do I do when I've made a mistake? How do I create
soft tonal gradations and edges? Let's take a look at
these last few questions before you get started!

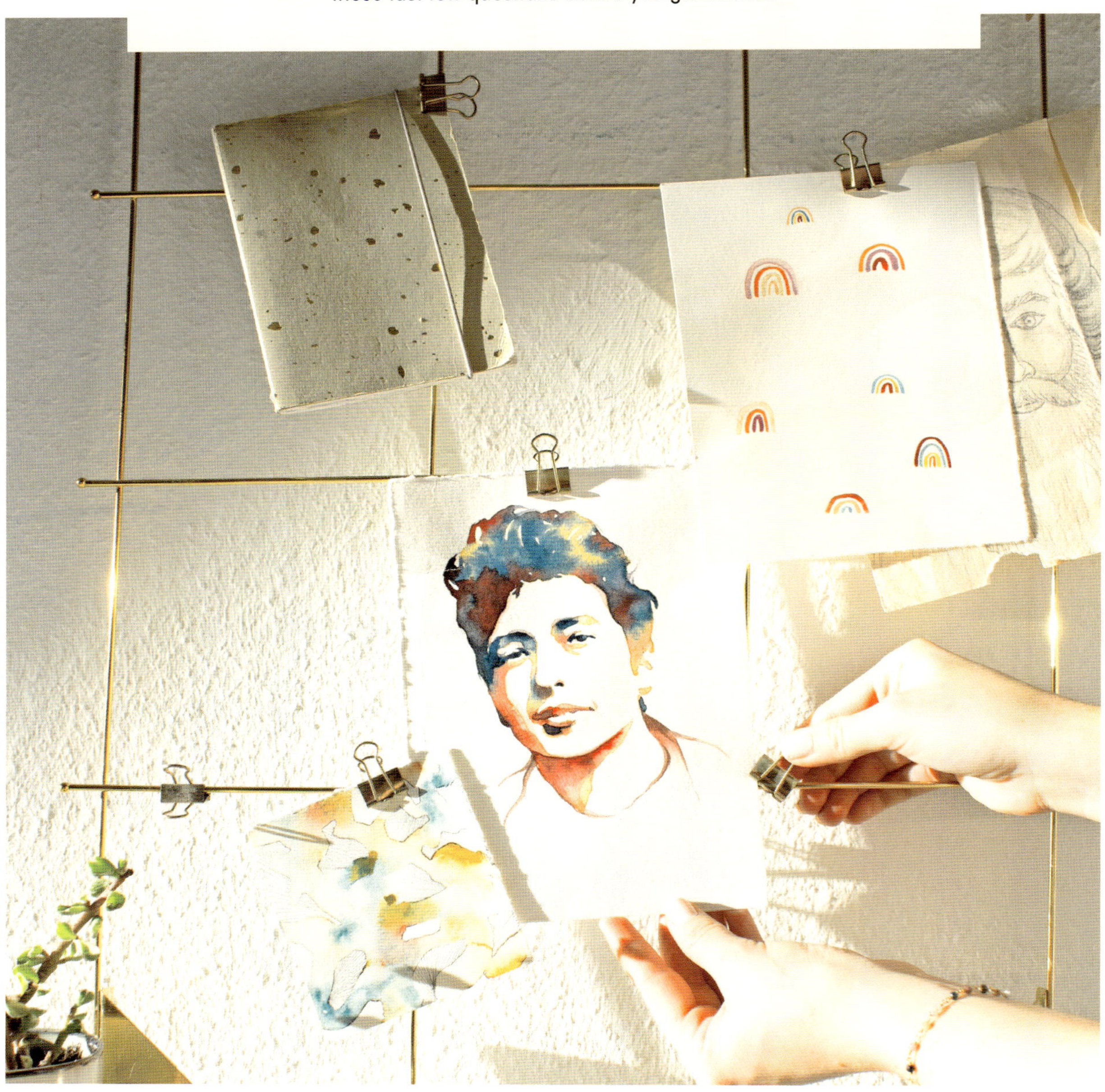

## GRADATIONS

Soft light gradations are best achieved with the wet-on-wet technique. Start by painting the only slightly diluted paint in one spot. Wash out your brush briefly, and go back to the dark spot with the damp brush and paint in the other direction. Wipe off the brush in between and use clear water again. The dark colored space will create a transition as if by itself with the water.

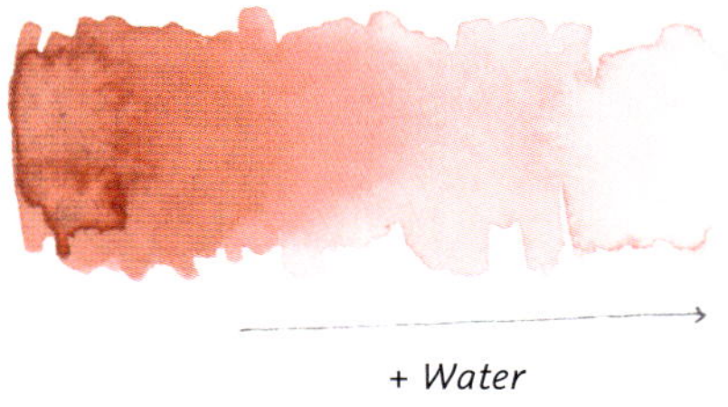



## CORRECTING BY REMOVING PAINT

As we know, the white areas of the paper will always remain the lightest parts of your picture, and since subsequent lightening of painted areas is only possible to a limited extent, you should consider beforehand which areas should remain white. Then start with a little pigment and gradually add more – figuratively speaking, paint from light to dark.

Don't worry if you do make a mistake! With a brush and a little water, you can tackle almost any blemish. For example, if you've used too much water or painted a wrong shade and want to remove the small puddles of paint on your paper surface, you can do this with a dry brush or paper towel. Dab over the space, and the excess paint will soak into the material by itself.

If you want to correct an area that has dried, use a damp brush and apply a little pressure – preferably in circular motions – to activate the area in question and then remove the excess using a brush or paper towel. (You can also apply the same technique to lighten or blend areas.)

**Tip:** *This trick is used far too seldom – yet it is basically the equivalent of erasing when drawing. Heads up: Watercolor paper can withstand a lot, but if you "erase" too much, the surface will eventually disintegrate.*

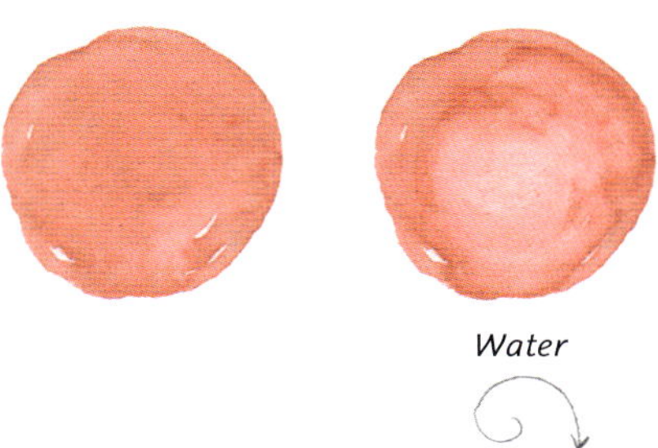



## BLENDING EDGES

When a colored space has dried, the edges usually look darker. To blend these in, take a clean brush with just water and activate the edge with a little pressure in circular motions. As described in Correcting by Removing Paint, the paint can then be removed very easily. Wipe the brush off several times on scratch paper so it no longer contains any of the removed paint.

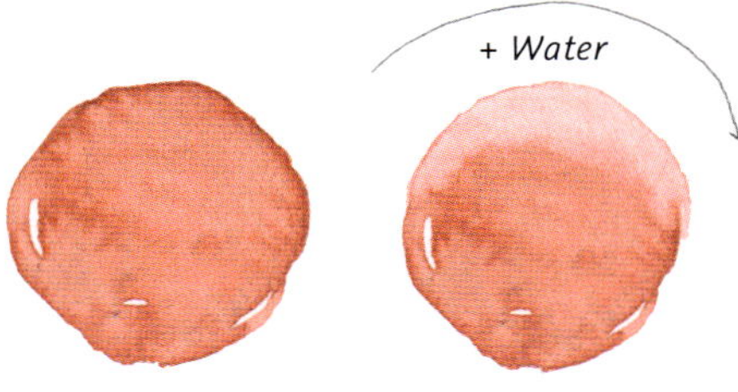

# A Flexible Approach

As you now know, watercolor always involves some adjustments. The time window in which the paint actually stays wet on the paper surface is limited, which can take a little getting used to. However, it is precisely this that lends excitement and spontaneity to any watercolor painting. To ultimately paint successfully with watercolor, you need a **flexible approach**. If in doubt, always listen to your gut feeling and do not become too attached to the original, because your portrait will deviate from it anyway. No two watercolors will ever be exactly the same, and that's what is so wonderful!

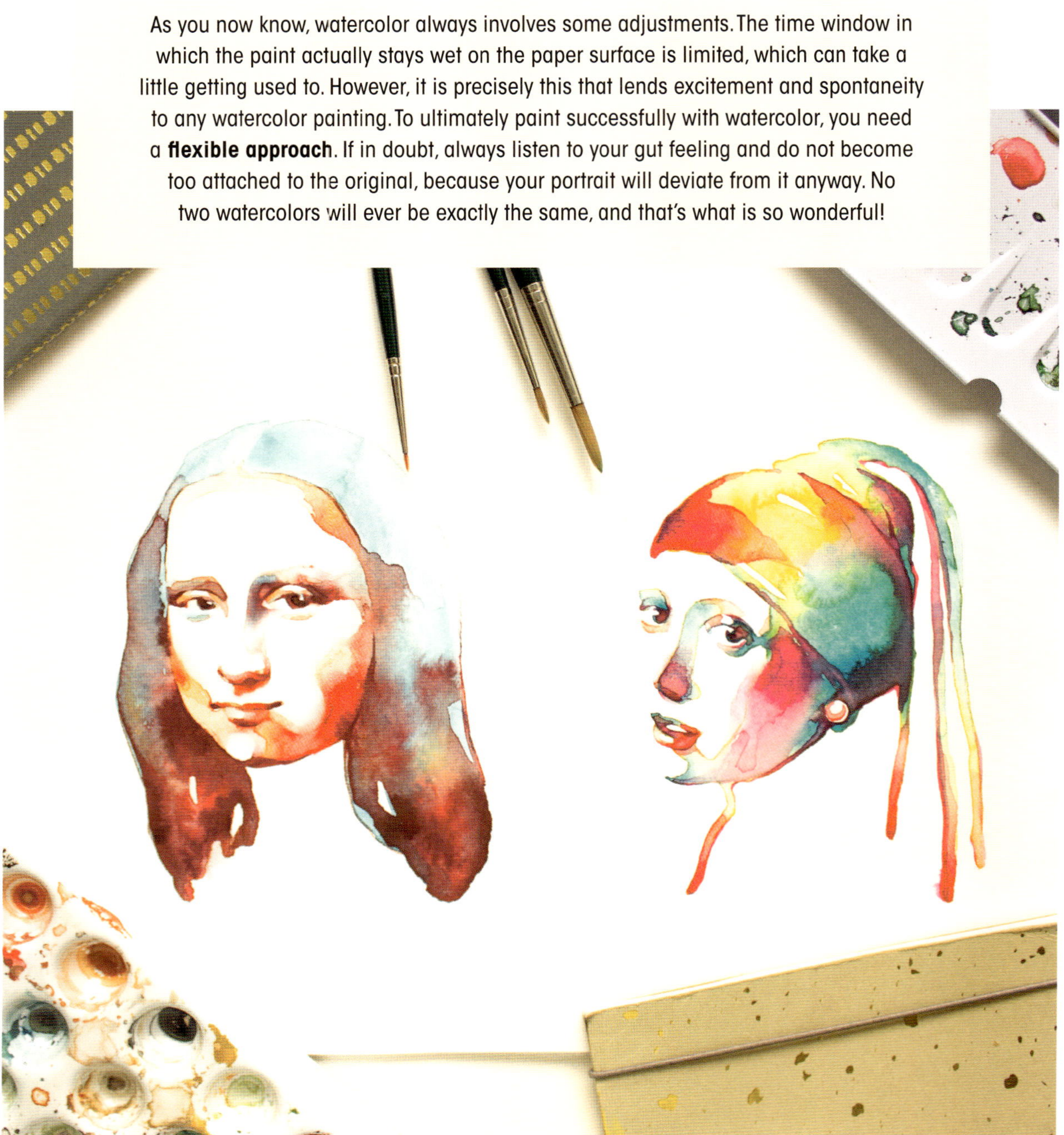

## IF IT DOESN'T WORK OUT

**"Have no fear of perfection – you'll never reach it."
Salvador Dali**

We often tend to have very high expectations of ourselves and look far too critically at our own pictures. When expectations are not met, our frustration can grow quickly. At the same time, striving for perfection is like aiming for a goal that we will never reach anyway!

If your picture just doesn't look as you had hoped, and it seems as if nothing is going to work out, take a break. Distract yourself. A walk, for example, can work wonders – or simply have another look at it the next day. Usually, you'll see your painting with different eyes, and suddenly you will see what the problem was.

You will keep your motivation to paint by having lots of little successes. You will only stay focused on it if it's fun and if you see progress, but at the same time it is important that you are still being sufficiently challenged.

**Tip:** *You can use the exercises included throughout the Basics section as such mini successes. And, if things don't work out as you had hoped, feel free to just improvise, and concentrate only on the colors and textures.*

**Tip:** *Always try to think in a* **solution-oriented** *way. If the paint runs into areas where it doesn't really belong, see it as an opportunity to make something great out of the supposed mistake. In a pinch, you can always remove the paint later.*

Discarding images and repeatedly giving it another shot is a process that can also be challenging at times. It takes a while to develop an open attitude, but when you do, it makes painting a lot more fun because you're more courageous with ideas and how to implement them!

The magic happens when you relinquish control to the paints, but still maintain an overview. With each painting, you'll become more sensitized towards the colors, and you will develop a feel for the appropriate water-to-pigment ratio at your own pace. Be brave, experiment as much as you can, and keep it fun!

**In your pictures, always make sure you strike a balance for the key points in the Conclusion list.**

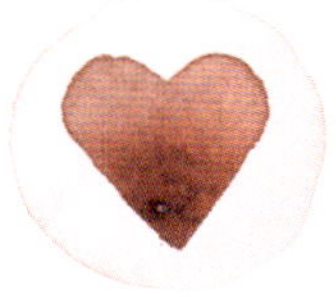

### CONCLUSION

→ **Color choice**: An exciting color focus, not just shade-on-shade

→ **Technique**: Wet-on-wet effects vs. clear spaces of glaze

→ **Sharpness and blurring**: Clear lines vs. flowing gradations – outlines partly feathered, partly very sharp

→ **Light-dark contrast**: A large tonal difference between the lightest and darkest spots in the picture provides for maximum expression

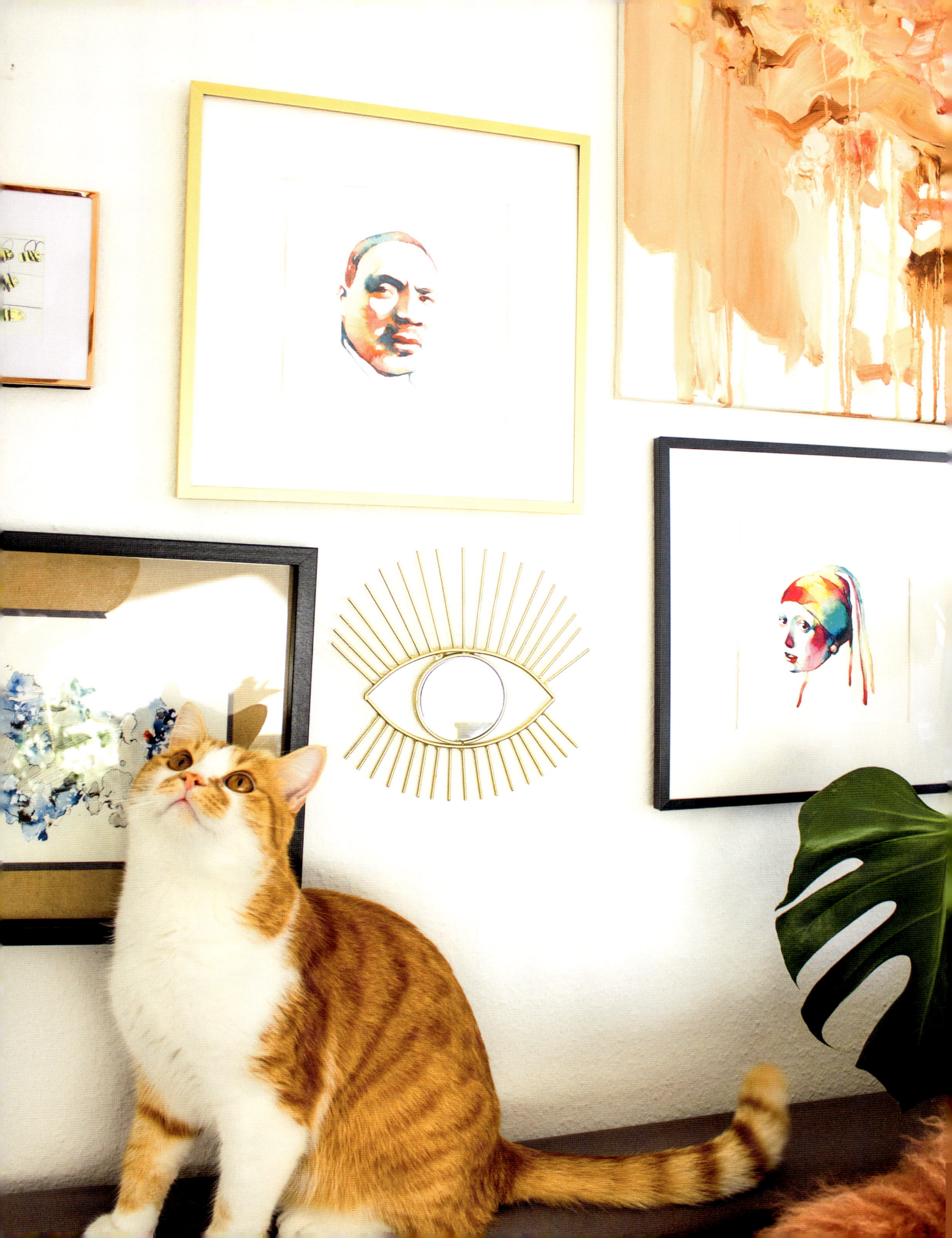

# Projects

# LEONARDO
## DiCaprio

Leonardo DiCaprio is without a doubt one of the most successful Hollywood actors of our time. He also uses this fame for his ecological activism, establishing the Leonardo DiCaprio Foundation, devoted to promoting environmental awareness and to producing documentaries about the protection and preservation of our planet.

A remarkable personality, DiCaprio is rendered here in an expressive way using warm colors and dark outlines.

**COLOR PALETTE:**

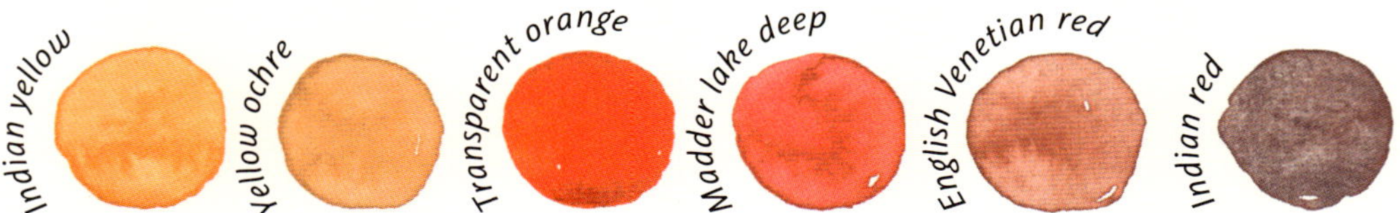

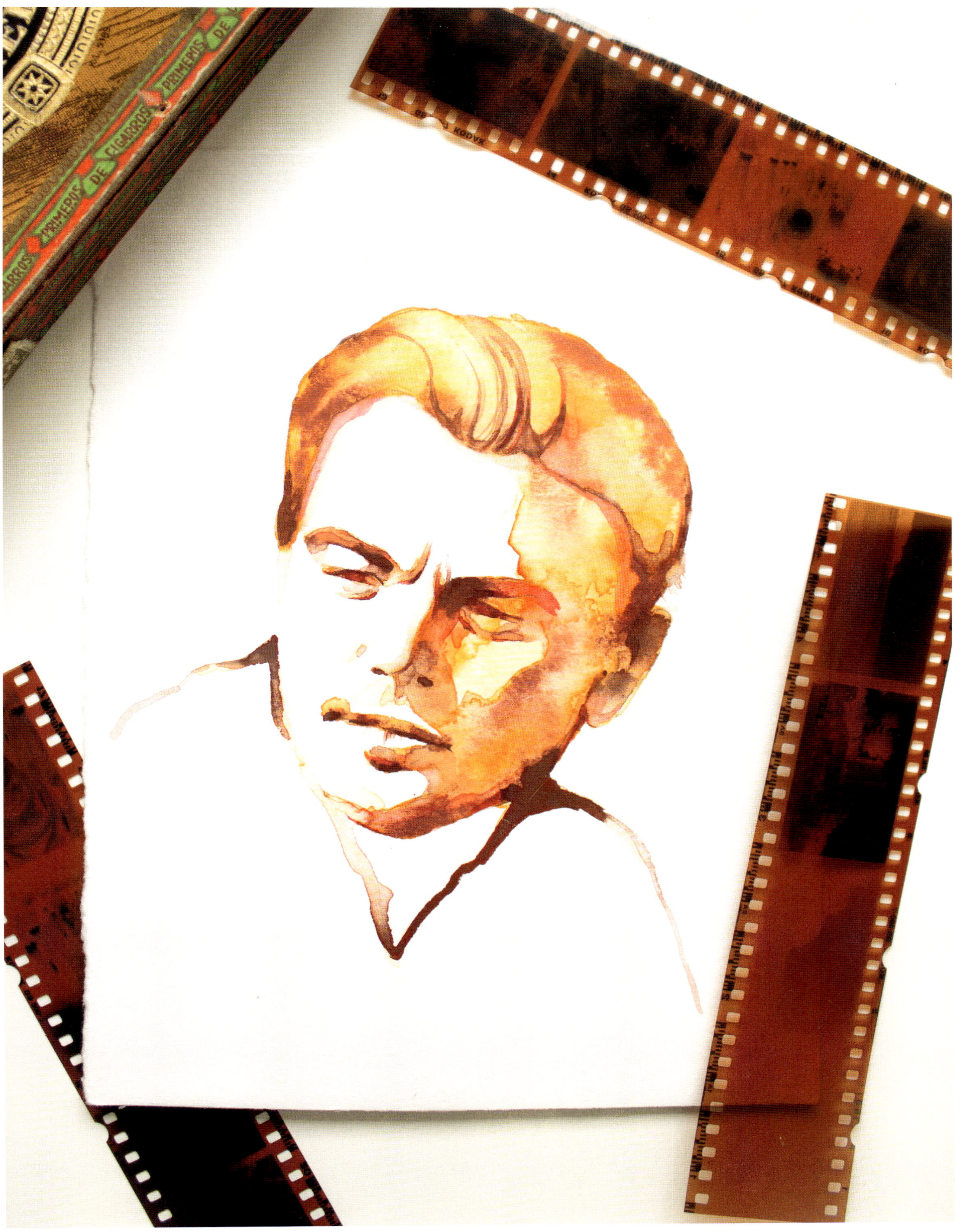

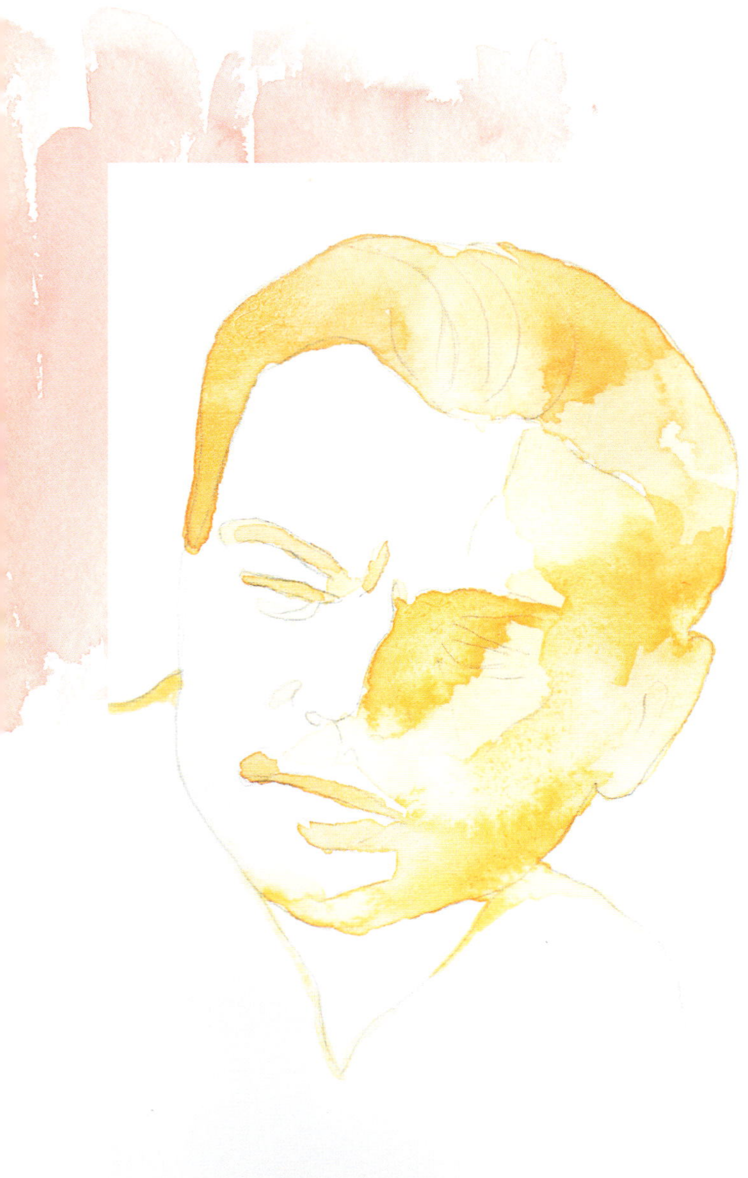

**1. Wet-on-wet:** Using a thick brush, mix a pale orange made up of lots of water and apply it liberally in circular motions to the hair space and right half of the face (it is very important, before you start painting, to make sure that you have plenty of paint prepared as the shaded space here is quite large). Then use the same pigment, undiluted this time, on the hairline, crown and eyebrow. Feel free to use larger amounts of pigment and work the same area several times to create beautiful textures. The area around the left eye and shoulder lines are also underpainted. Now wait until everything dries.

Leonardo DiCaprio

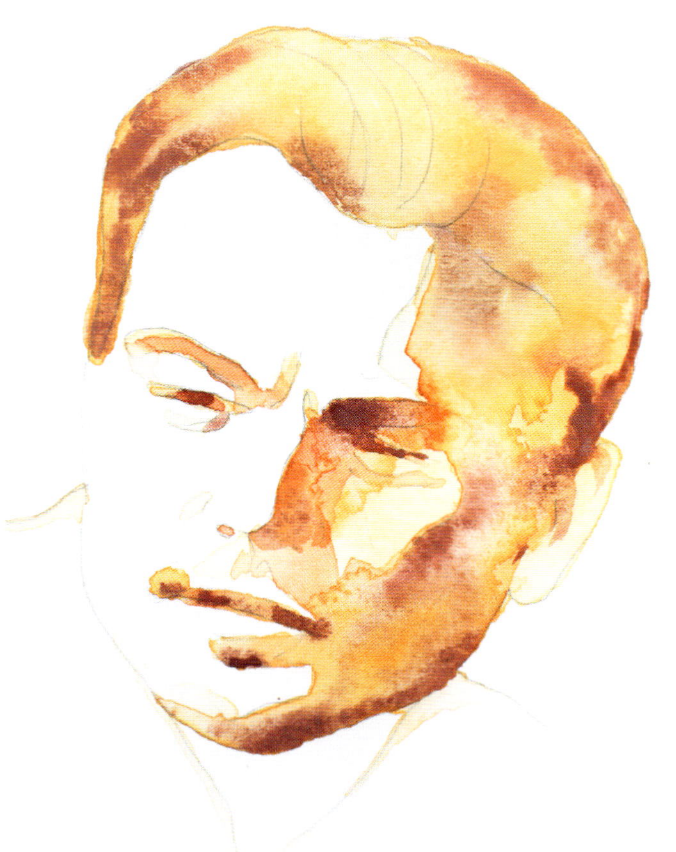

**2. Wet-on-wet:** When your paint is dry, use a clean brush to carefully paint a clear wash of water onto the dry, painted space. Do not go over the ear or the triangular area under the right eye.

**Tip:** *If you look at your picture from the side, you can see better where you have already applied water.*

Now switch to your finest brush and dab a bold brown onto the hair, eyebrow, corners of the mouth, jawline, and most importantly, on the edges of the cheekbone. Try not to use any additional water, because the dark color spaces should not run too far. Wait until some of the water has been absorbed – then you will have the most control over the color gradations.

**Tip:** *Add a little pink or orange to the brown. By combining the pigments with each other, you can achieve harmonious nuances of color.*

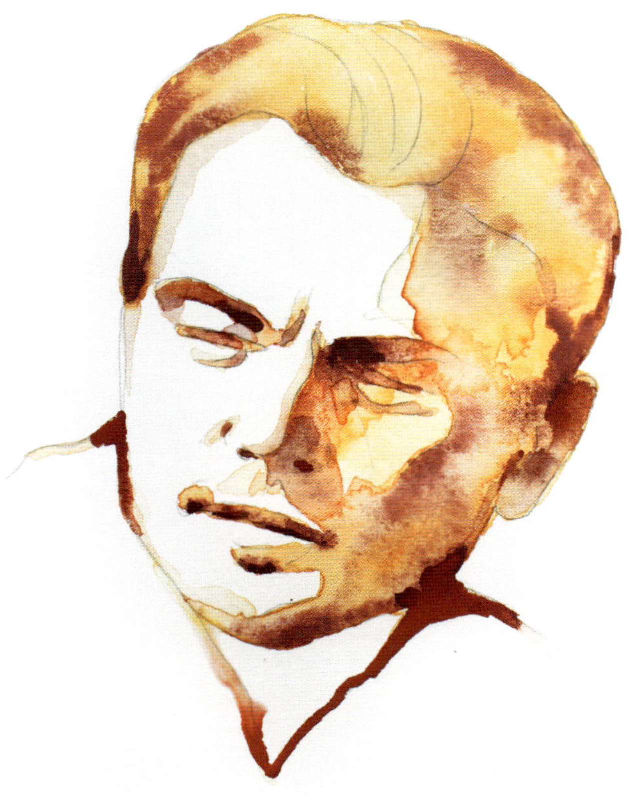

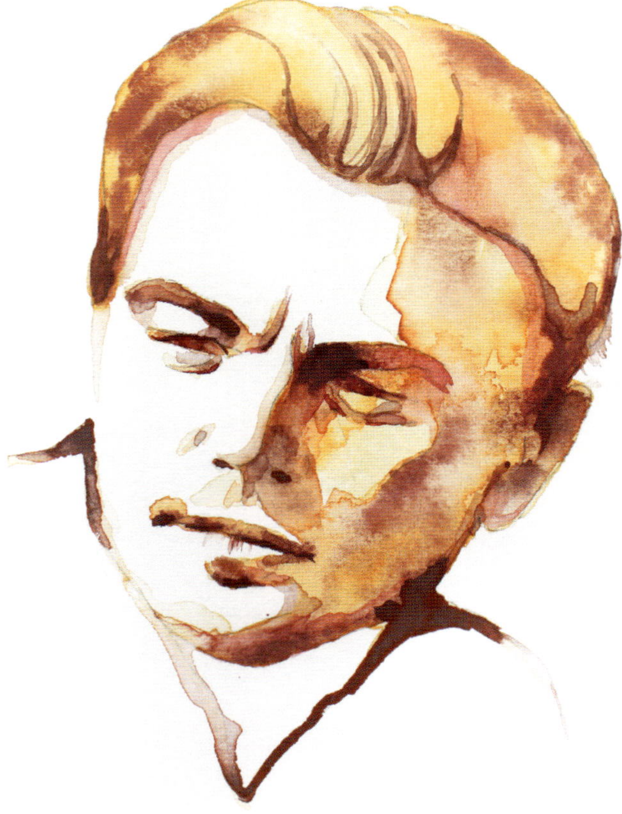

**3.** *Glaze:* The layer of paint should be dry when you darken the eyebrows with a deep brown glaze. Take care to use a relaxed brushstroke and layer several spaces on top of each other. Try to let the shadows look casual overall, and not "painted in". Trace the shoulder and neck lines with clear water, wait a moment, and then dab in individual areas with the boldest shade so that the color runs on its own. For the nostrils and eyes, use your finest brush. Paint along the bridge of the nose and the hairline with very diluted orange, which provides the transition between the light and the shaded areas. Use the same color to complete the shadow on the left side of the forehead. The eyelid creases and the ear are also darkened.

**4.** *Glaze:* This is very similar to the previous step, but now we intensify all of the dark areas a bit more. The eyes are defined, as are the lower lip and chin. Using something of a lighter glaze, fill in the lower eyelid and the shadow at the hairline. To create some color tension, paint a thin glaze of a rich pink over the right eyebrow, jawline, and hairline. Add some very thin lines for the lip and frown lines. Finally, go over the pre-drawn strands of hair. These can run together a little more at the base without any problems.

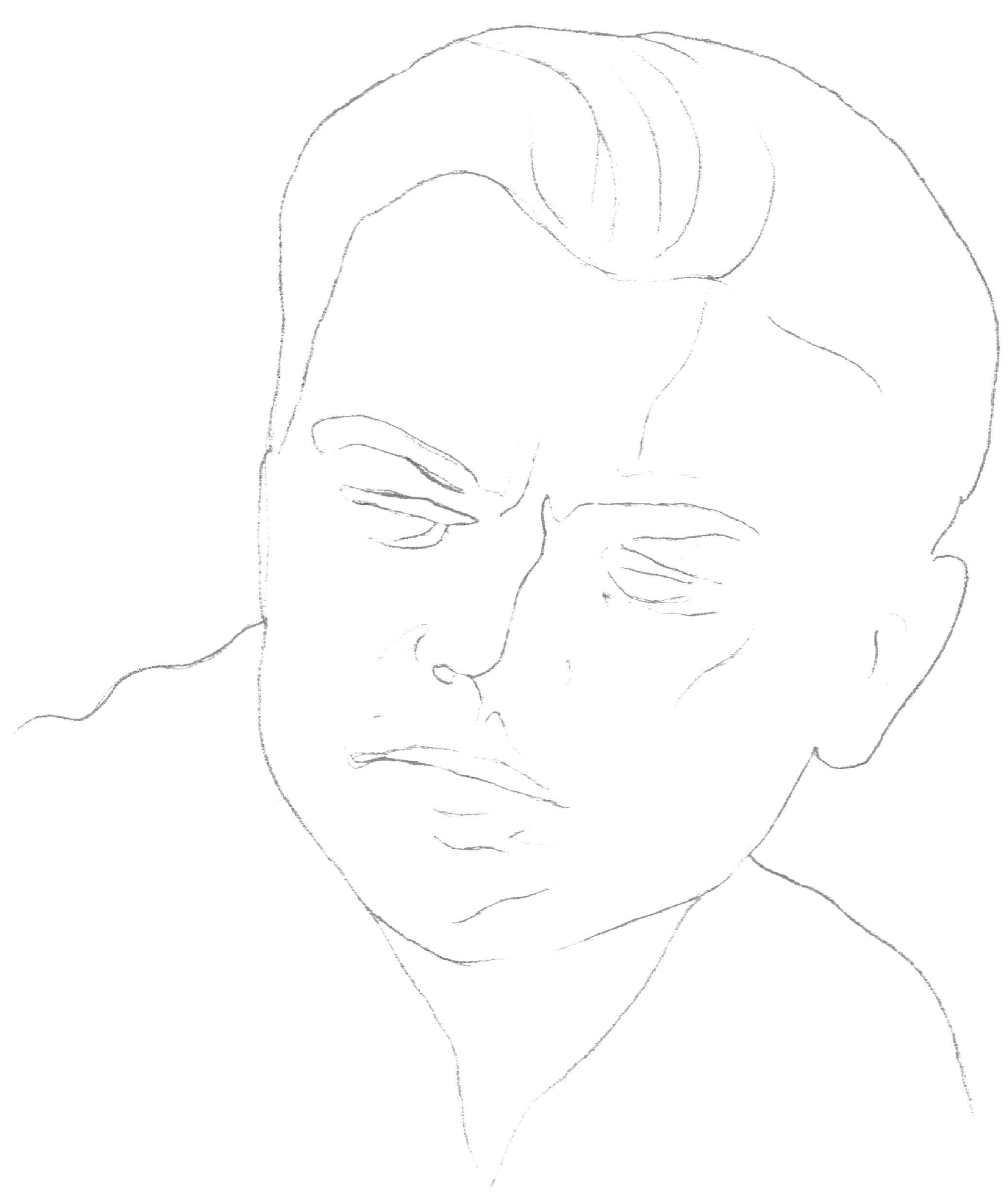

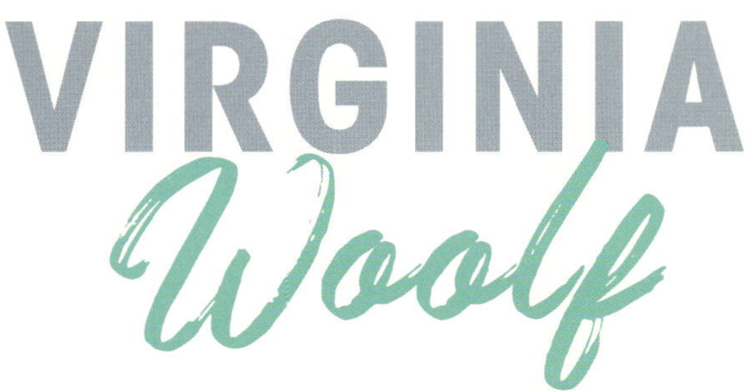

# VIRGINIA
## *Woolf*

Her porcelain-like features might be deceiving at first impression, because this is a rather opinionated personality!

Virginia Woolf, born in London in 1882, was an author, publisher and a pioneer of feminism. In her essays and novels, she talks about the image of women, demands equal opportunities and free artistic expression – all way ahead of her time! Today, almost 150 years later, she is regarded as a visionary of modern feminism.

## COLOR PALETTE:

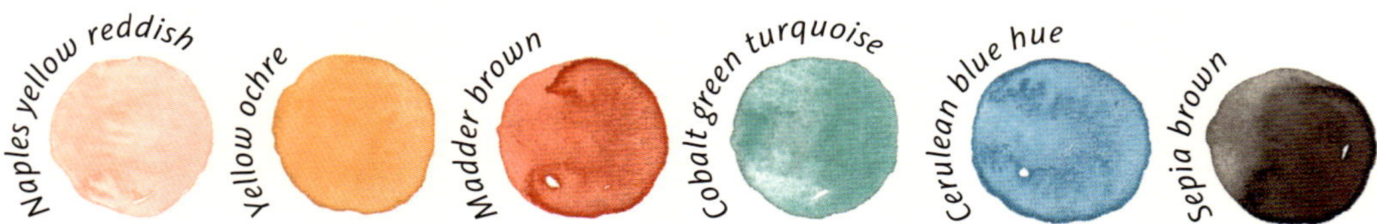

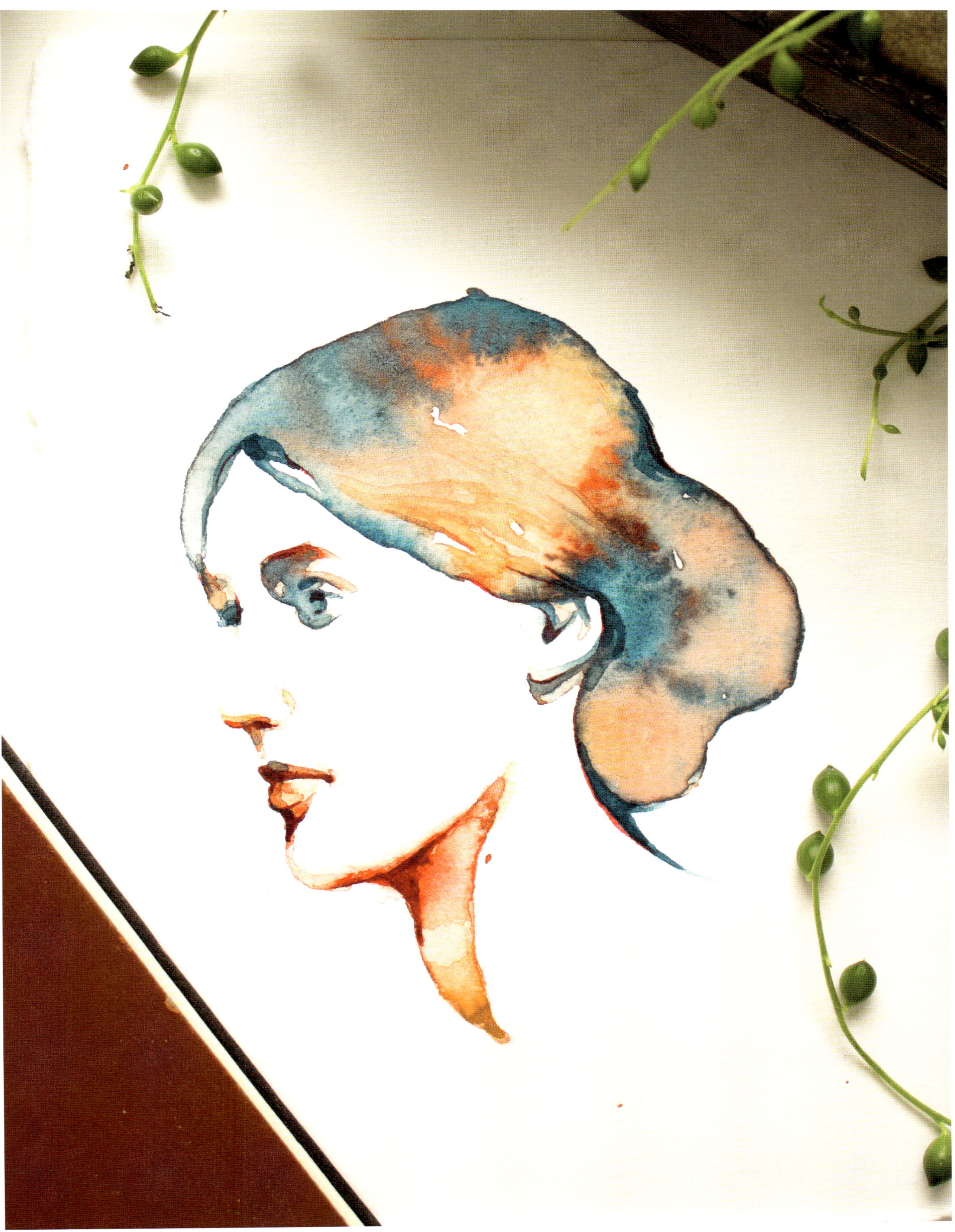

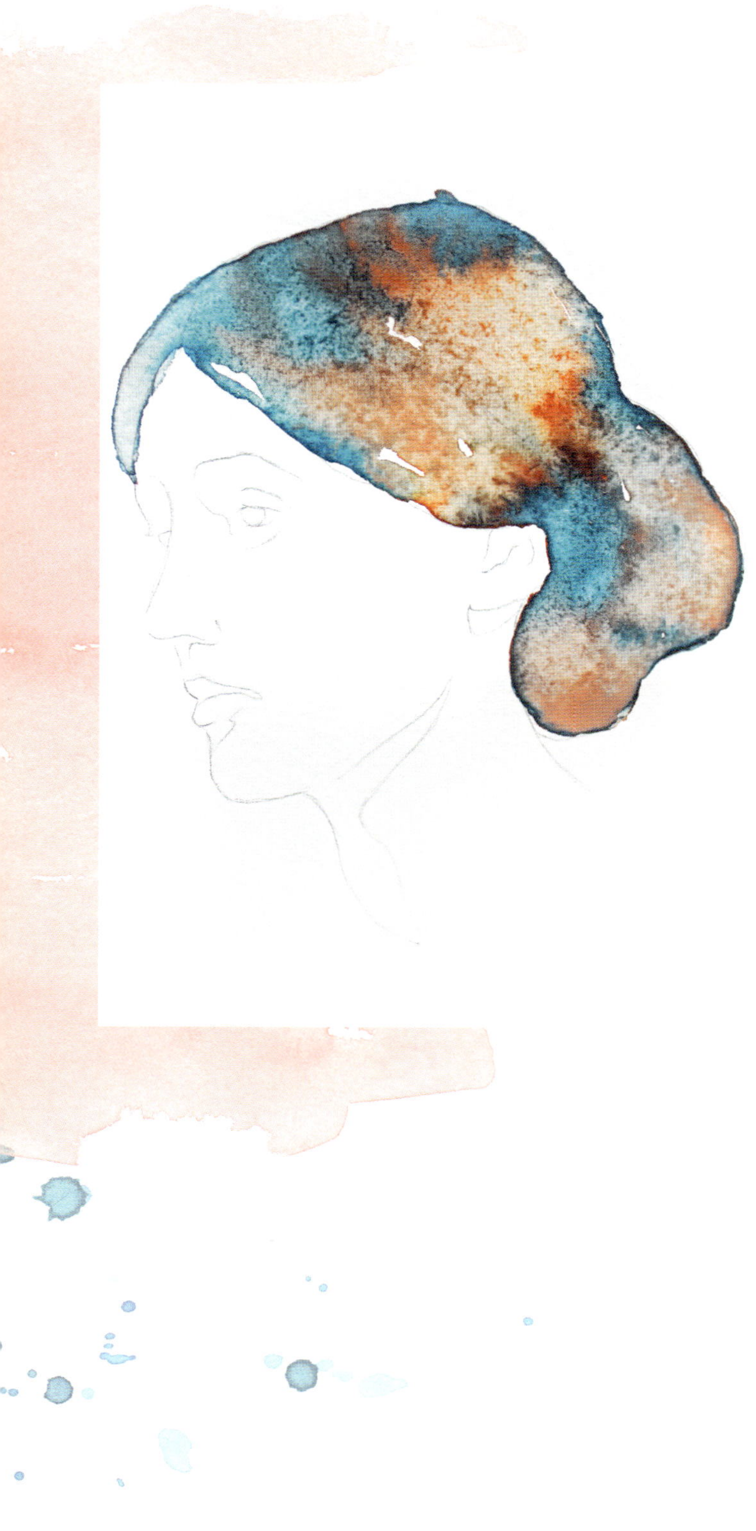

**1.** *Wet-on-wet:* The hair is painted completely wet-on-wet. To do this, mix a reddish orange with plenty of water, and apply a wash quickly over the entire space. Leave a few gaps though, because this breaks up the space and provides some texture. Now, using the same brush, add your undiluted blue pigment to the outer edges of the ear. Repeat this step with a bold orange, applying it more centrally – but let both colors run on their own without moving them with the brush. Since the hair is not going to change much, take your time and play with the colors until you are satisfied.

**Tip:** *Match your brushstrokes to the strands of hair. Start from the crown and paint downwards with a slight sweep. This will help you in "leaving gaps".*

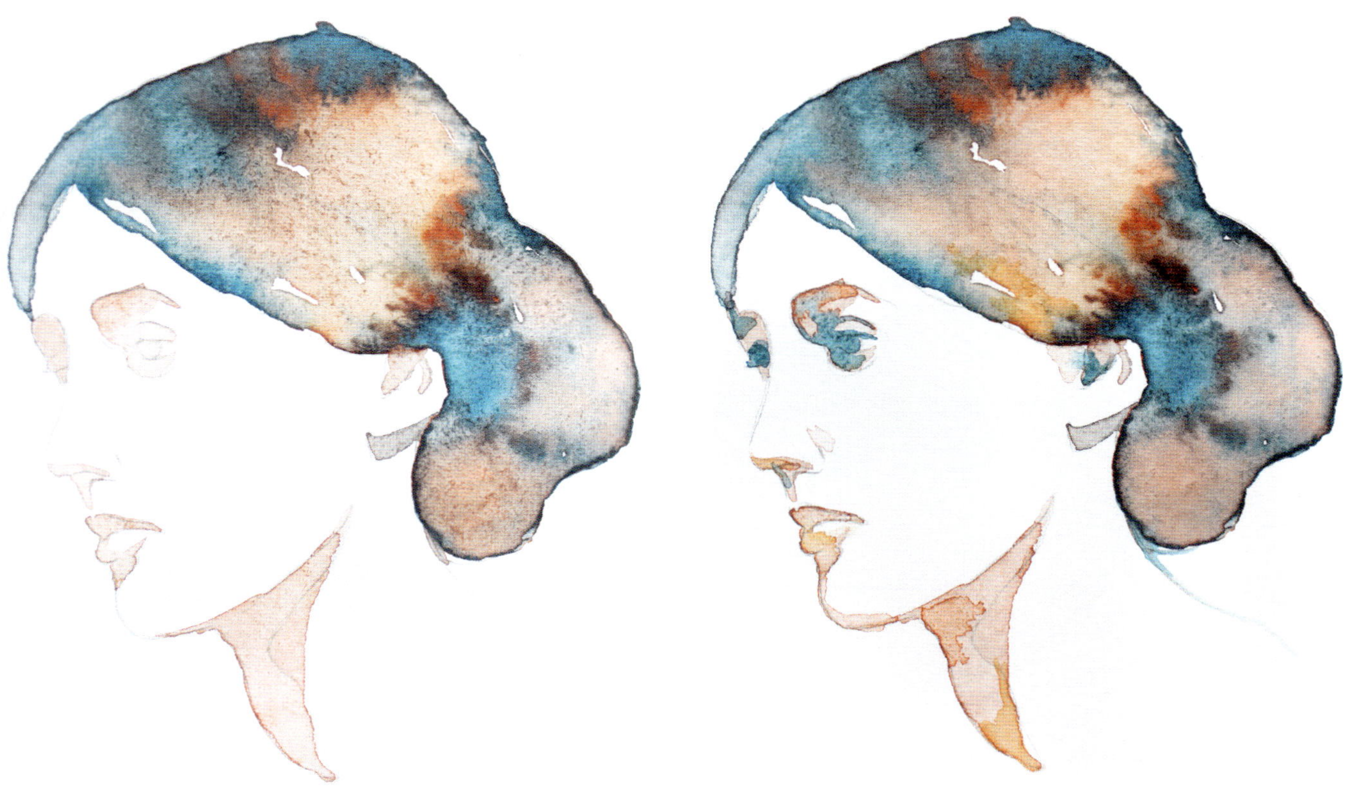

**2.** *Wet-on-dry:* Now switch to a finer brush and underpaint the facial shadows with a similar orange to the beginning of the first step. Emphasize the darker shadows, such as on the eyebrow and upper lip, by using more pigment and less water, and accurately trace the jawline with your brush tip to make it easier to paint in the neck space.

**3.** *Wet-on-wet & glaze:* Now paint semi-transparently over the tip of the nose, lower lip, chin and neck. Dried areas won't run, but wet areas will, so you are using a combination of both basic techniques. The ochre, which you apply to the lower lip, the nose shadow, the neck and the hair transparently, gives the portrait a warm glow. The blue on the eyes creates an intriguing warm-cold contrast.

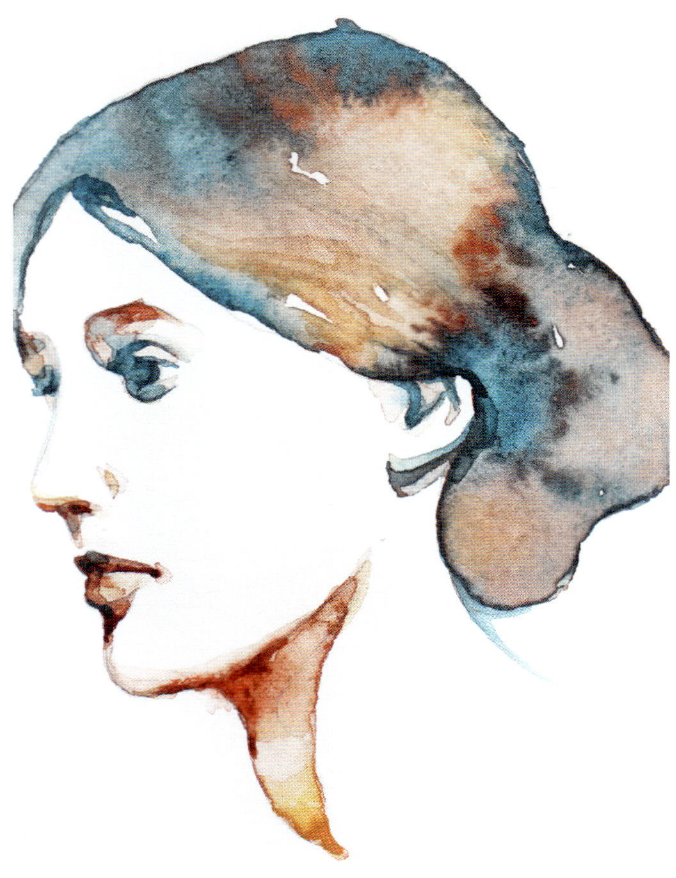

**4.** *Wet-on-wet & glaze:* Repeat the previous step with all parts of the face, and now also use a dark red. Use a brush with clear water to re-moisten the dried areas a little – on the neck, eyebrows and lip – to then dab in with the undiluted shade. Mix another dark shade using blue and a little black, and apply this to the area around the ear. From there, draw a sharp line down the nape. Now, intensify the iris and eye wrinkles with a bold blue. Just a few brushstrokes on the upper part are enough here. Complete the delicate shadows at the corner of the mouth, the bridge of the nose and the nose wing with a very diluted orange. Finally, you can layer a few strands of hair with an ochre glaze.

Virginia Woolf

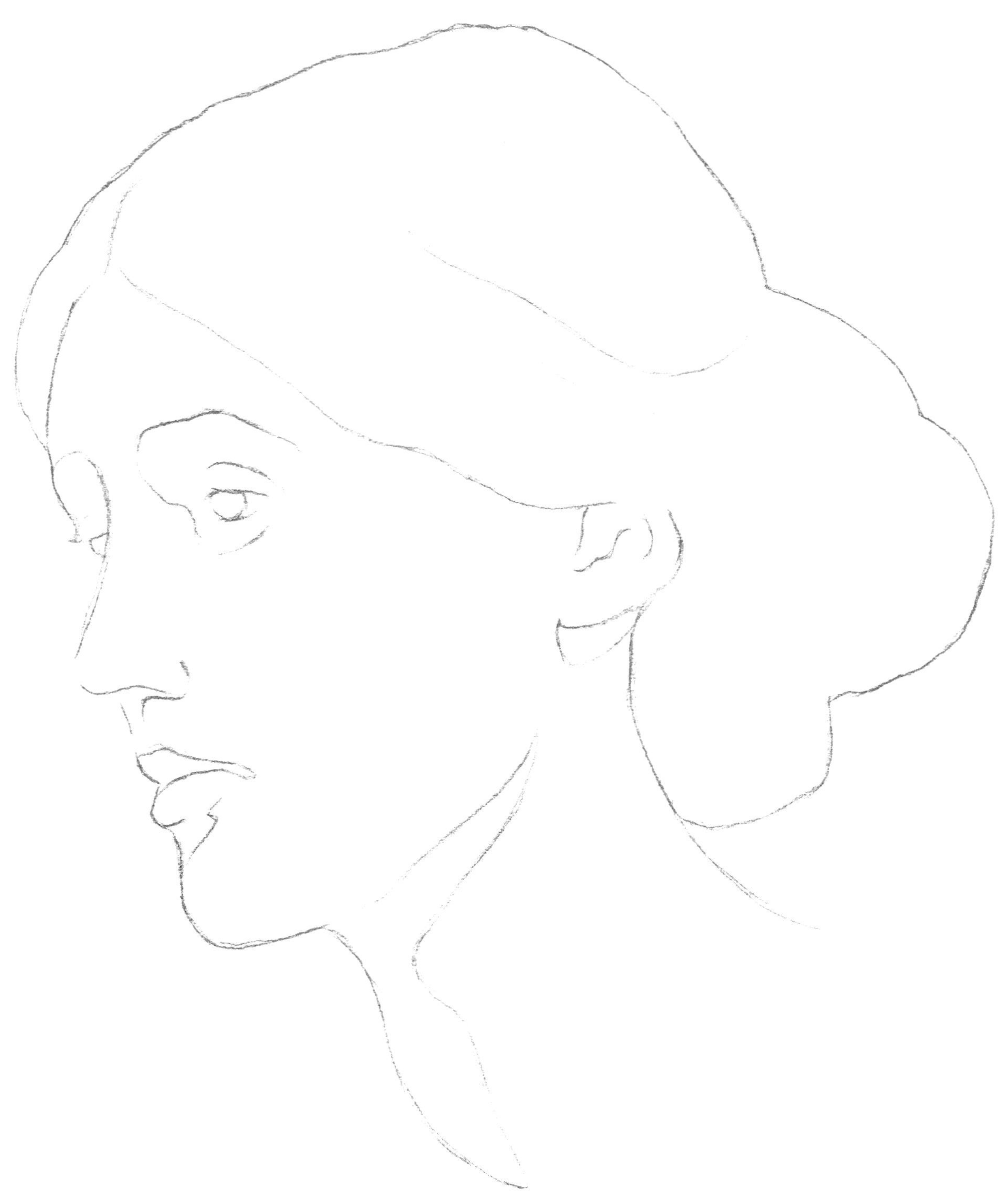

# JAMES
## *Dean*

This American actor was just 24 years old when he was involved in a fatal car accident. In his short life, James Dean nevertheless managed to prove himself as a gifted performer. He loved the unconventional and broke with the conservative fashion trend of the 1950s – which eventually made him a style icon. A perfect white T-shirt and blue jeans: We have him to thank for that classic look.

**COLOR PALETTE:**

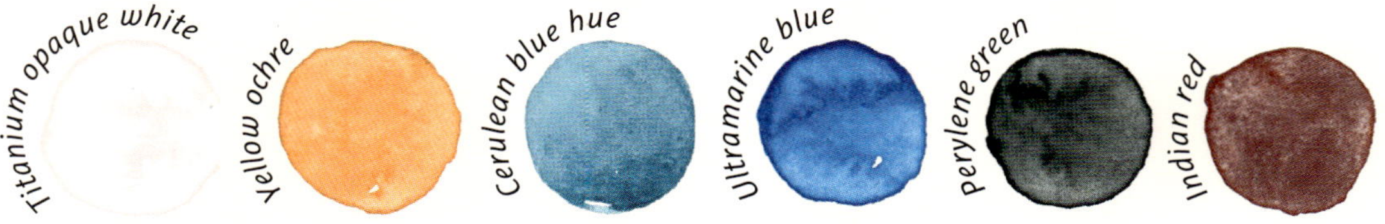

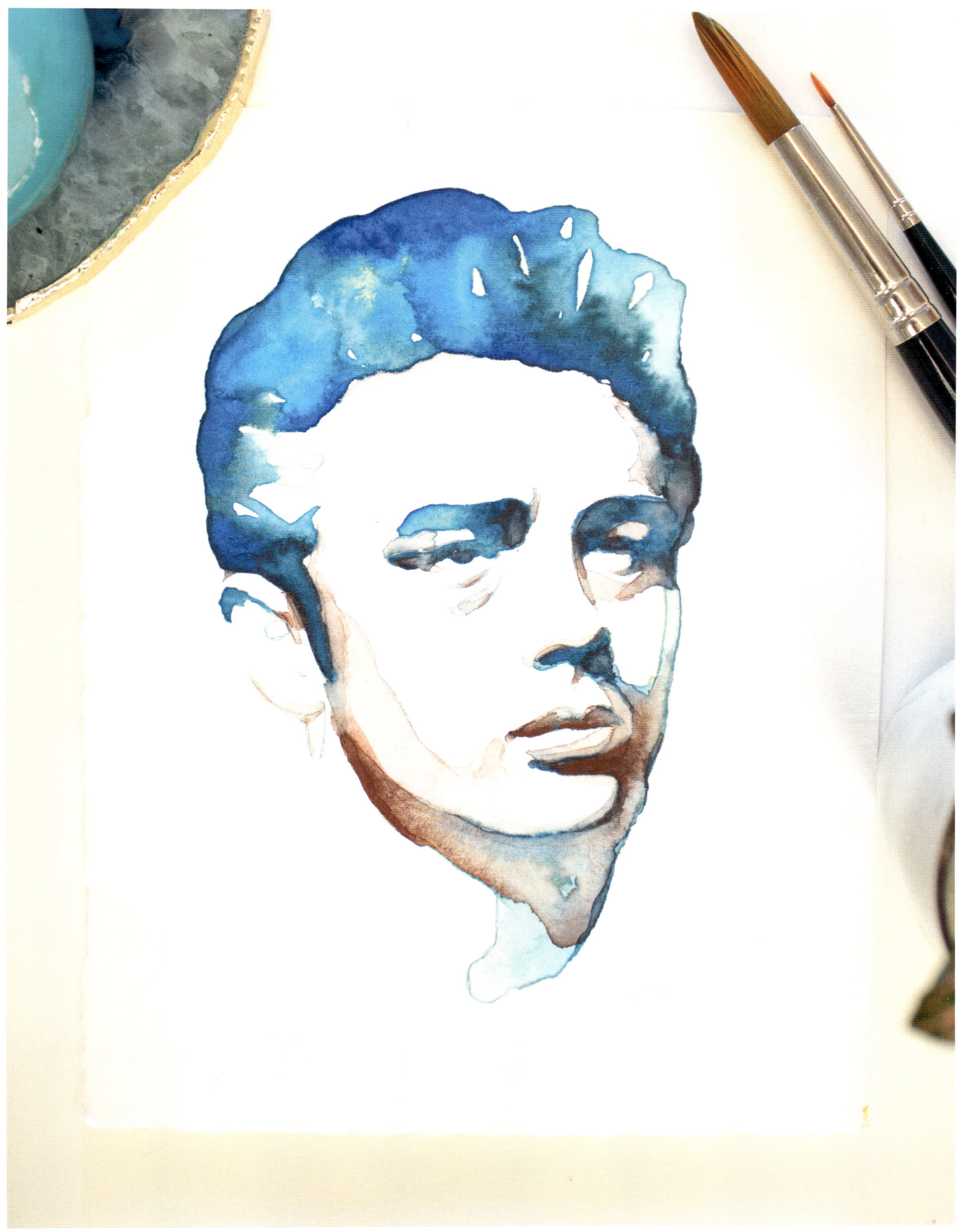

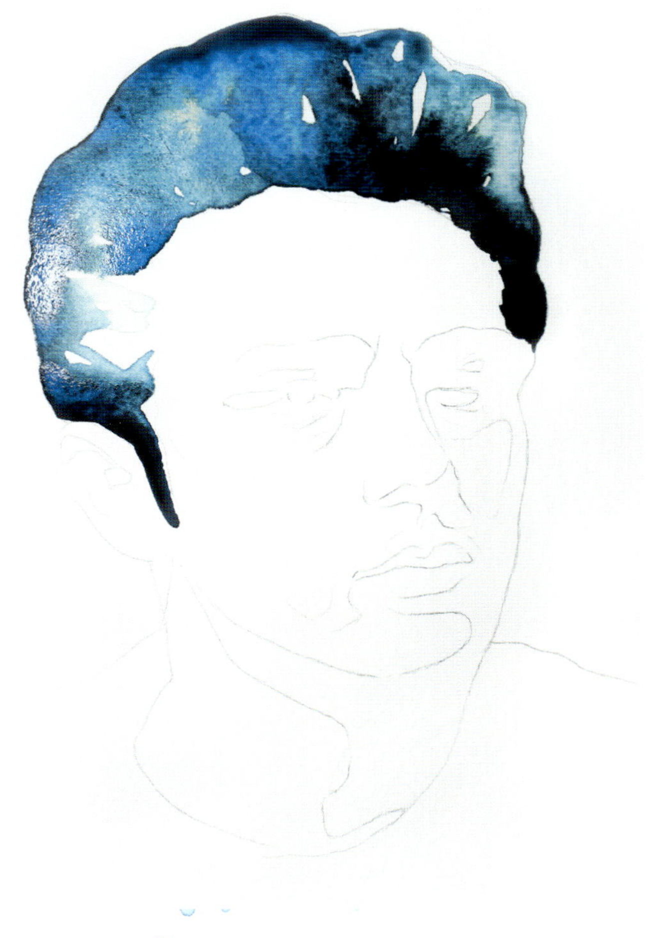

James Dean

*1. Wet-on-wet:* Underpaint the hair first with a glaze consisting of ochre, blue and a little white. Starting at the hairline, paint upward, leaving some teardrop-shaped gaps for some texture.

**Tip:** *You can also map out the gaps in pencil first to better focus on the painting.*

Now you're going to paint with two different shades of blue. Be sure to use more paint, especially on the hairline on the right side, and dab on the outer line as well. Some areas, on the other hand, will not be worked on at all, leaving the bright turquoise to shine through. Take up a lot of blue, and add some perylene green, or even black, with as little water as possible, so that you have a dark, almost undiluted shade. Dab this several times over the ear and on the opposite side, along the hairline. Wait until the color runs, then repeat this step until the areas are looking very bold.

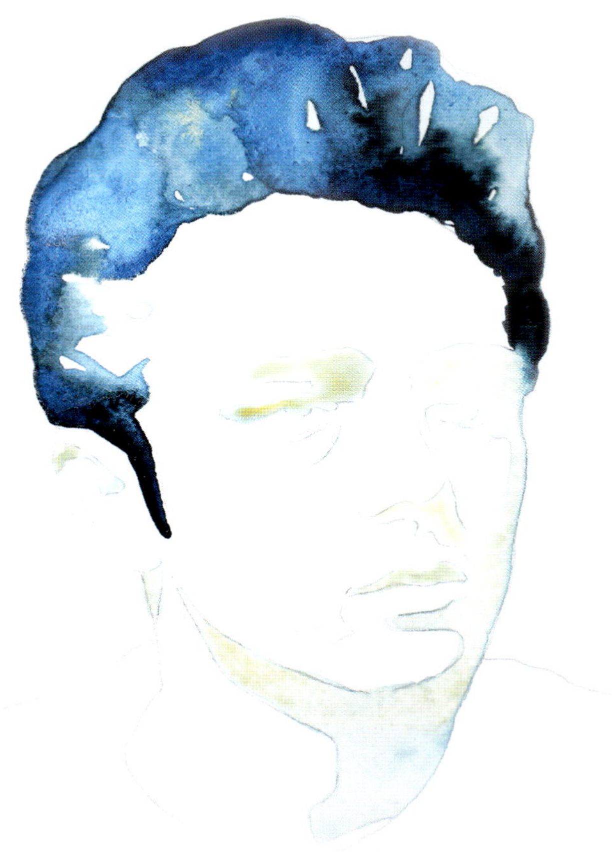

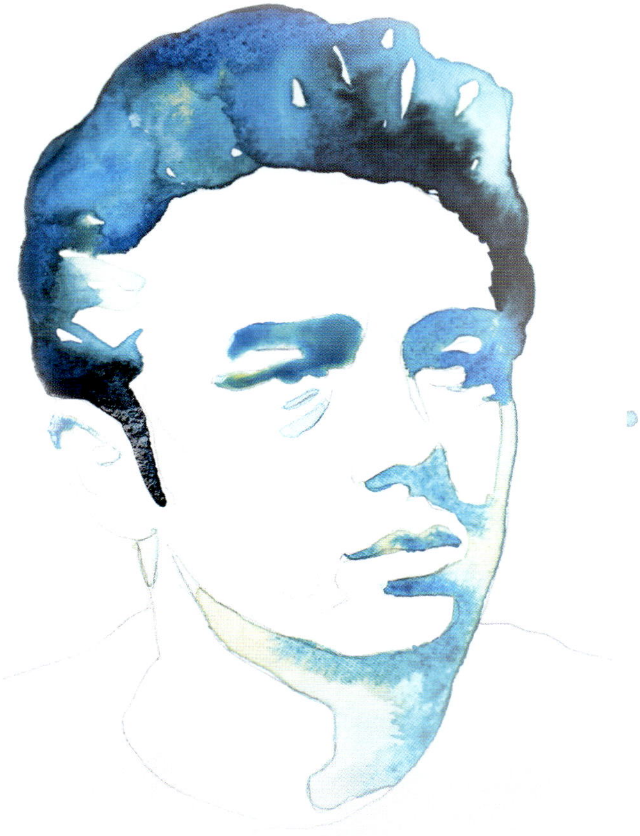

**2.** *Wet-on-wet:* When the hair is sufficiently dry, it's time to start on the facial shadows. Underpaint them with a diluted pale blue. In addition, paint some ochre into the paint layer, and the two colors will blend on the paper into a wonderfully soft turquoise.

**3.** *Wet-on-wet:* Wash out your brush, then start dabbing a little blue on some areas, such as the chin line, eyebrows and nose shadow – not too much, as the underlying layer should still be discernible. The color spreads out by itself, but to better control the flow of color, the drying stage of the paper needs to be right! If you have any doubts, refer to Basic Techniques (see Condition of the Surface).

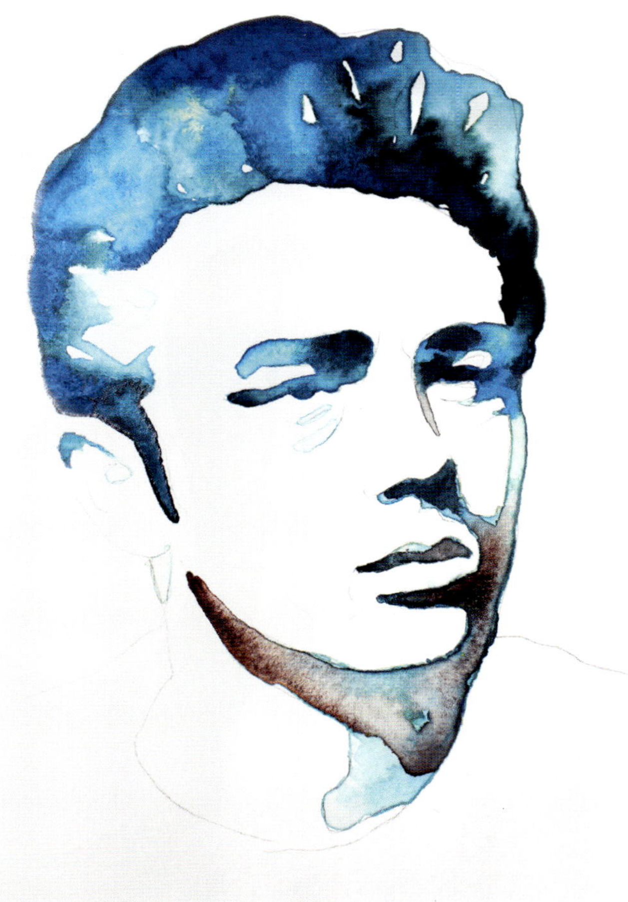

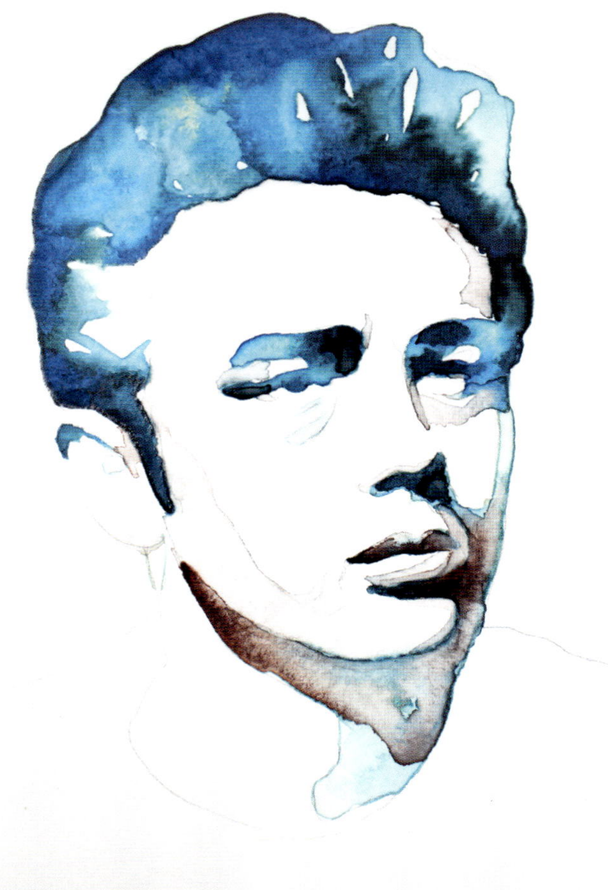

**4. *Wet-on-wet:*** If any parts have already dried, wet them in small steps with a little clear water. Take up the dark blue that you used for the hair with a thin brush, and dab it just lightly on the inner corners of the eyebrows and eyelids. The paint needs to be very strong, so it should contain hardly any water. Moisten the nose shadow as well and go over it with the blue.

This is where it gets exciting: Paint a strong red-brown, thin glaze onto the upper lip so that some of the blue underneath remains visible at the left edge. Wet the lower lip shadow with water, and draw the water layer down to the neck and up towards the eye. The shadow will become darker if you blot in some undiluted dabs of color.

**5. *Glaze:*** Wait until your portrait has dried; this is important because you will now be painting just with glazes. Dilute the red-brown with plenty of water and keep testing it on a piece of scratch paper so that the color is not too dark. Paint spaces which will serve as intermediate shadows on the forehead, eyes, nose, ear and mouth. Paint in the left cheek shadow with a thick brush, too. You can also create more darkness on the eyebrows and nose by using a stronger brown. The chin line and lip shadow are emphasized. Finally, use a narrow brush to add smaller details to the lower eyelids, ear and the crease of the upper lip.

**Tip:** *Add in the shoulder lines if you like.*

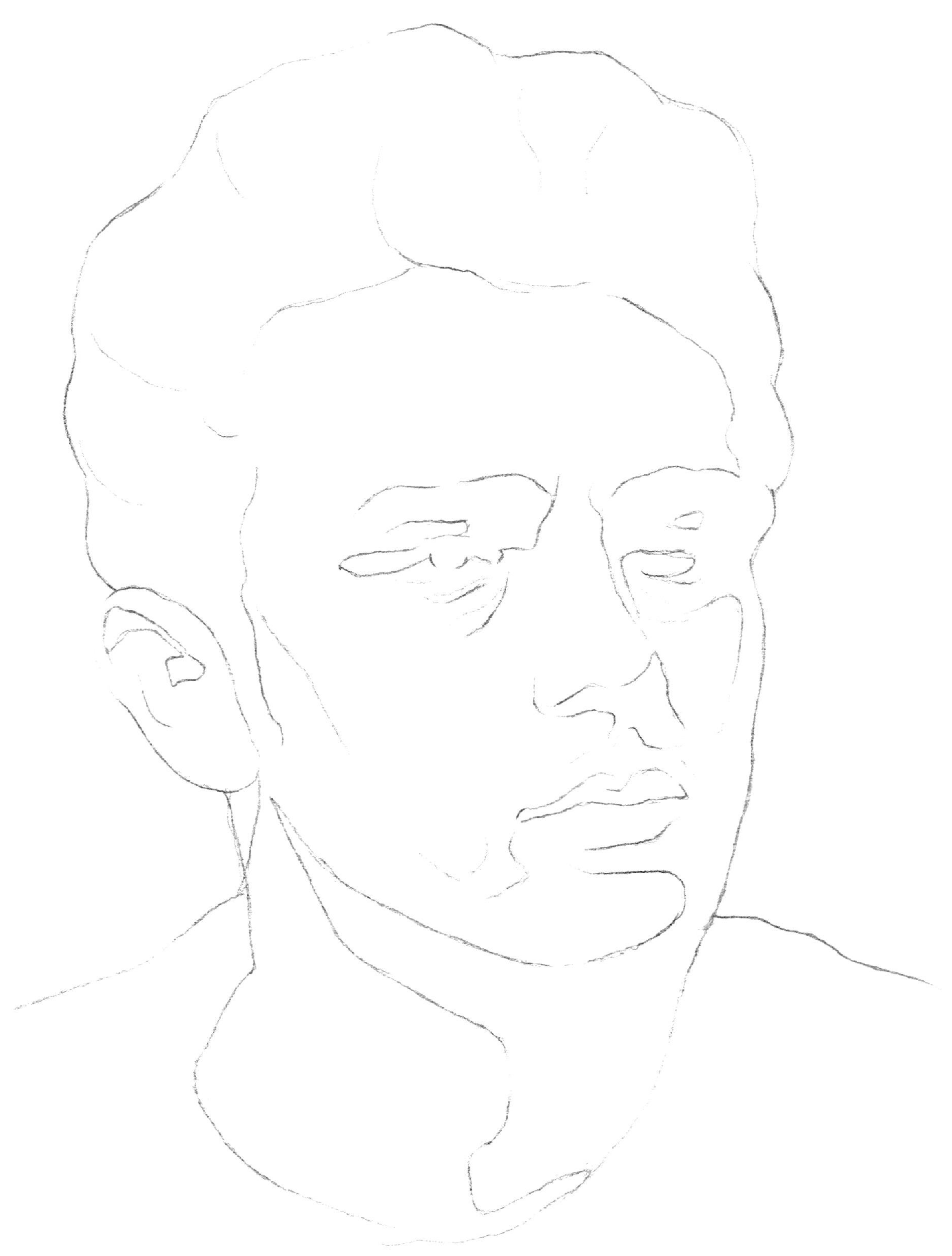

# LANA
## Del Rey

Lana Del Rey's songs always induce a specific feeling that is hard to explain – as if you were in a dream gone by, shrouded in clouds of nostalgia. Melancholy, romance, poetic lyrics and a longing for places and people you don't even know – all of this makes her an extraordinary artist.

**COLOR PALETTE:**

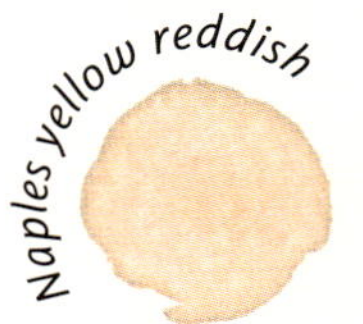
Naples yellow reddish

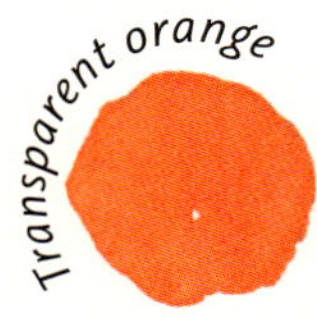
Transparent orange

Madder lake deep

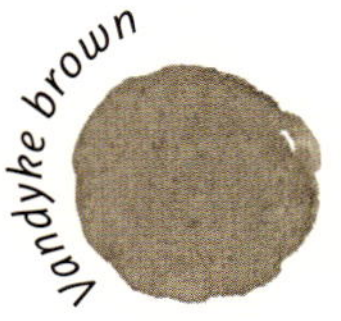
Vandyke brown

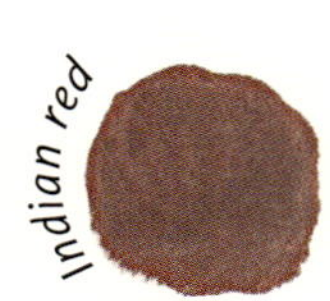
Indian red

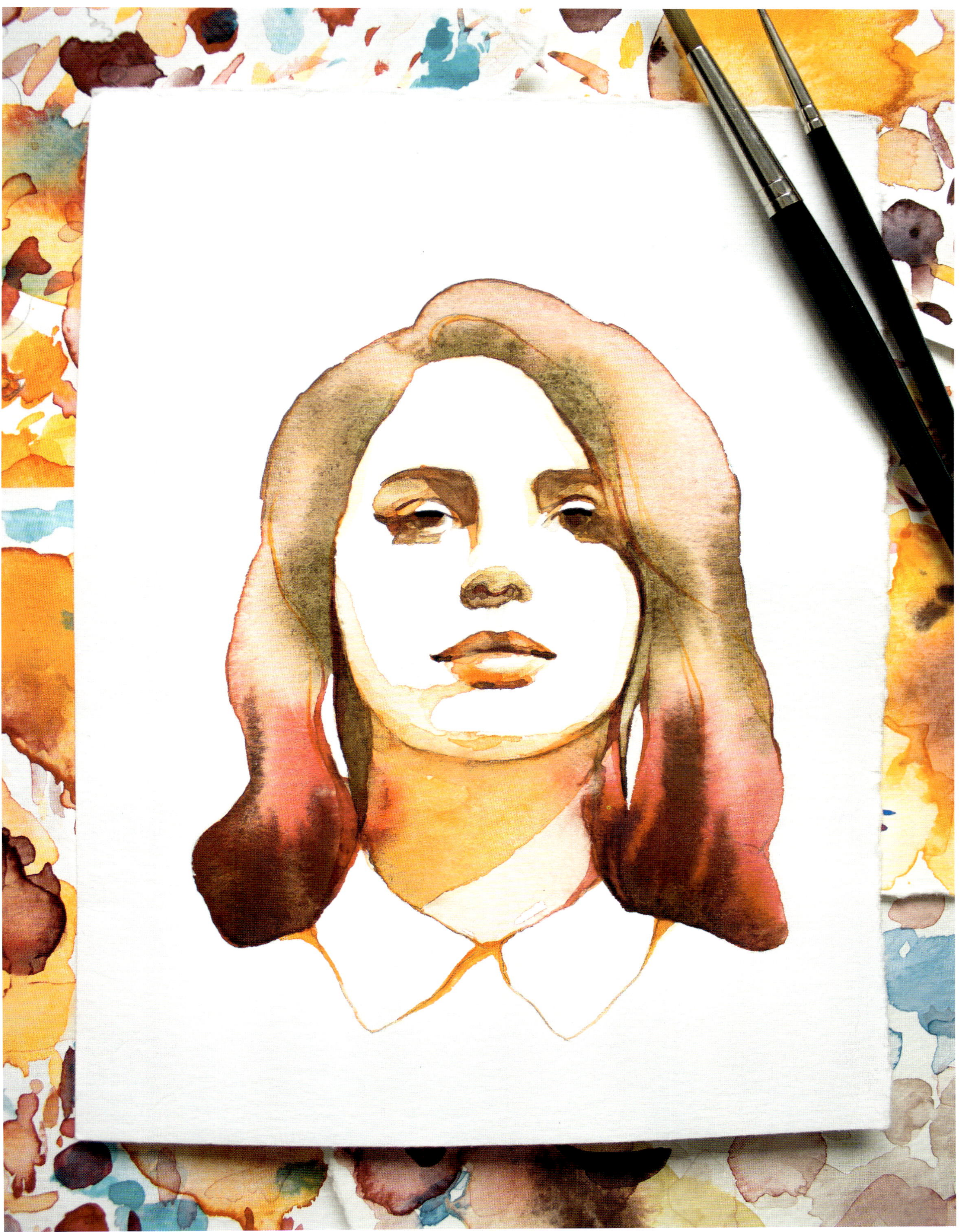

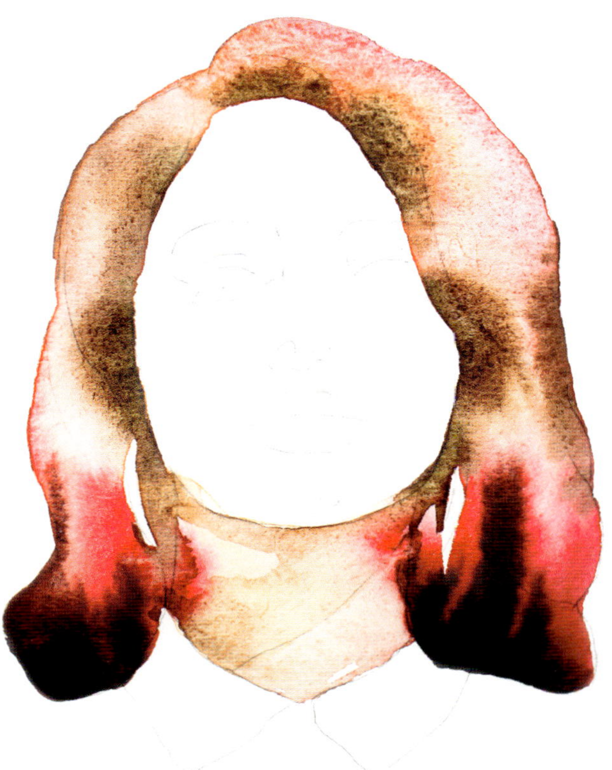

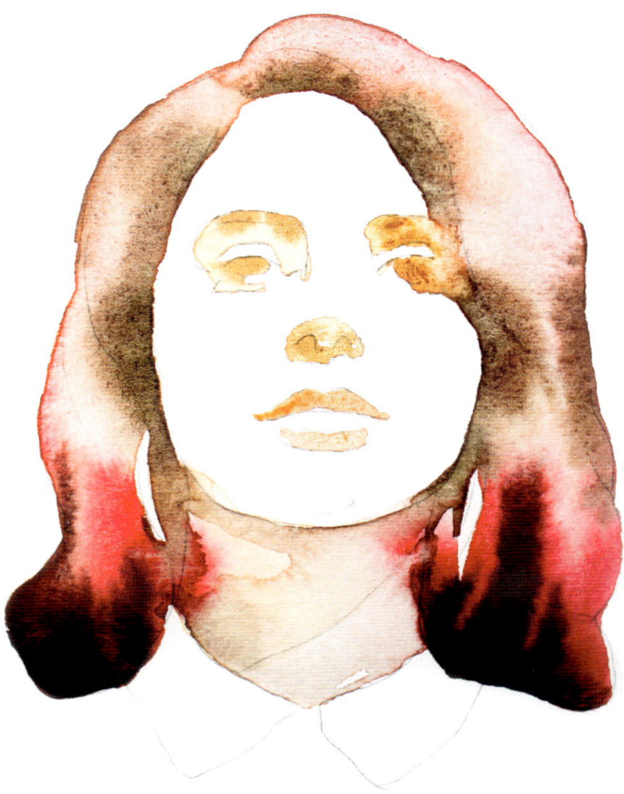

**1.** *Wet-on-wet:* Start by mixing an orange-pink with a lot of water and applying it liberally to the hair and neck, just leaving two narrow areas for the earrings. Now, using a thick brush, pick up lots of pink pigment directly from your tray and apply it, unmixed, to the lower hair area. Repeat this with a very dark, opaque red-brown, and also dab a paler brown on the inner and partly on the outer edges of the hair. You will need to use a lot of pigment for this step, as the hair will not change much afterwards.

**Tip:** *Tilt the sheet away from you so that the paint runs towards the hairline.*

**2.** *Wet-on-wet:* Now underpaint the facial shadows. Use a number of related shades here, as I have in this example by painting the lips in red and the eyes in brown hues. You can create a beautiful wash over the dark hair space bordering the right eye. Note: Be sure to leave white areas around the eyes. Use a fine brush to dab the undiluted orange-brown, wet-on-wet, onto the eyebrows, eyes, nostrils and upper lip.

**Tip:** *If you have made a mistake, you can easily remove the wet paint with a piece of paper towel.*

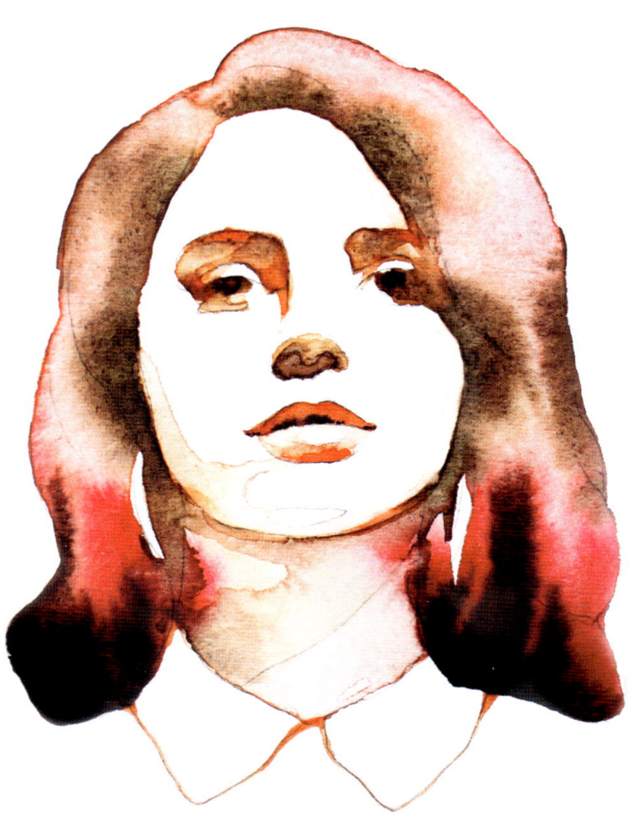

**3. *Wet-on-wet:*** Before you continue, the paint layer should still be a little wet. If not, wet the dried areas again with a little water. Paint the upper lip darker, and emphasize the shadowy areas around the eyes with undiluted paint. Define the mouth line and iris with a fine brush and an opaque shade of brown.

***Glaze:*** When the paint has dried, paint a layer of orange on the inner and outer corners of the eyes. You will notice that from hereon you are just going to be using glazes. Use the same color for the lines of the collar. Emphasize the lower lip with a similar, only more diluted orange, leaving a small oval area white for the light reflection. Using the same color, give the face more definition by adding shadows to the left side of the cheeks and chin. On the right side, create a transition between the edge of the face and the hair in the same manner.

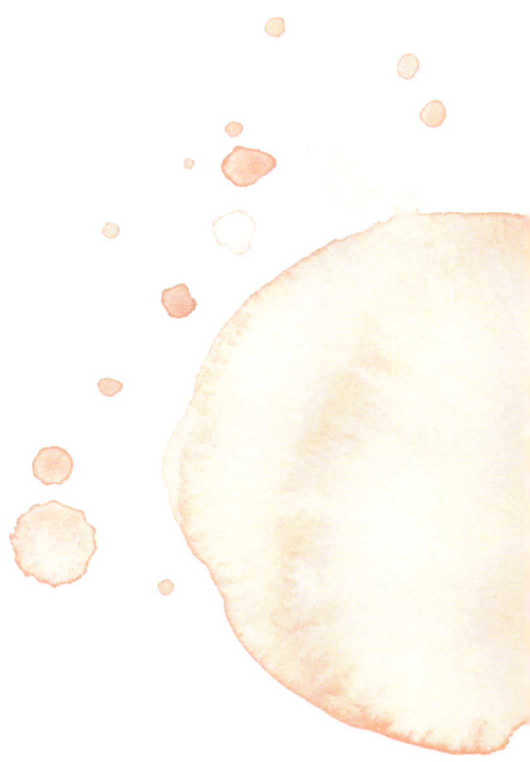

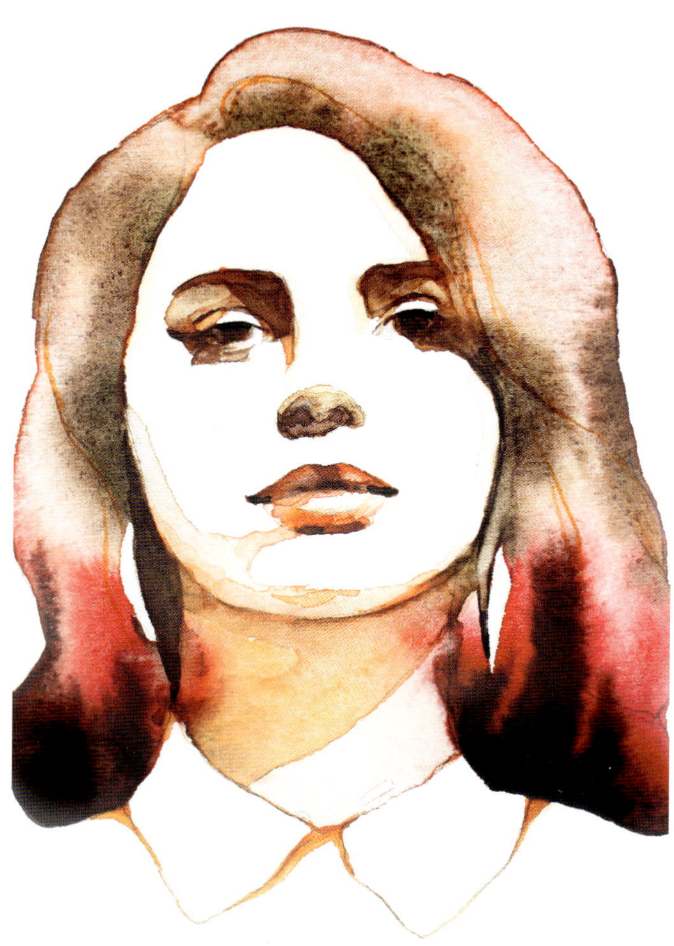

**4. *Glaze:*** Paint a dark brown glaze on the eyebrows, the inner corner of the eyes, the eye crease and the eyelash line, and draw sharp lines along the creases of the eyelids. Darken the shadows on the lower lip and nose in the same way. Finally, blend the eye outlines with orange and warm up the neck shadow. Paint the lines on the shirt partially thicker, and pick up the linear element in the hair by picking out a few strands.

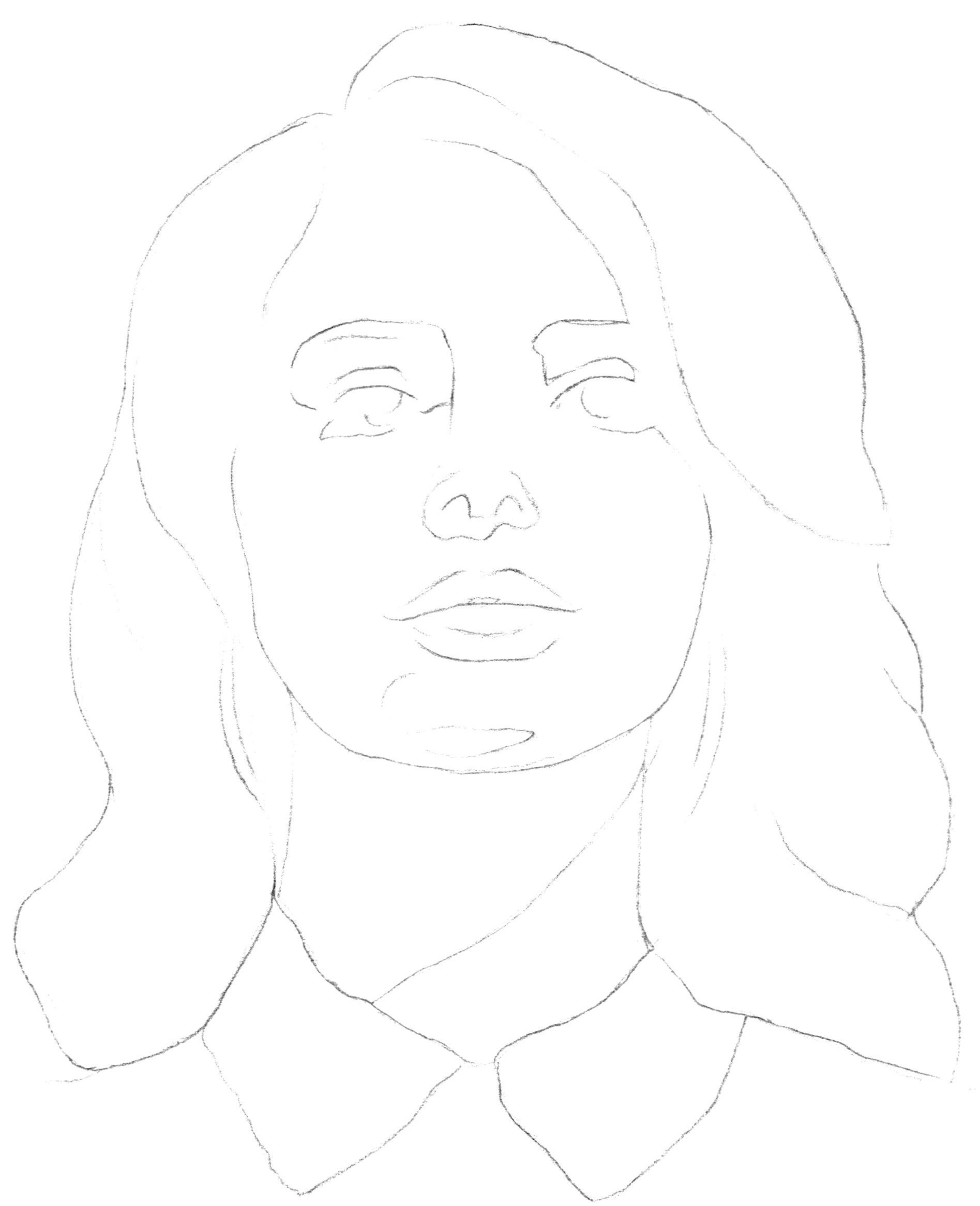

# BOB
# *Dylan*

"Knock, knock, knocking on heaven's door …" – Yes, this song was originally penned by American musician, Bob Dylan, a leading light in the history of music in the 20th century, whose extraordinary talent as a lyricist saw him become the first musician to win the Nobel Prize in Literature in 2016.

The portrait shows him at a younger age. His characteristic curly hair and mischievous look are depicted here through the use of highly contrasting color values.

**COLOR PALETTE:**

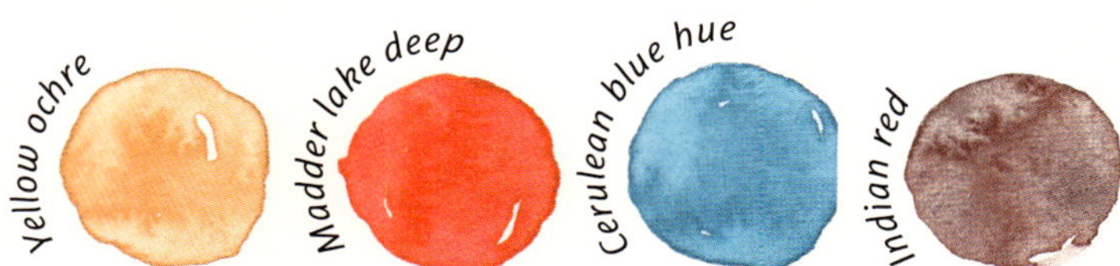

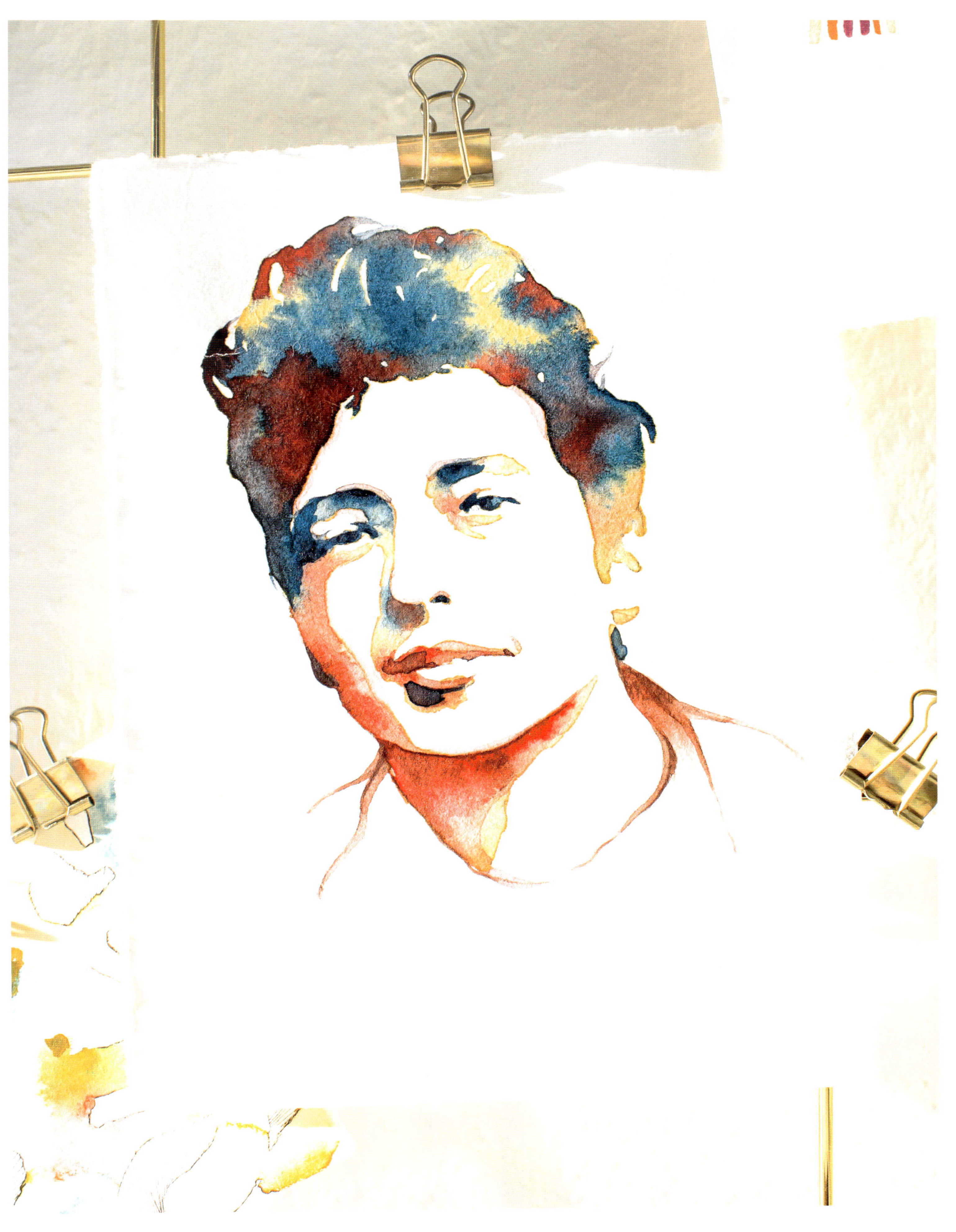

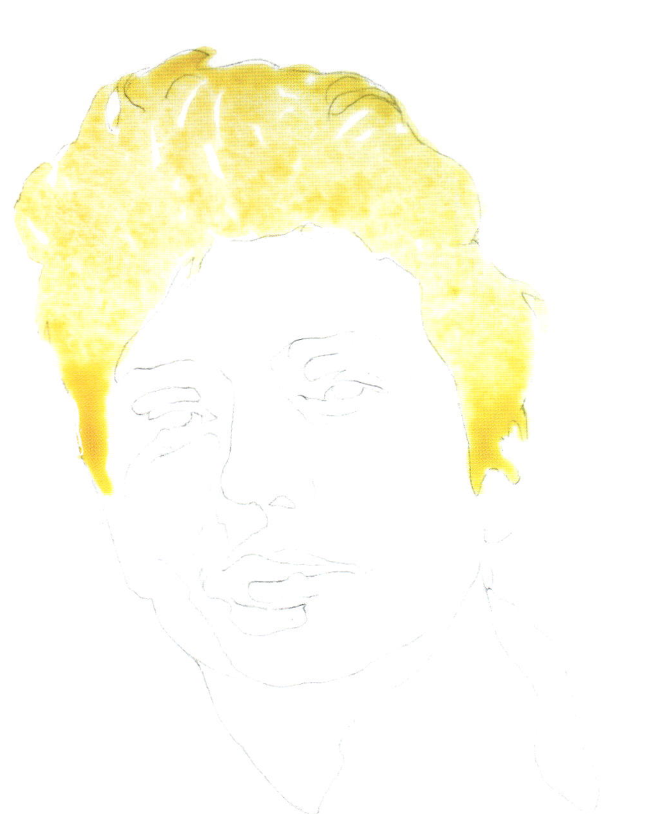

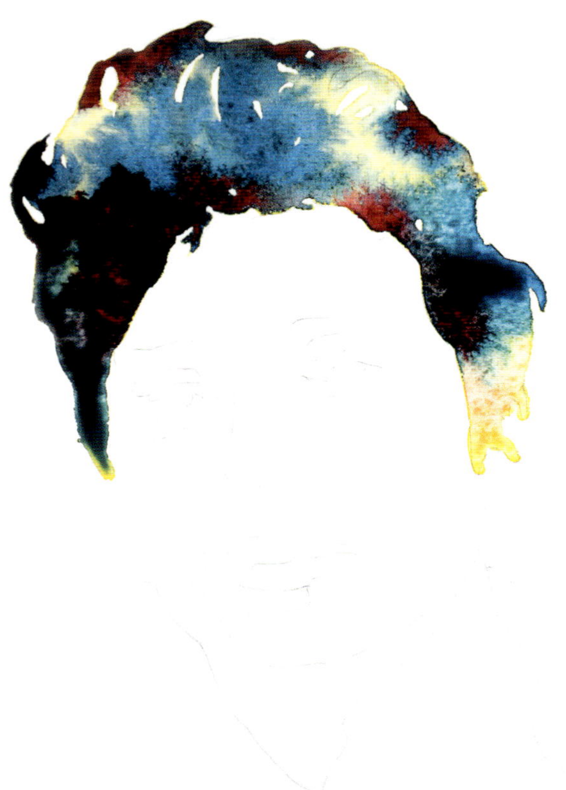

**1. *Wet-on-dry:*** Dilute some ochre with plenty of water and fill in the hair space with it. Make sure to leave several short white areas. This is easier if you paint with momentum, starting from the hairline, following the strands of hair.

**2. *Wet-on-wet:*** When the water has nearly been absorbed into the paper, take up a good amount of blue paint with a thick brush, and dab this into the damp space. The layer of yellow paint underneath will mix with the blue, resulting in nuances of green developing on the paper. Wash out your brush and add another color, red-brown. It is important that darker areas are created especially at the hairline on the left, so straight afterwards, paint in with a vibrant red, which will provide even more saturation. Dab it on the outer edges of the hair as well.

**Tip:** *Play with the stages of wetness. Take your time and dab several times with short breaks in between until you have achieved the desired depth.*

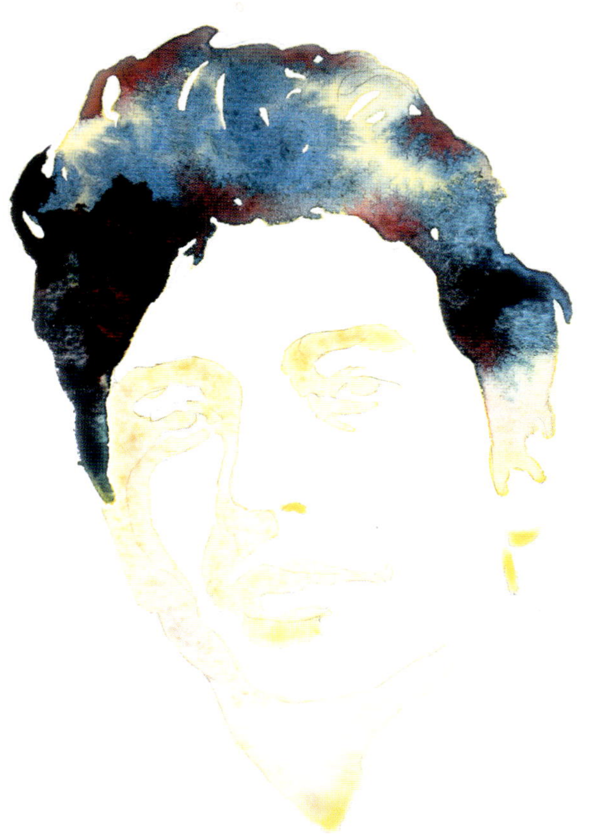

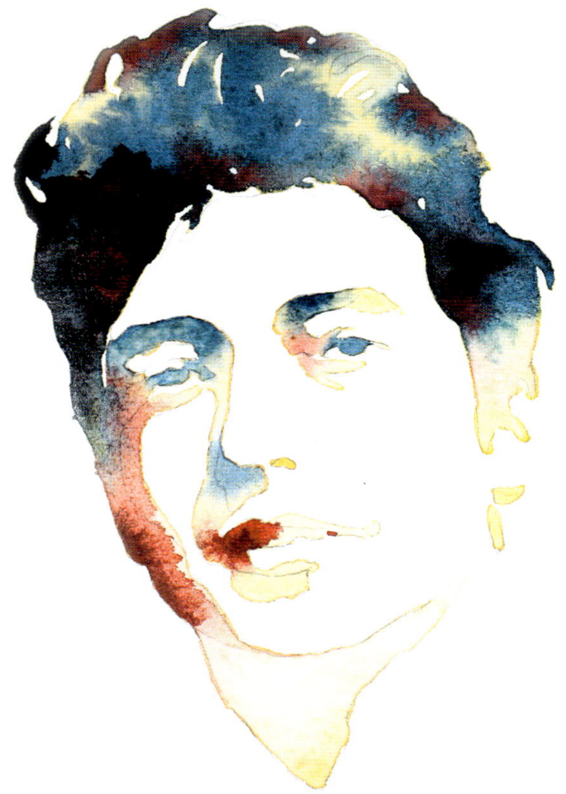

**3.** *Wet-on-dry:* You can continue as soon as the hair space is dry. Now underpaint the facial shadows using a thin brush, and pay attention to the white areas when painting in the eyes. Use the tip of the brush to paint more precisely. Also, paint in the neck. For more color variation, you can add a bit of red.

**Tip:** *If you are painting the facial shadows while the hair is still wet, be sure to leave a narrow border around the hair so that the dark colors do not mix into the light spaces.*

**4.** *Wet-on-wet:* Using your finest brush, dab a little blue onto the eyebrows and eyes, but really just a little, so that you can see how far the color runs. Depending on this, you can dab several times to gradually build up depth. Do the same with a mixture of red-brown and pink, slightly diluted, on the outer corner of the left eye, washed in downwards towards the chin.

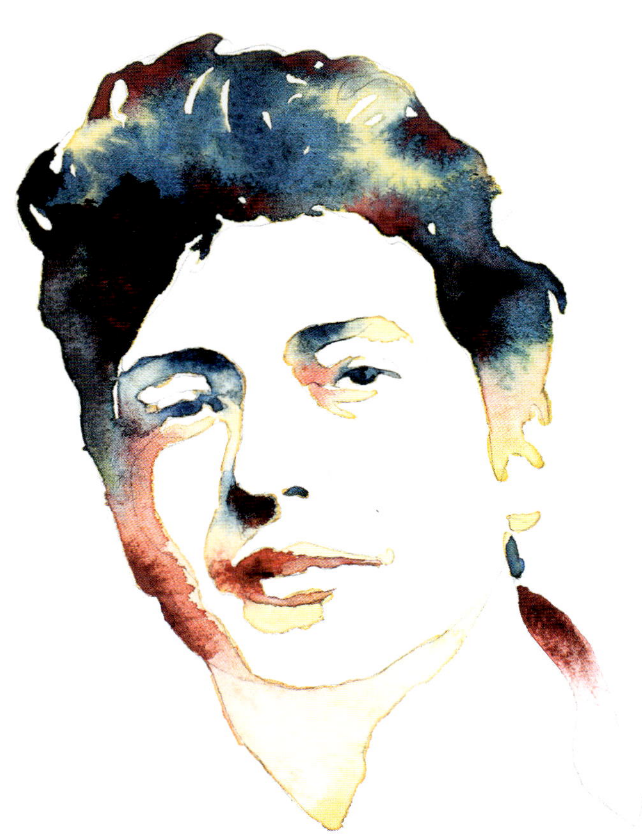

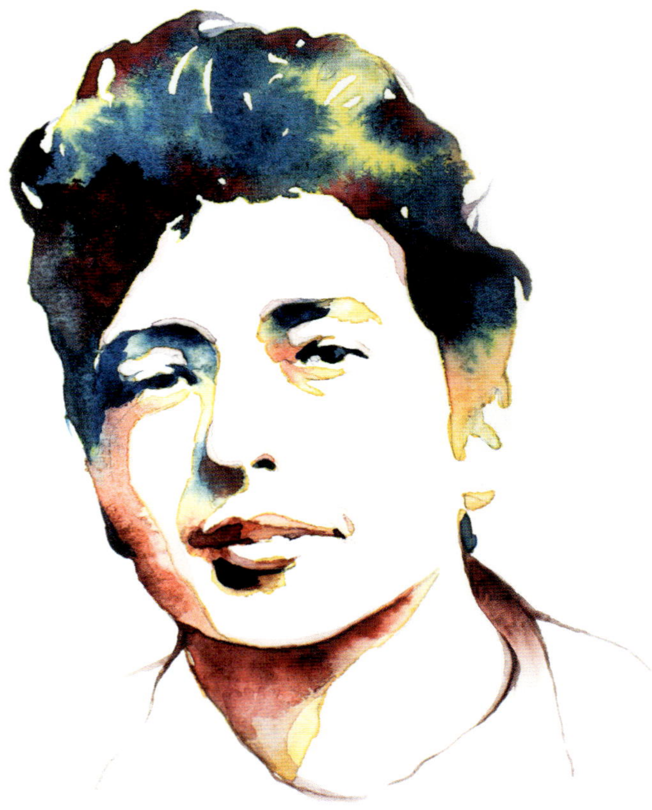

**5. *Wet-on-wet & glaze:*** Since a few areas are sure to have dried, but you are about to continue painting wet-on-wet, you will need a brush with clear water to moisten the dry areas. Use your other brush as normal for painting in the color. So, you'll continue to paint wet-on-wet, but this time you'll moisten the areas of the face in stages instead of painting them all at once. Start with the eyes and paint them in immediately afterwards with a strong pigment. Glaze the lips, and paint part of the upper lip in red-brown. Fill in the shoulder line with a pale pink first, then add a splash of undiluted red.

**6. *Glaze:*** Now we continue with glazing. Delicate, and therefore, well-diluted shades are applied to the corners of the mouth, nose wing, tip of the nose, temple and eyelid as shadows. The eyes are darkened with a stronger blue glaze, which is painted on the dry layer with only a little water, especially the left eye, both outside and inside. Paint into the hair space for a better transition. For the lower lip shadow and the upper lip, use a red-brown. Wet the shadow under the chin with clear water and dab a very strong red pigment on the edge. Finally, highlight the edges of a few hairs with a fine brush and draw some thin hairs coming out of the hairline with the leftover paint residues. Complete the portrait by adding the shoulder lines.

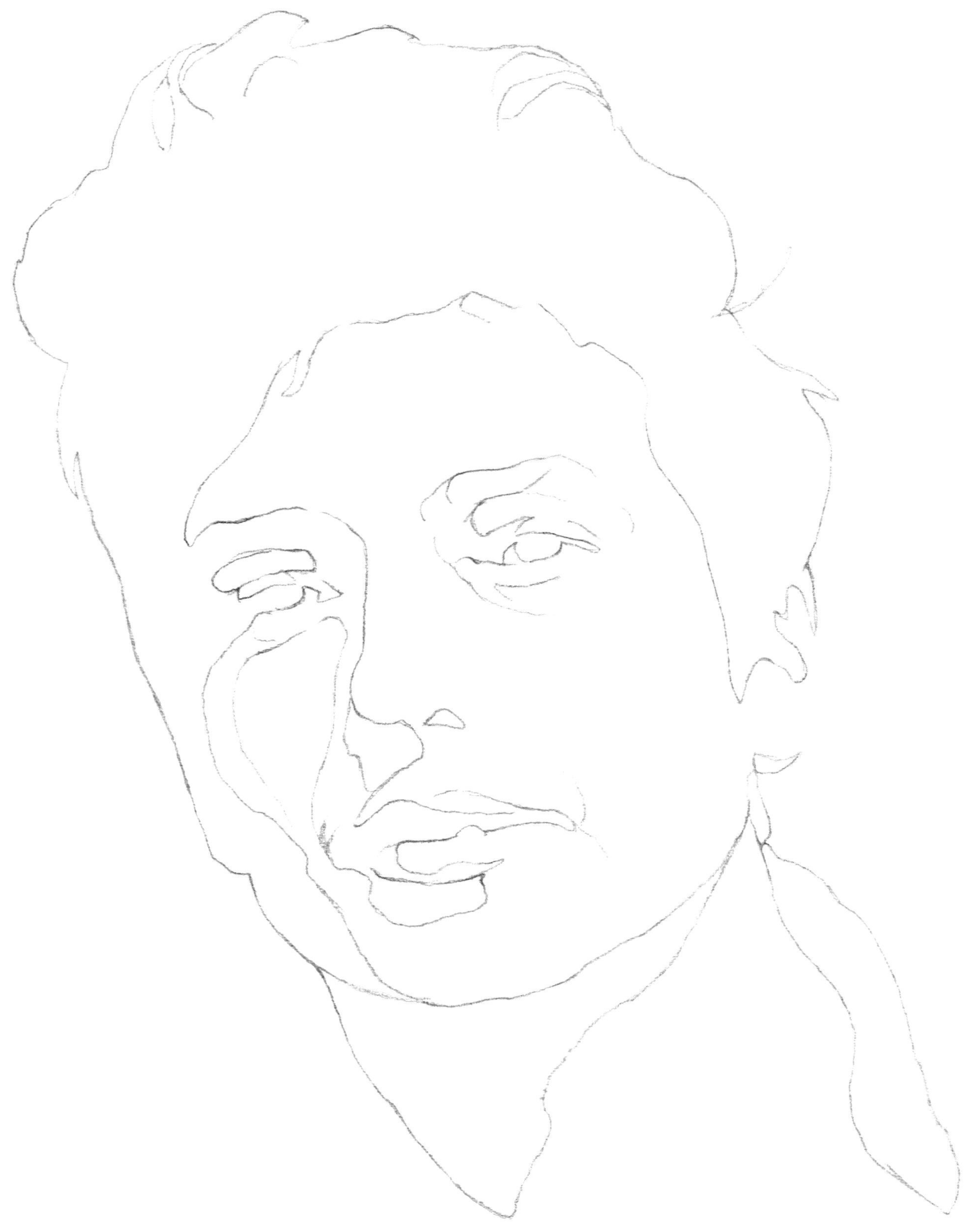

# MICHELLE
## *Obama*

Michelle Obama was not only the first African-American First Lady in the history of the United States, but also a lawyer, author, mother and style icon, someone who encourages young women to believe in themselves from the bottom of their hearts. She has a radiant personality and her smile is simply infectious!

**COLOR PALETTE:**

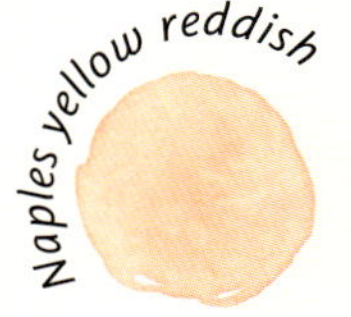

Naples yellow reddish

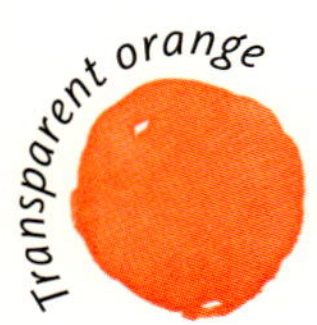

Transparent orange

Madder lake deep

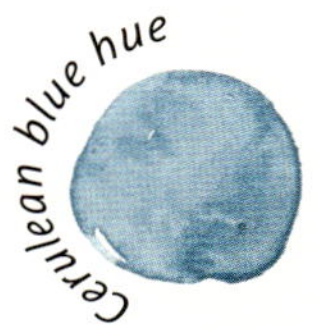

Cerulean blue hue

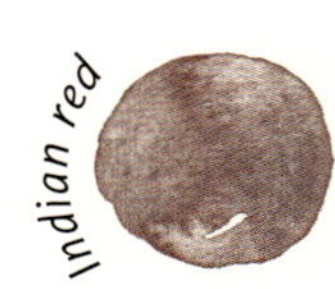

Indian red

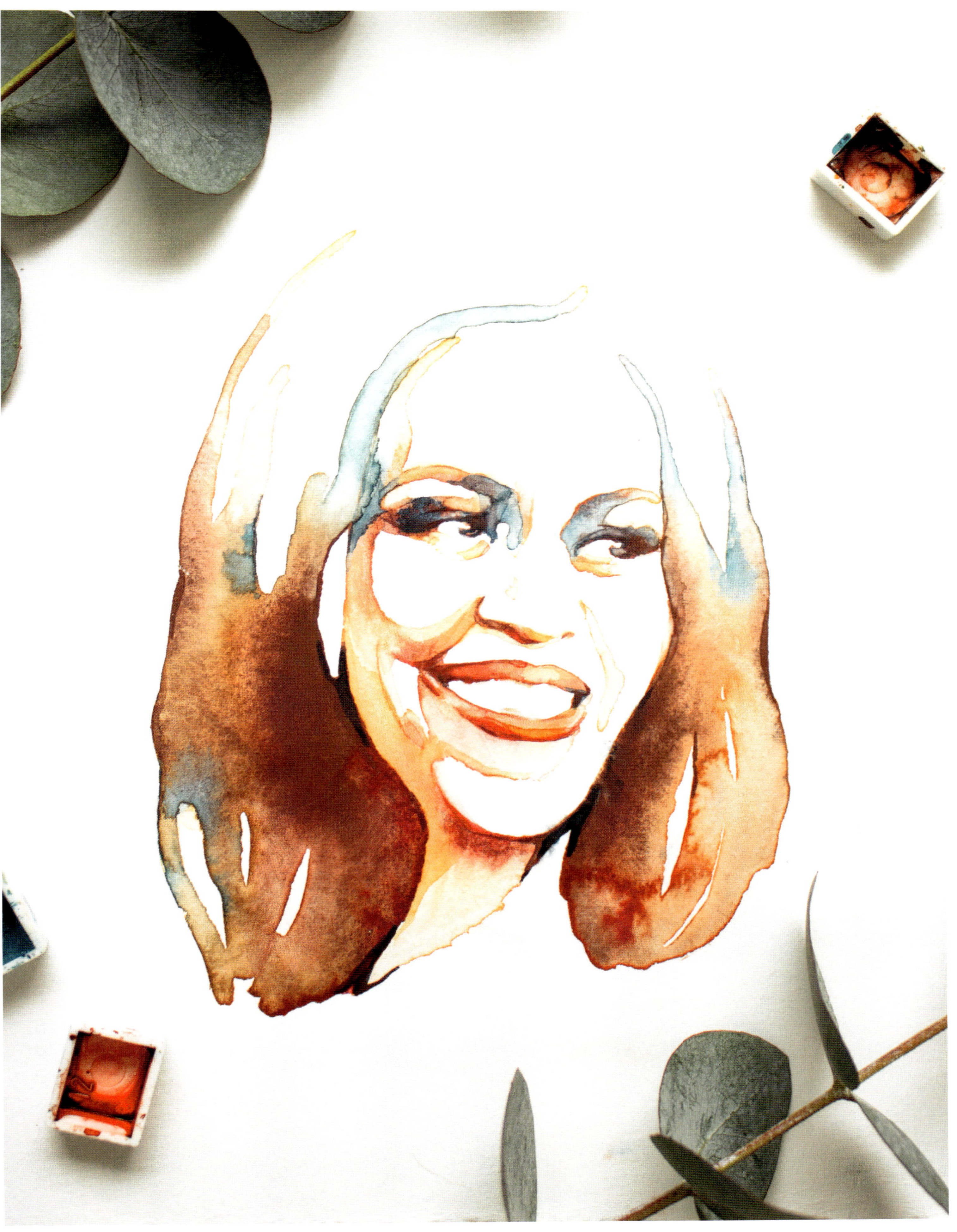

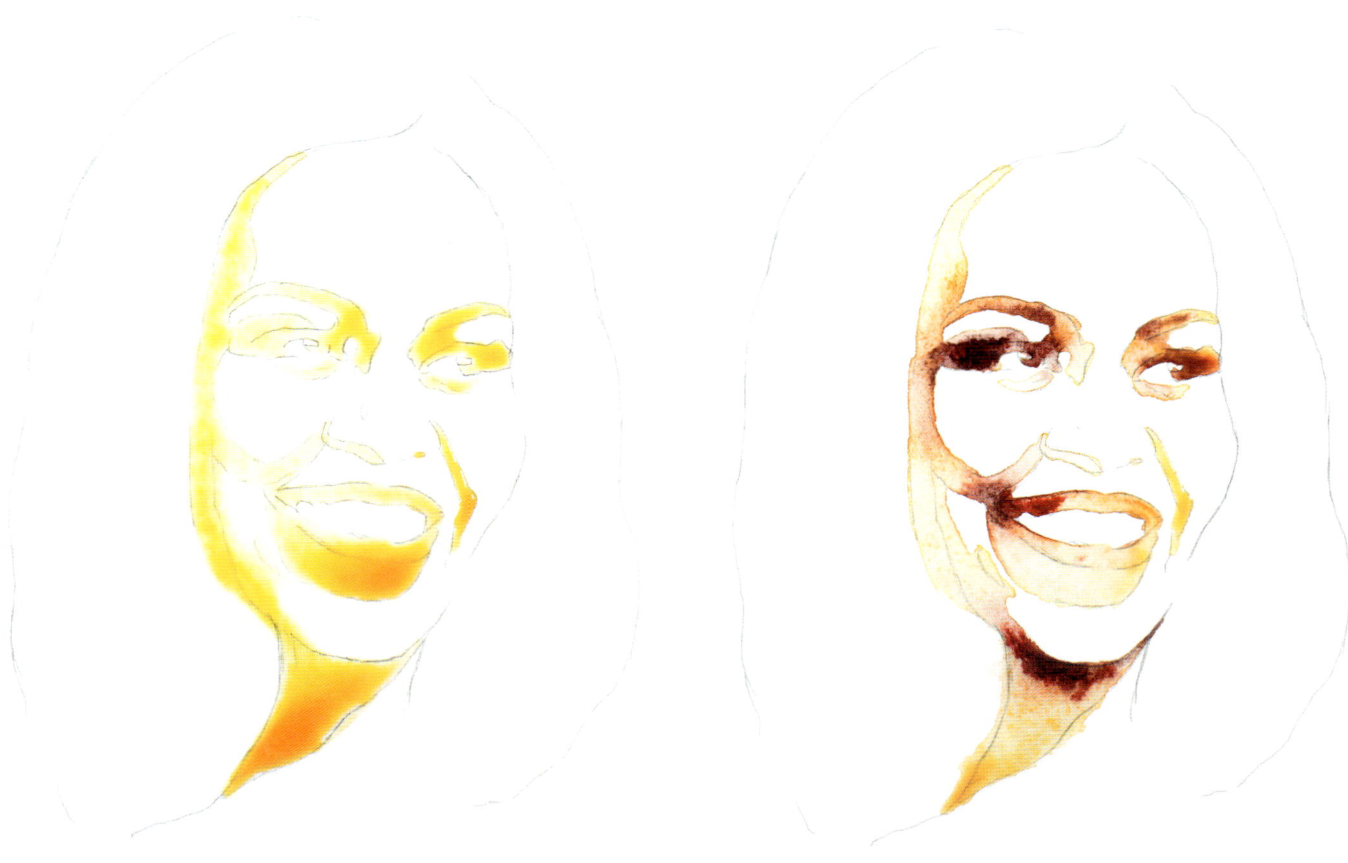

**1. Wet-on-dry:** Mix an orange that you wash quite well-diluted on the face shadows. Make sure to use the tip of your brush, especially for the eyes, to better leave out the light spots and the whites of the eyes. Use a fine brush for the small shadows and switch to a larger one for the cheek shadow.

**Tip:** *If you feel the space is going to start drying, just dab again onto the mixed shade to keep it constantly wet. This is very important because you will continue painting wet-on-wet in the next step.*

**2. Wet-on-wet:** Now switch back to your finest brush, and go with a mixture of red, brown and orange selectively over the eyebrows, the outer corners of the eyes, the corners of the mouth and the chin. Use little water – your paints should be applied almost undiluted, since the background is still wet.

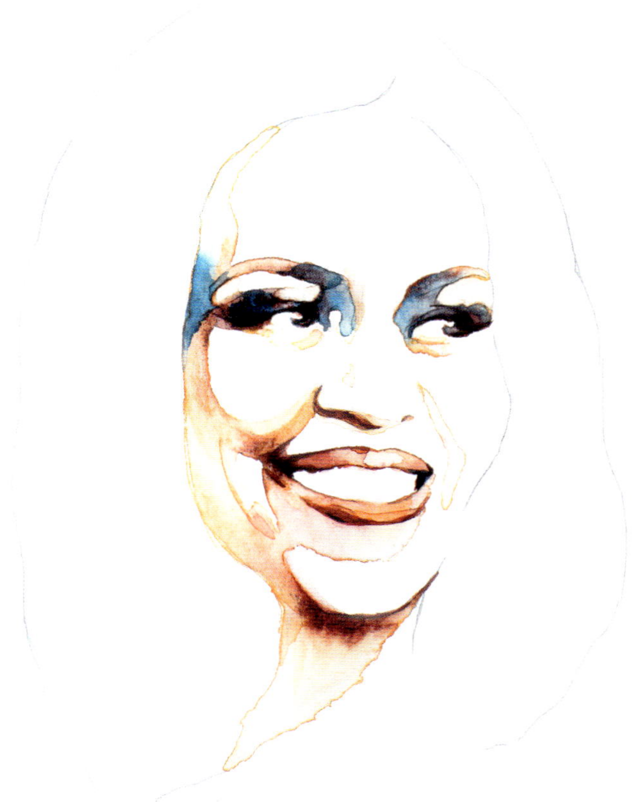

**3. *Wet-on-wet & glaze:*** Now continue painting with blue, partly glazing and partly wet-on-wet. You can clearly see that the temple and the outer corners of the eyes have been painted wet-on-wet. Look at which areas are still damp and go in there with a bold blue. Wash your brush out, then darken the lips with a glaze of orange and red. Also, emphasize the lower eyelid creases and shadows on the lower lip and nose with a thin layer.

To make your portrait look softer and more detailed, you will need a very thin brush. Mix a pale transitional shade for the finer shadows and apply it under the eyebrows, above the eyelids, on the frown lines, the tip and wings of the nose, and to the entire left shadow of the face. Also, hint at the gums with just a few brushstrokes.

**Tip:** *Be careful with teeth and whites of the eyes! Less is definitely more here. It helps here to wipe your brush on a piece of scratch paper and to paint with only the residues of the paint.*

Now you can take care of the required sharpness and darkness. Again, choose a thin brush for this. Start with the eyes, and with the tip of the brush, paint a rich blue on the eye wrinkles and eyebrows. Draw clear lines. The iris in particular should look very dark, as this draws attention to the eyes. Use a similar approach for the mouth and nose, but using strong shades of red and brown. Both the corners of the mouth and the edge of the lower lip should stand out prominently.

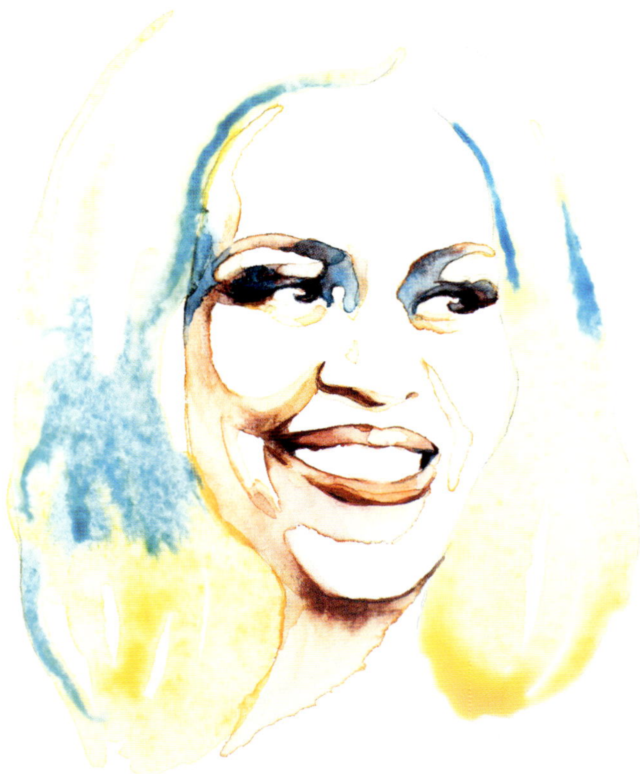

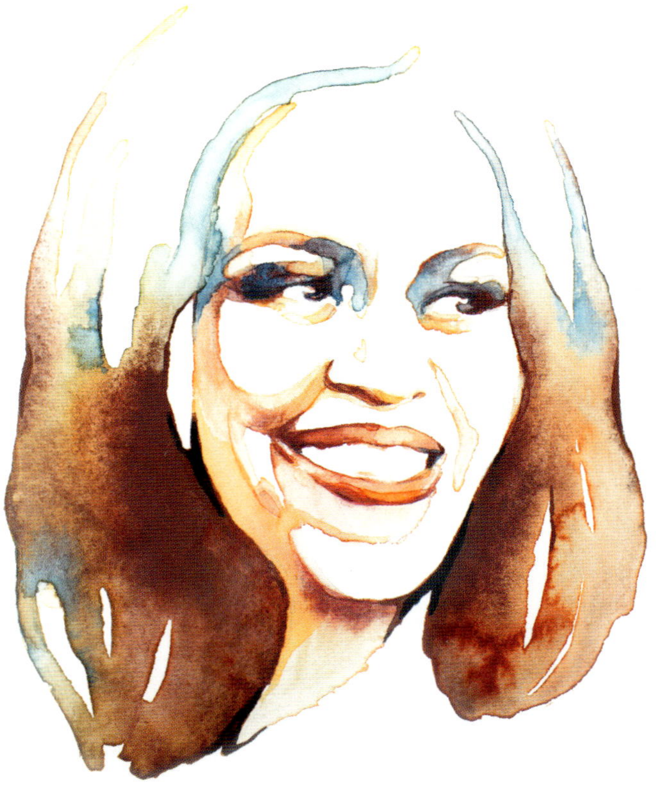

**4. Wet-on-wet:** Now mix a pale orange with a lot of water, and then apply a generous wash to the hair. Start with the lines at the top, and build up the color layer towards the bottom. Leave a few narrow gaps for the texture of the hair. Then dab a bold blue into selected areas.

**Tip:** *Alternatively, paint in the entire hair space.*

**5. Wet-on-wet & glaze:** Repeat the previous step with a lush brown and red. In the areas around the face, use pure, undiluted pigment to accentuate the face through a strong light-dark contrast. For more liveliness and warmth, at the very end, paint a thin orange glaze wash onto the chin, cheeks and mouth.

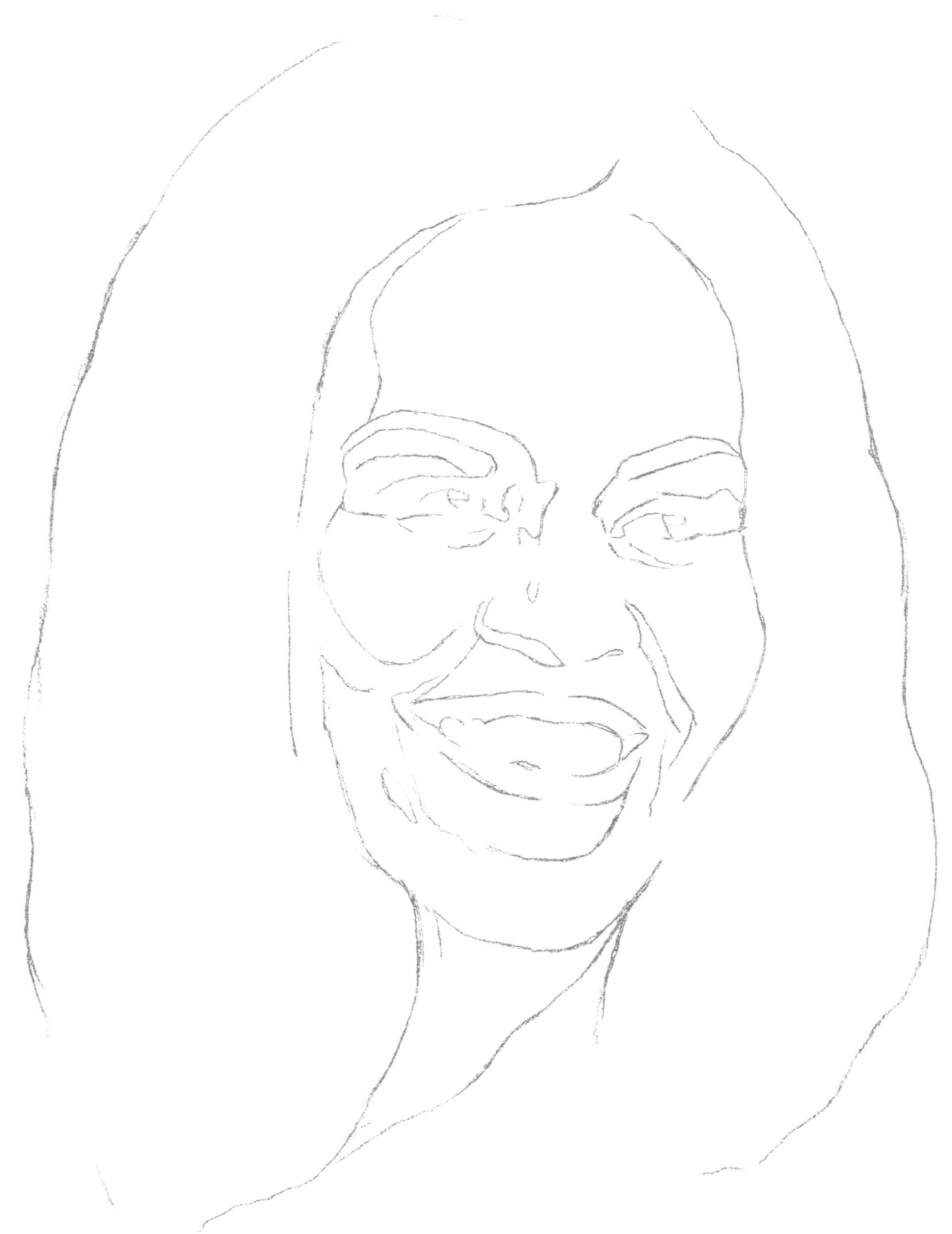

# ALBERT
## *Einstein*

Albert Einstein is known worldwide as one of the most significant scientists of the 20th century. In his work on the theory of relativity, he published the well-known formula $E=mc^2$ in 1905. His unmistakable charisma, perseverance and curiosity eventually made him an intellectual icon of the modern era.

Einstein's eyes have a warm and gentle expression. However, by contrast, they are painted here in a deep blue, and although the rest of the portrait is also composed of predominantly cool shades, a little warmth still shines through in some places in the form of a rich yellow.

## COLOR PALETTE:

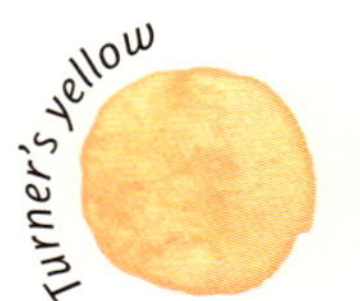
Turner's yellow

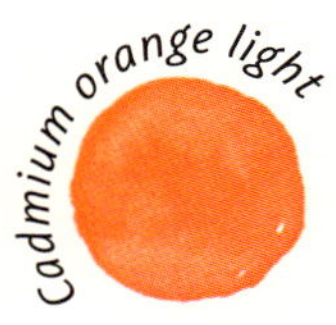
Cadmium orange light

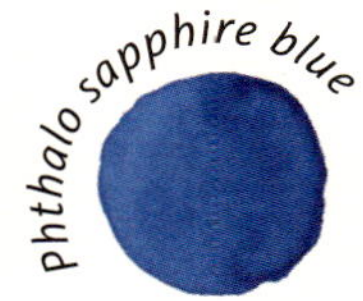
Phthalo sapphire blue

Indigo

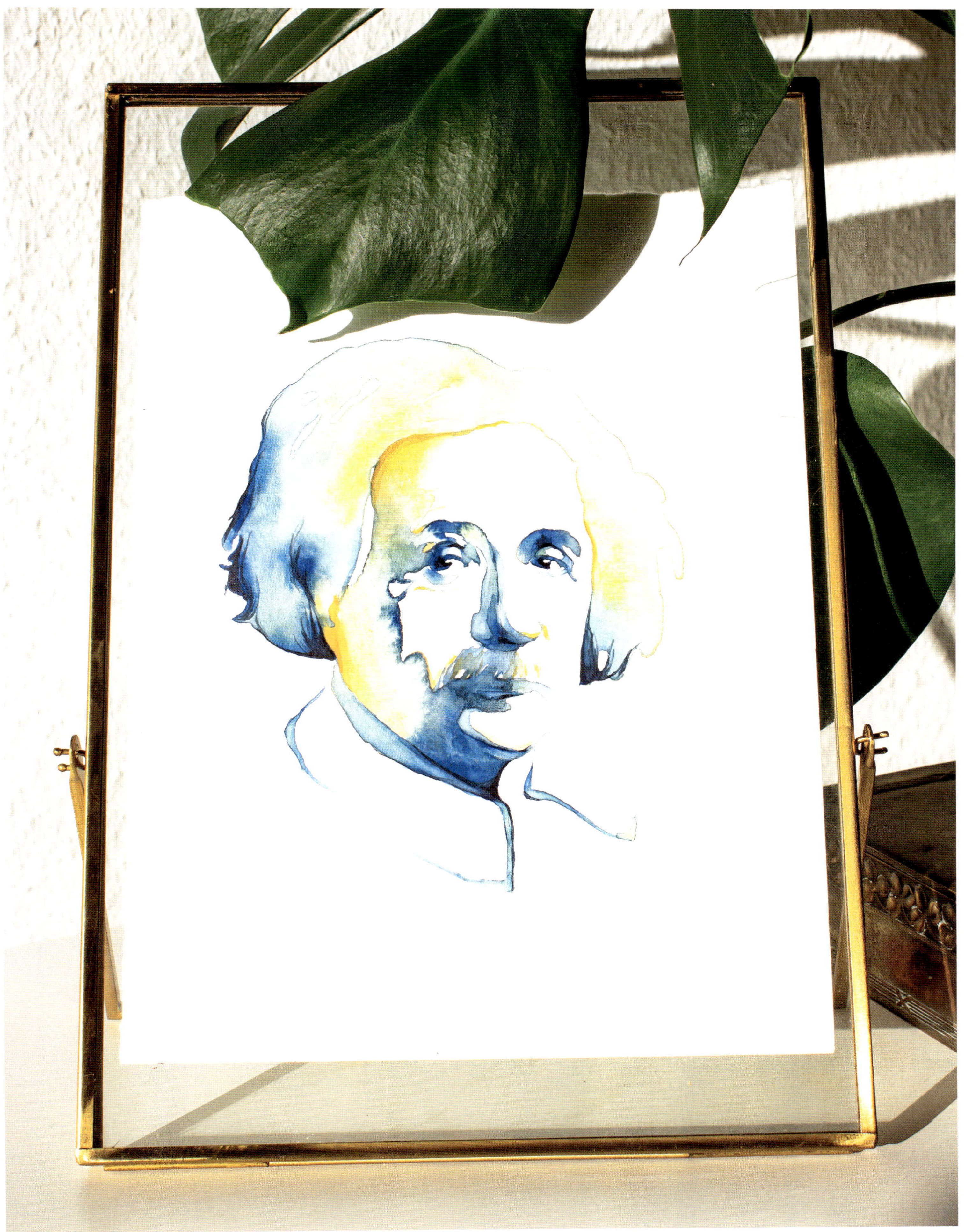

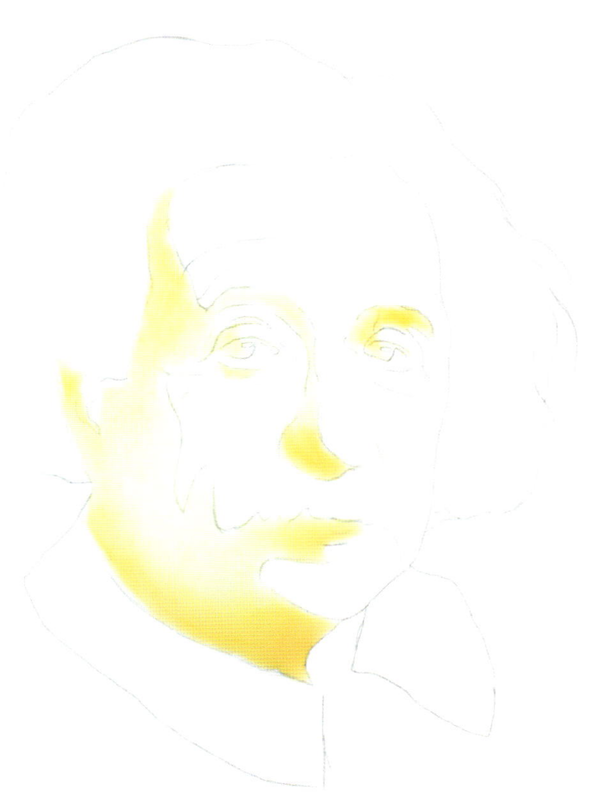

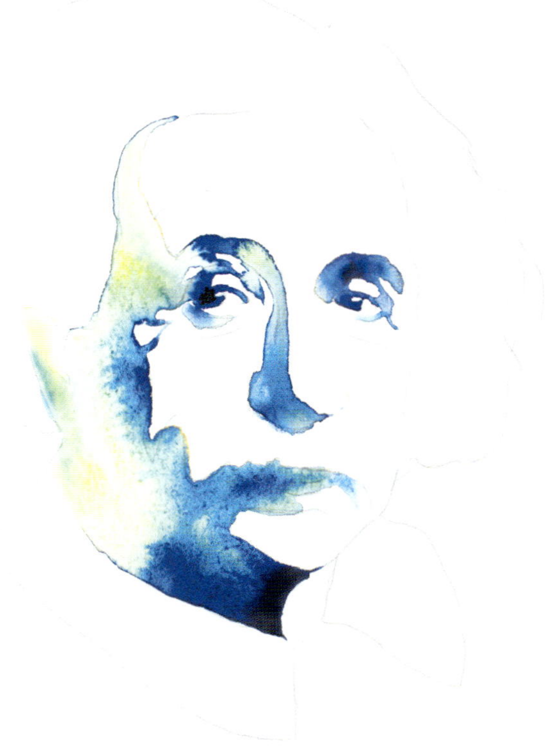

**1.** *Wet-on-dry:* Start with the facial shadows, which you paint in swiftly using a well-diluted yellow. For the eye area, just use the tip of your brush to better leave out the light reflections and to make it easier to paint along the eyelid crease.

**2.** *Wet-on-wet:* Take a strong blue, and paint in the yellow space with it. Dab it on only briefly at first and then apply a wash into areas that need to shine completely in blue. However, be careful not to move the pigment back and forth too much, because the yellow should still show through in some places. Switch to a narrower brush for the eyes and use an almost undiluted pigment for the iris so that it acquires expression. The neck can also be accentuated, nice and bold.

**Tip:** *Try to regard the upper and lower lip as one space, and paint just the shadow of the lower lip a little darker.*

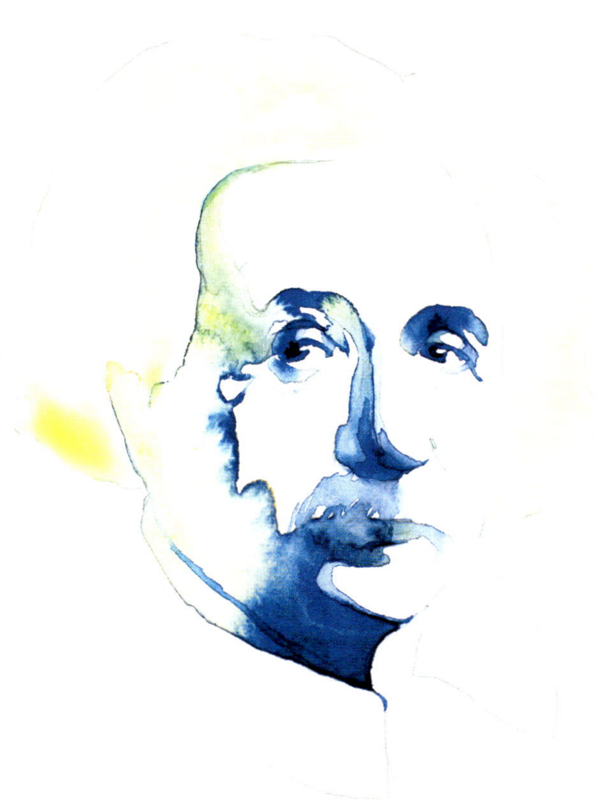

**3.** *Glaze & wet-on-dry:* Once dry, add a few softer shadows in a pale blue glaze to the upper and lower eyelids. Don't forget also the bridge of the nose, chin and forehead. Now connect the mouth and nose area with the mustache. Be sure to leave a few gaps between the whiskers here, and then paint in the eyelid creases and nose shadows with a bold blue for more sharpness. Also, draw a thin jawline for more definition.

Now casually and swiftly paint the hair area in with a well-diluted yellow, in a similar way to the first step, again leaving a few gaps here and there.

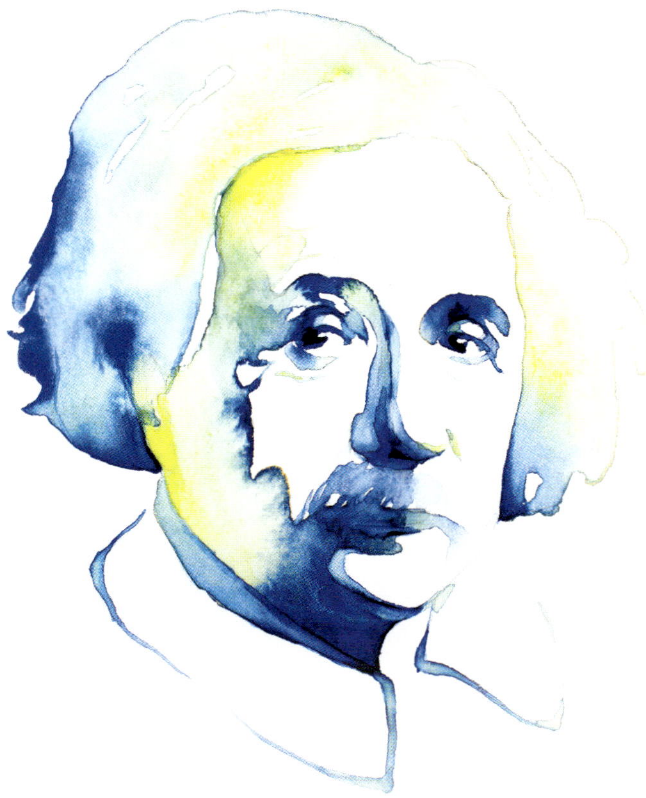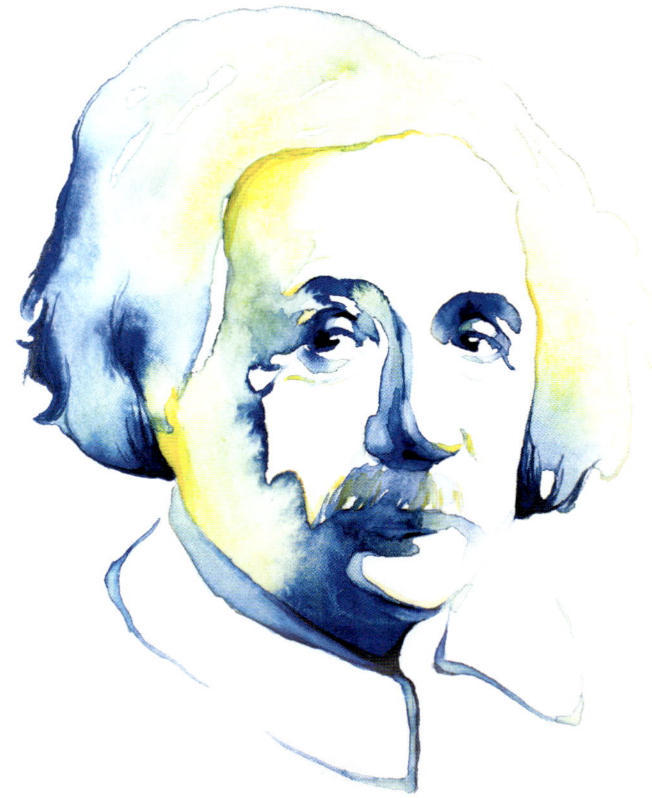

**4. Wet-on-wet:** Take some blue again and apply it to the bottom of the outer and inner edges of the hair. Tilt your page away from you so the color runs more easily and conjures a soft gradient. The upper part of the hair space should remain light so that the attention is entirely on Einstein's gaze, so apply a little more of the yellow paint – especially where the hair and forehead shadow meet. When you're happy with the coloring, complete the neck, and hint at the collar with a loose brushstroke.

**Tip:** *You can also paint in the collar, or paint the lines in other colors.*

**5. Glaze:** You can achieve more luminosity in the face with a yellow-orange glaze on the tip of the nose, forehead, mustache and a few of the wrinkles. If you want even more light-dark contrast and hair texture, you can add some final highlights to the neck, edges of the hair and eyes with a bold indigo.

**Tip:** *For the strands of hair, start with a dark spot and from there, draw a few lines upwards with very little pressure. Really try to use only the tip of the brush.*

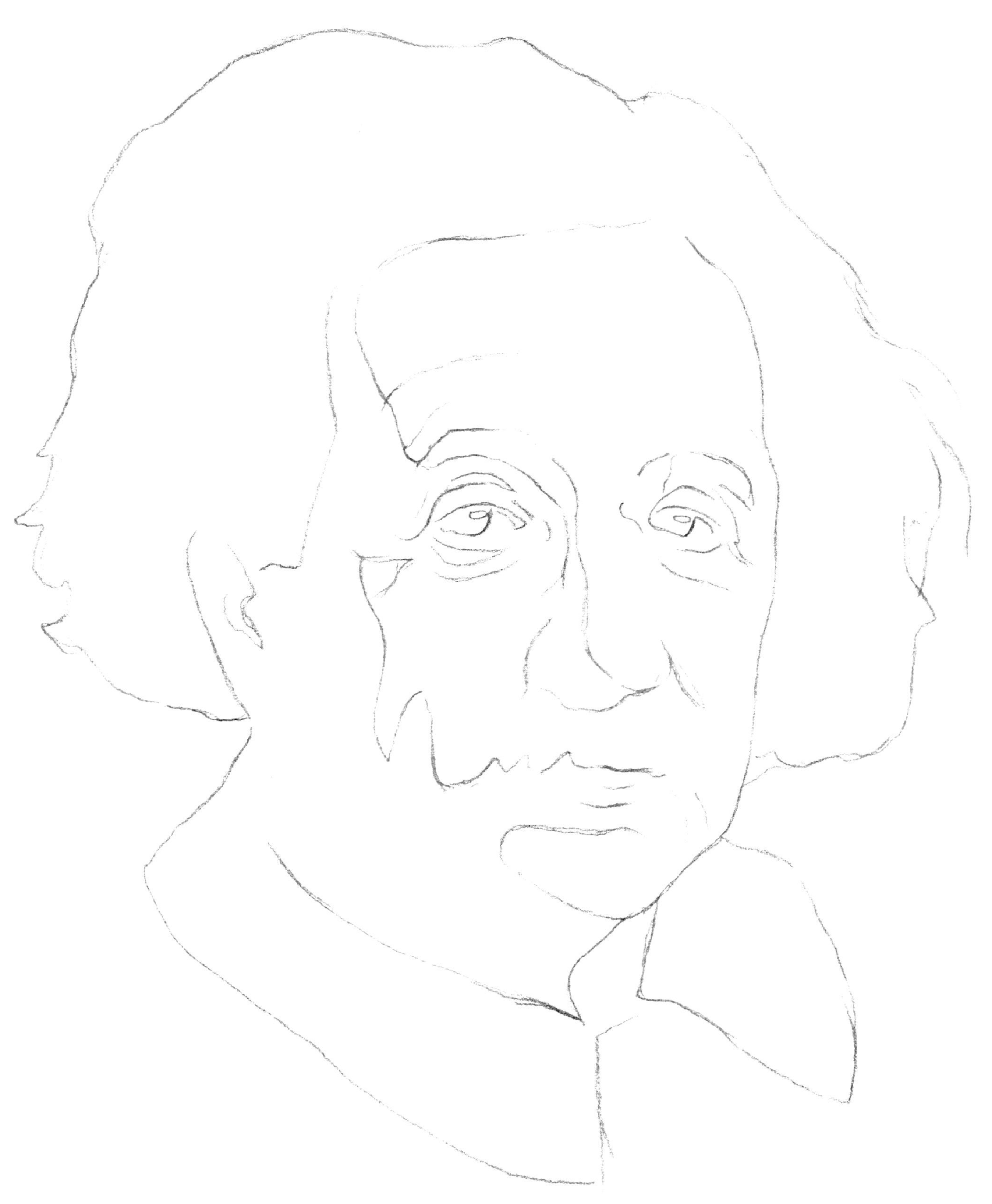

# MARILYN
## Monroe

From an unhappy childhood and a very humble background, Norma Jeane Baker worked her way up to become probably the most famous actor of all time, the iconic Marilyn Monroe. In addition to her film performances, she has also had an enormous impact on art and music and still inspires us today with her manner.

Here, her fine face is painted in detail. Standing in contrast to this is her characteristically wavy hair, created with bold sweeping lines.

## COLOR PALETTE:

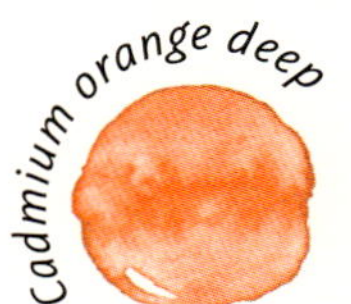

Cadmium orange deep

Madder red dark

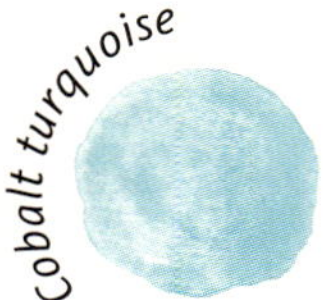

Cobalt turquoise

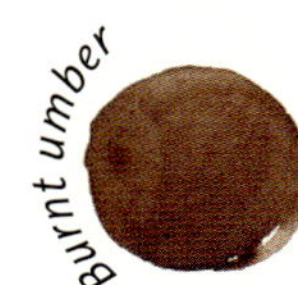

Burnt umber

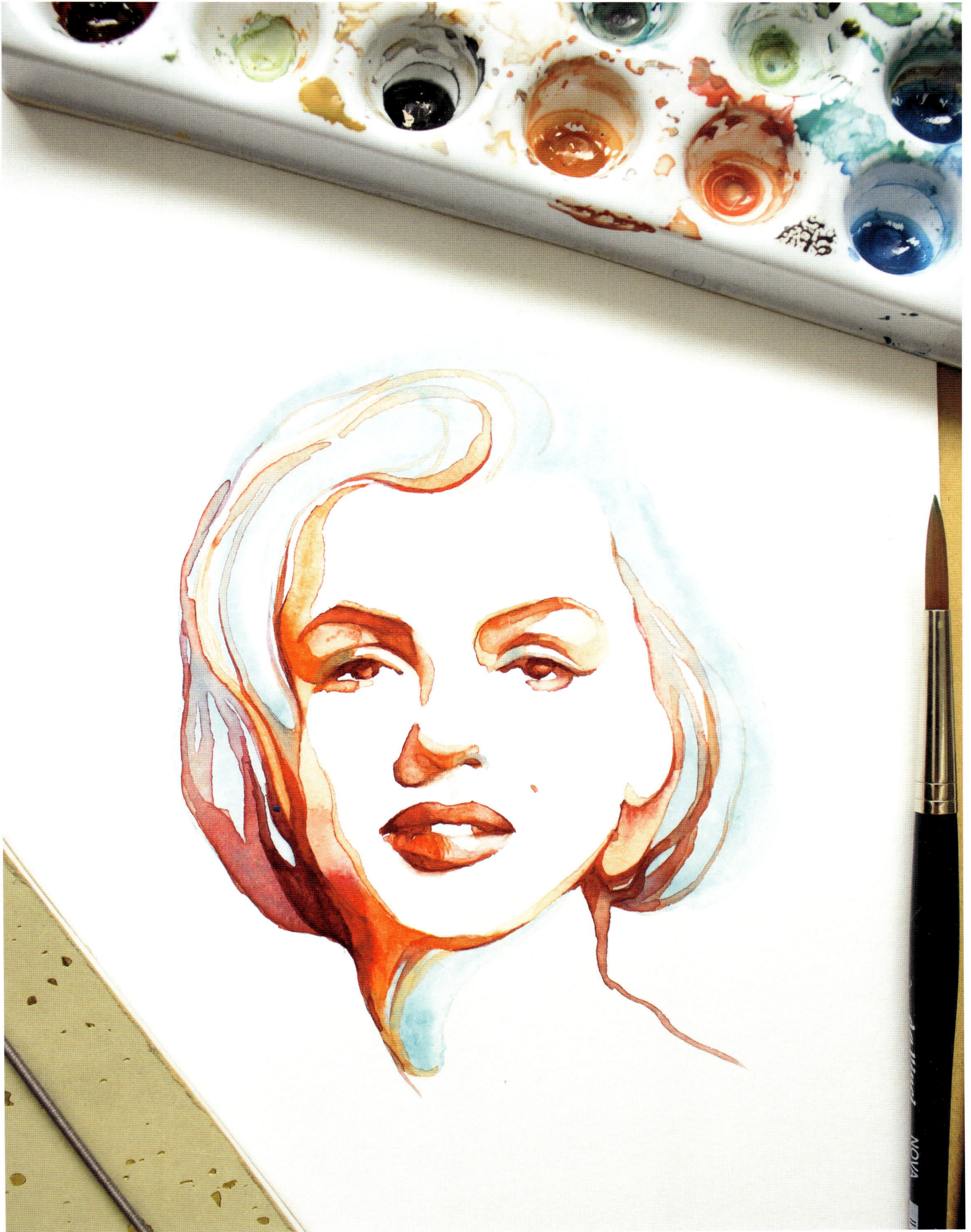

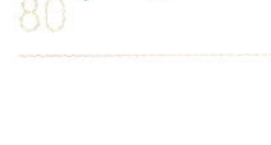



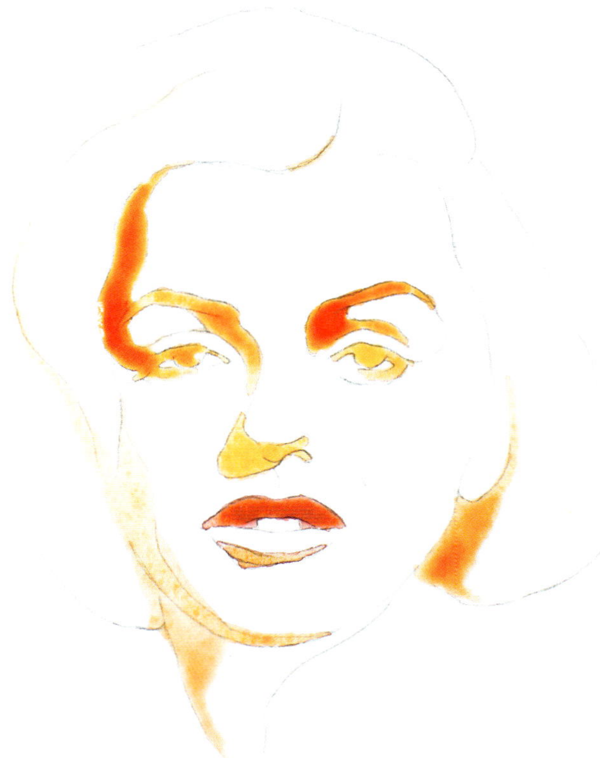

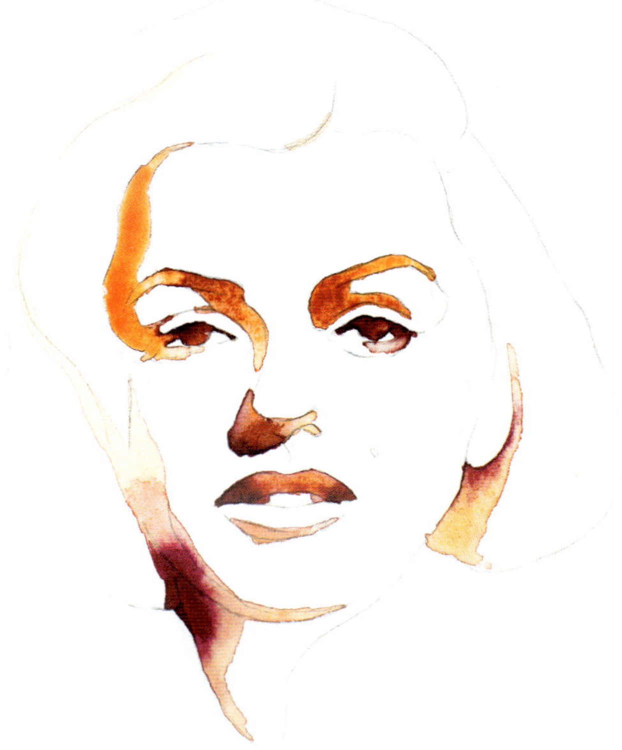

**1. Wet-on-dry:** Mix a pale shade out of orange and some red, which you paint as a wash onto the facial shadows. For the mouth, use generally more red. Work on areas like the eyelash line with your narrowest brush. Starting from the left facial shadow, hint at the hair texture with sweeping lines.

**Tip:** *To prevent the lower eyelids from looking too dark, wipe off the brush on your scratch paper beforehand, and continue painting only with the paint residue.*

**Tip:** *Be careful with the mouth area. Try to paint the lips in as accurately as possible, and leave out the teeth especially.*

**2. Wet-on-wet:** Since you are now continuing wet-on-wet, the colored spaces should still be damp. If they have dried in the meantime, you can moisten them with a little water. A strong pigment provides the required depth. Paint a lot of dark red with a fine brush onto the corners of the mouth, eyes, nose shadow and chin. Wait a moment and, if necessary, go over it again with a stronger pigment so that the areas stand out nicely.

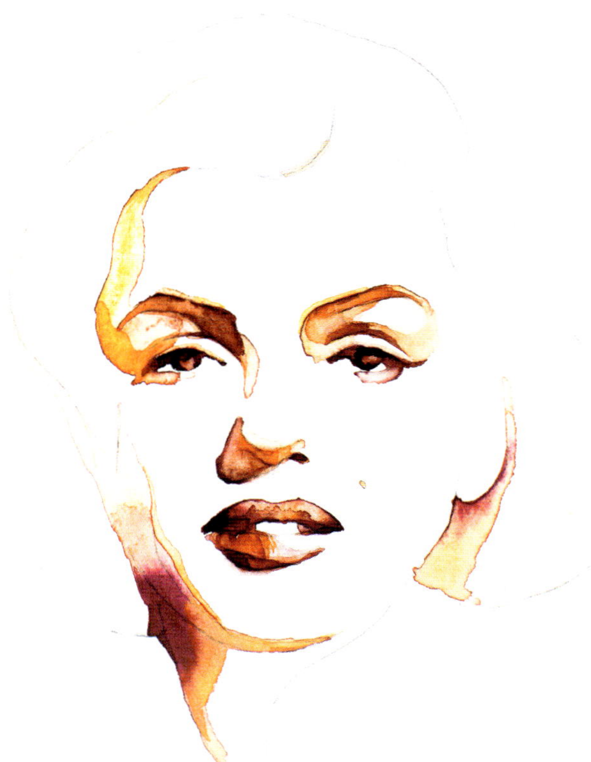

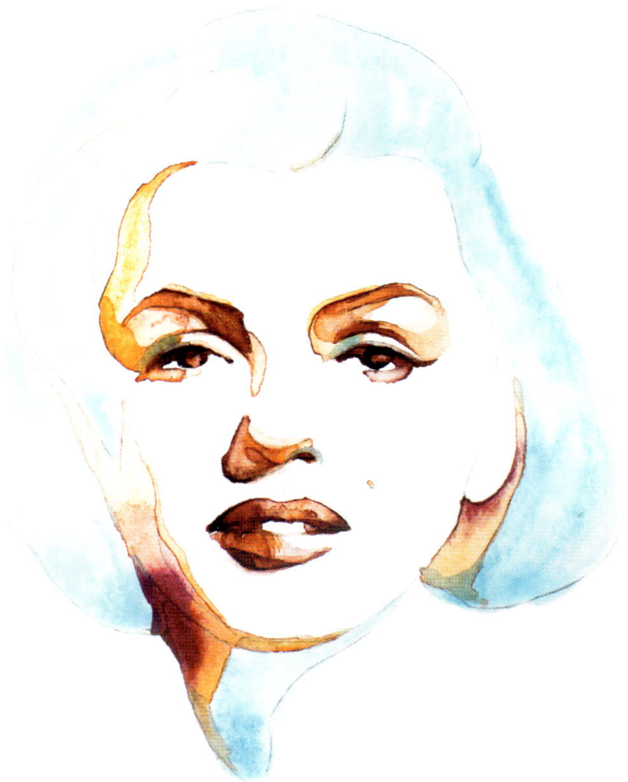

**3.** *Glaze:* Your portrait should be dry before you continue. Now come the intermediate shadows that connect the light and shaded areas. Since the left half of the face has a more pronounced overall appearance, darken the area above the left eye as well. Don't forget the lower lip and the outer corners of the eyes. Blend the shadow of the left cheek with a fine line in pale orange. Using the same brush, but with a different color, complete the dark creases of the eyelids and the eyelash line. The upper lip and iris are also accentuated with very strong areas of glaze.

**4.** *Wet-on-dry & glaze:* Underpaint the hair surface and neck with a radiant turquoise, while leaving a few gaps. Add quite a bit of water to the turquoise before you start painting in a wash. Then, add a slight color highlight to the eyelids and nostrils using a glaze.

**5.** *Glaze:* Paint the lines of the hair in layers on the dry surface – preferably from the bottom up, so that they are denser at the bottom and fade away towards the top. Follow the waves of the hair, and use different shades. You will get more saturation with an orange glaze over the temple and chin. Afterwards, frame the neck with two thin lines.

**Tip:** *Switch to a narrower brush sometimes to occasionally add finer lines of hair.*

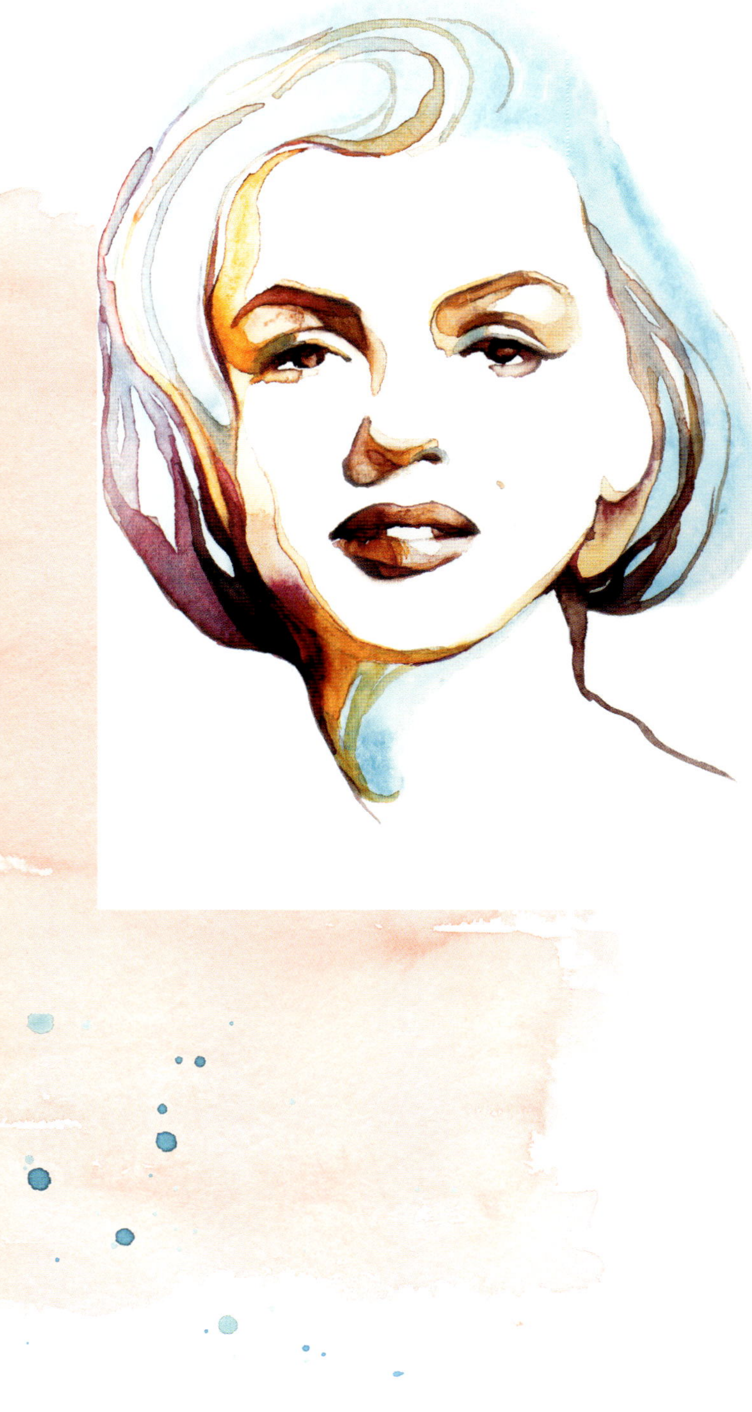

Marilyn Monroe

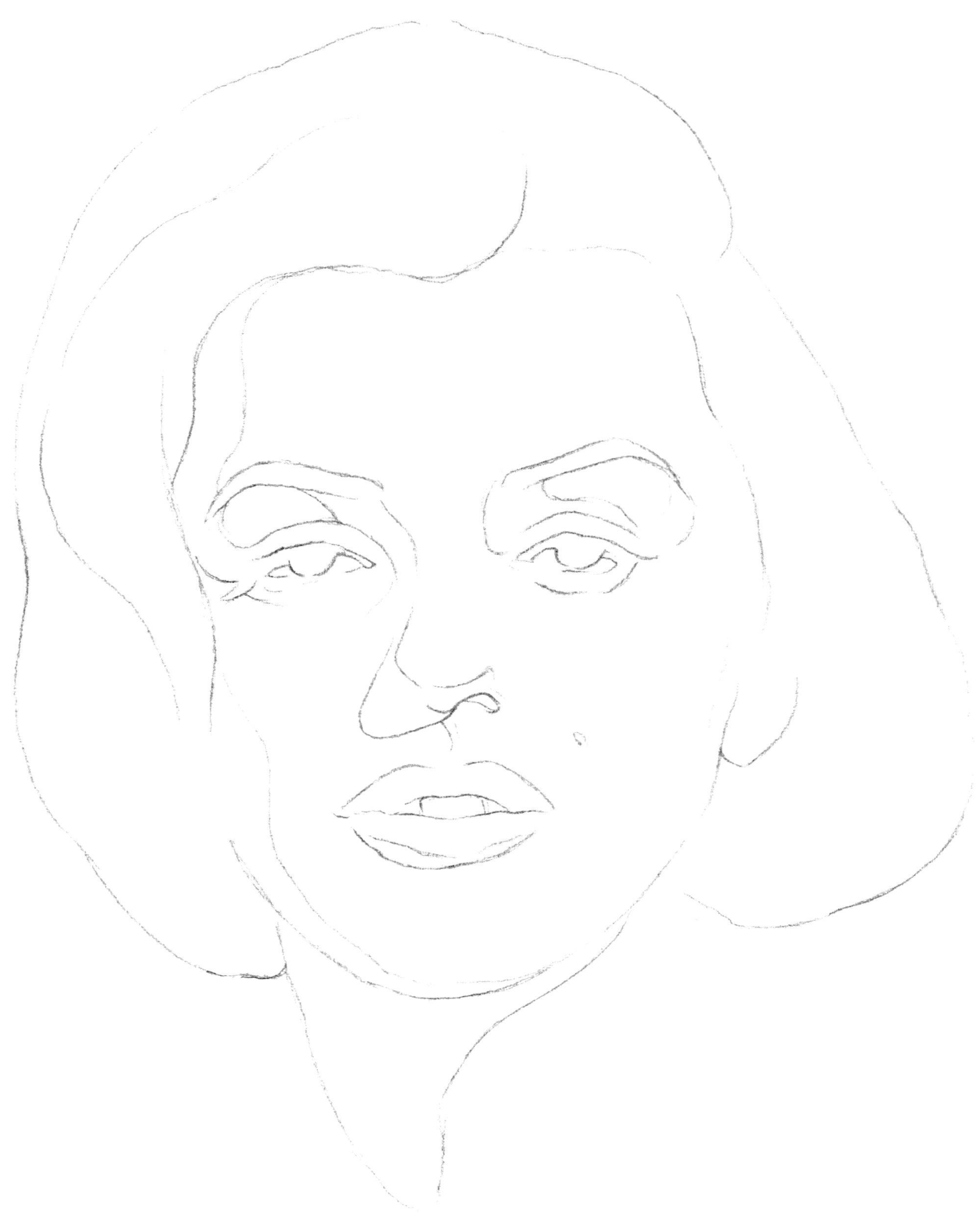

# GIRL WITH A
# *Pearl Earring*

The "Girl with a Pearl Earring" is an oil on canvas painting by the Dutch painter Vermeer, created around 1665, in the style of the Old Masters. By the way, the identity of the girl is still a mystery today!

This portrait is a reinterpretation with expressive colors and sharp lines. It could hardly be more different from the original painting! Only the delicate facial expression has remained the same.

**Tip:** *Transport yourself to the Dutch Baroque age by watching the film of the same name directed by Peter Webber!*

## COLOR PALETTE:

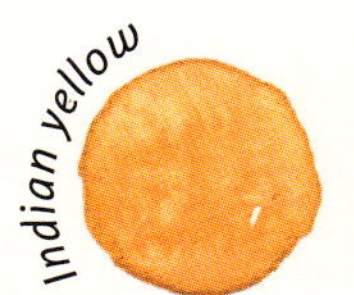


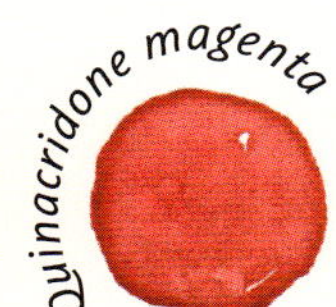


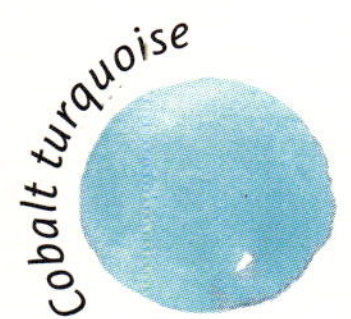


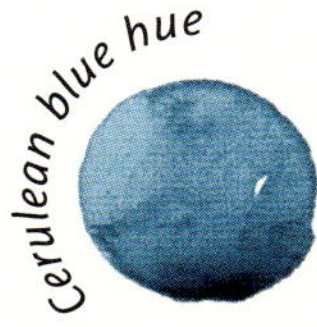

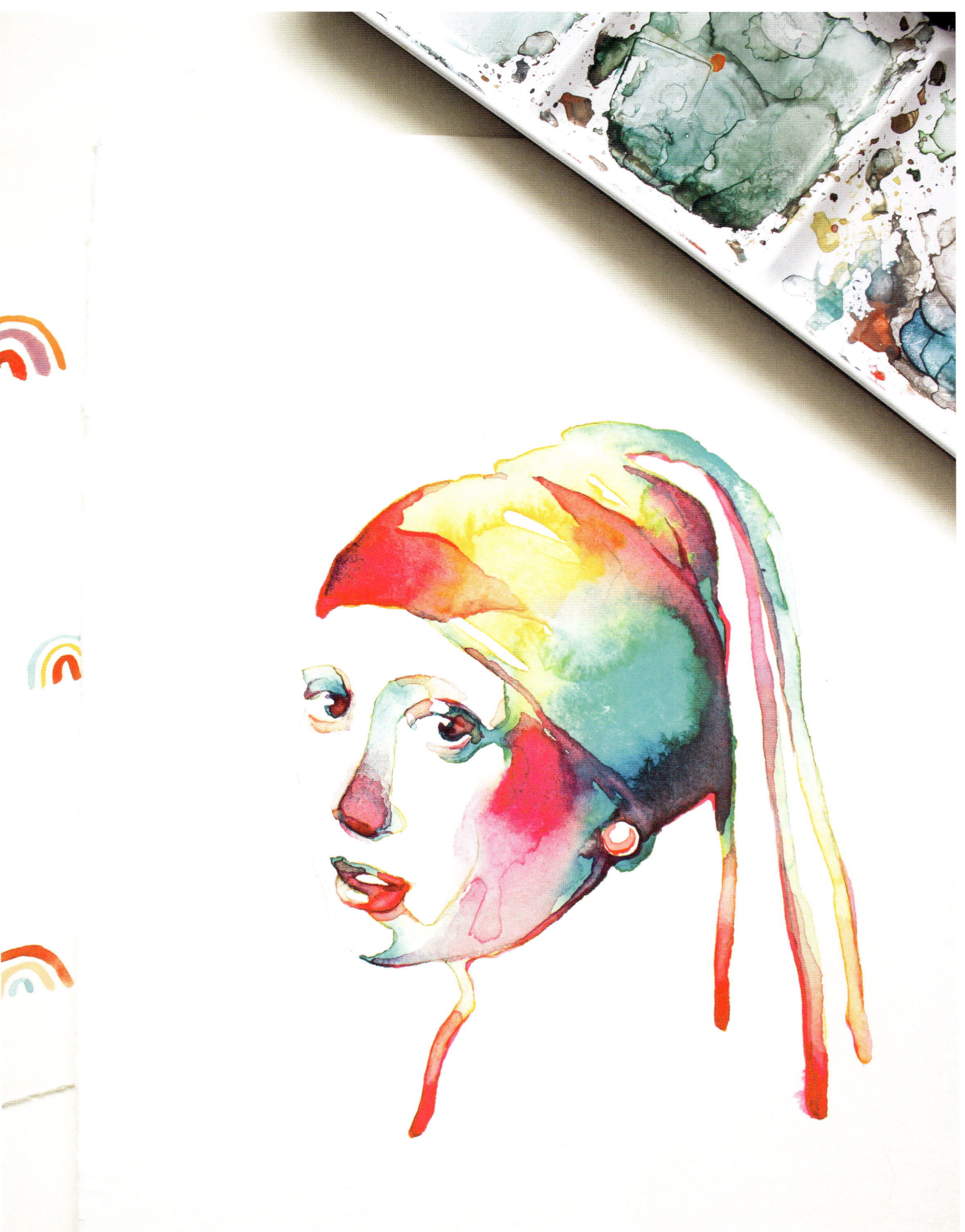

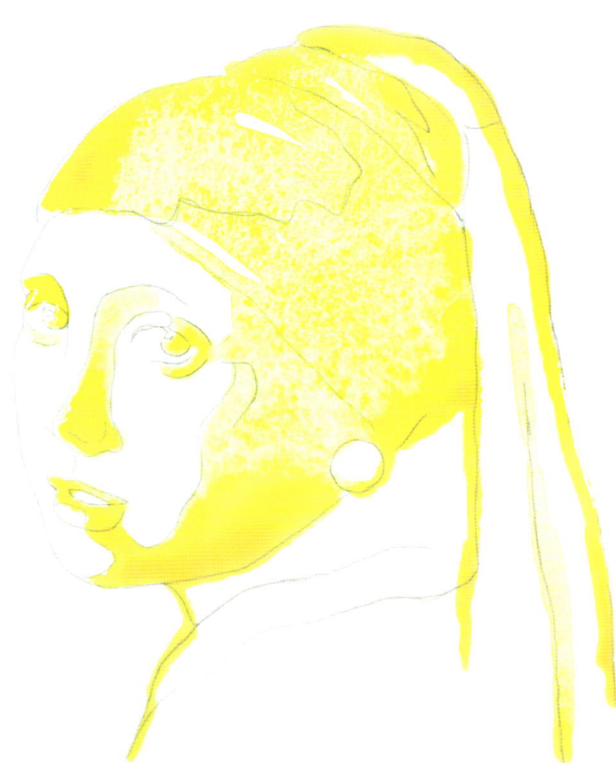

*1. Wet-on-dry:* Using plenty of water, apply a rich yellow to the entire head area and facial shadows. Start with the large spaces, and draw several lines downwards from the crown of the head, hinting at the fabric of the turban. Leave out the earring space. Then switch to a finer brush to make it easier to paint in the facial shadows.

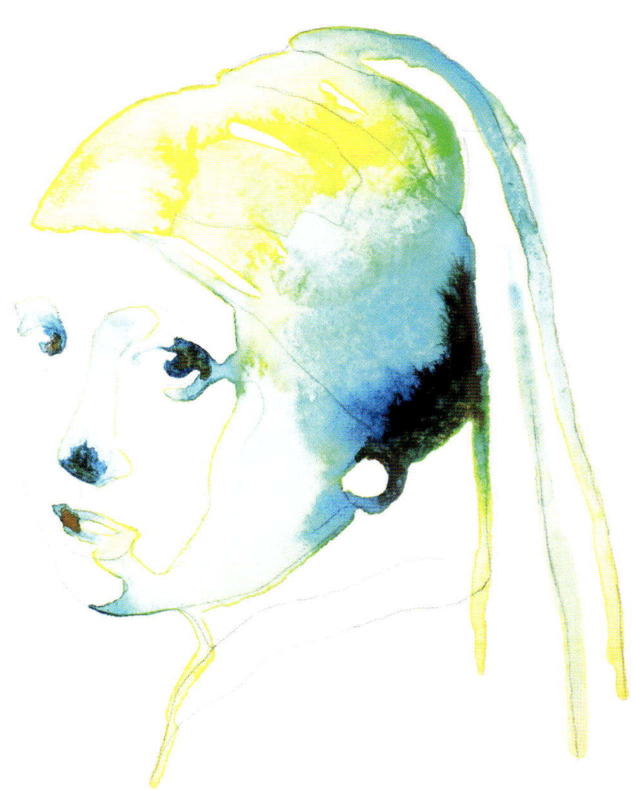

**2.** *Wet-on-wet:* Wash out your brush, and take up some pure turquoise pigment, which you apply to the lower edge of the head. Tilt your page so that the majority of the yellow space mixes with the turquoise and creates a gradation around the head. Add the same color to the fold lines of the turban as well, letting it run along the lines on its own. For the eyes, choose a smaller brush size and dab briefly instead of applying a wash over a large area. Wait for the correct stage of dryness, then dab on the tip of the nose, the eyes and the corners of the mouth with plenty of blue – these areas can be really dark.

**Tip:** *Don't wash the colors together too much, but just dab them onto the surface and leave them – otherwise mixing too many different colors can quickly turn them gray.*

**Tip:** *I previously corrected the shadows of the nose and cheeks with some paper towel, removing the excess yellow pigment and then painting over it with a pale turquoise, otherwise it would have become too gray.*

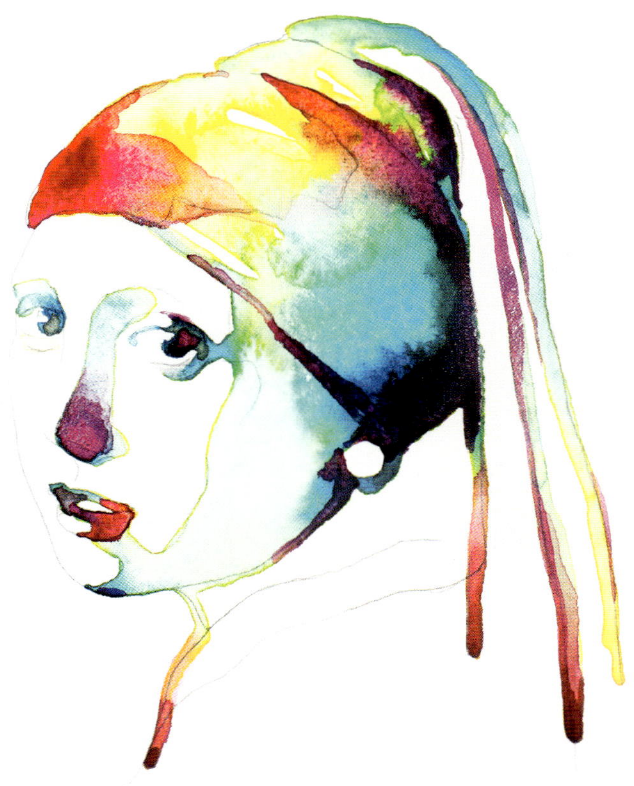

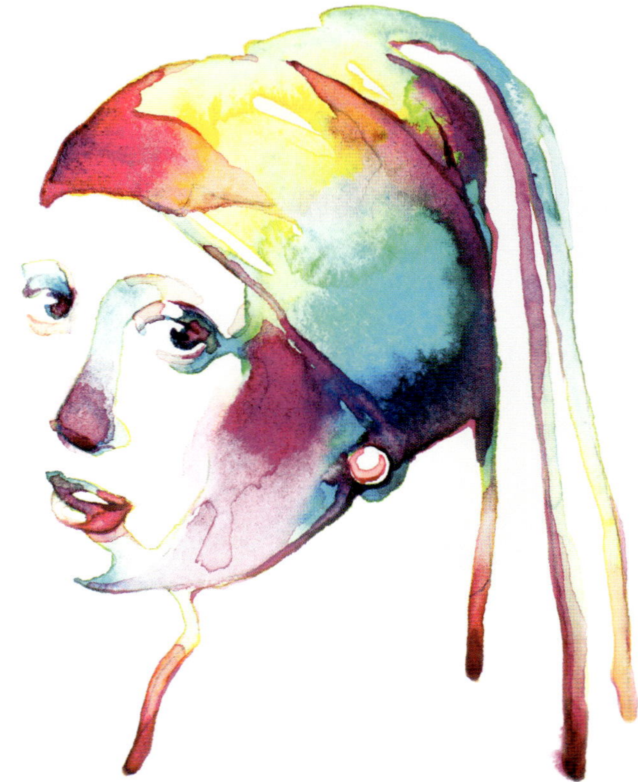

**3.** *Wet-on-wet & glaze:* Now, when the color is dry, paint over it in some spots with a red. Here, for example, I have emphasized the lower lip and eyes. Moisten the nose shadow with a thin layer of water beforehand, so that you only have to dab on the tip of it afterwards. This will create a soft gradation. The head area was still a little wet, so the spaces are feathered in some places. Trace over the folds of the fabric with your brush tip using as little pressure as possible. Use more paint at the ends to make it look like it is running down.

**4.** *Wet-on-wet & glaze:* Wet the cheek shadow with a layer of clear water. Wait for the right moment and then dab on a strong magenta, especially on the cheekbone. While the color evolves, use the time to define other parts like the lips, and draw finer lines for the eyelids and the pearl earring. Complete the left edges of the face with a soft, well-diluted red. Then return to the cheek shadow and, if necessary, dab in more undiluted paint so that the area appears nice and bold.

Apply the last brushstrokes to the bridge of the nose in light tones, along with very fine, flashy lines on the eyelids, earring, wrinkles, chin and nostril.

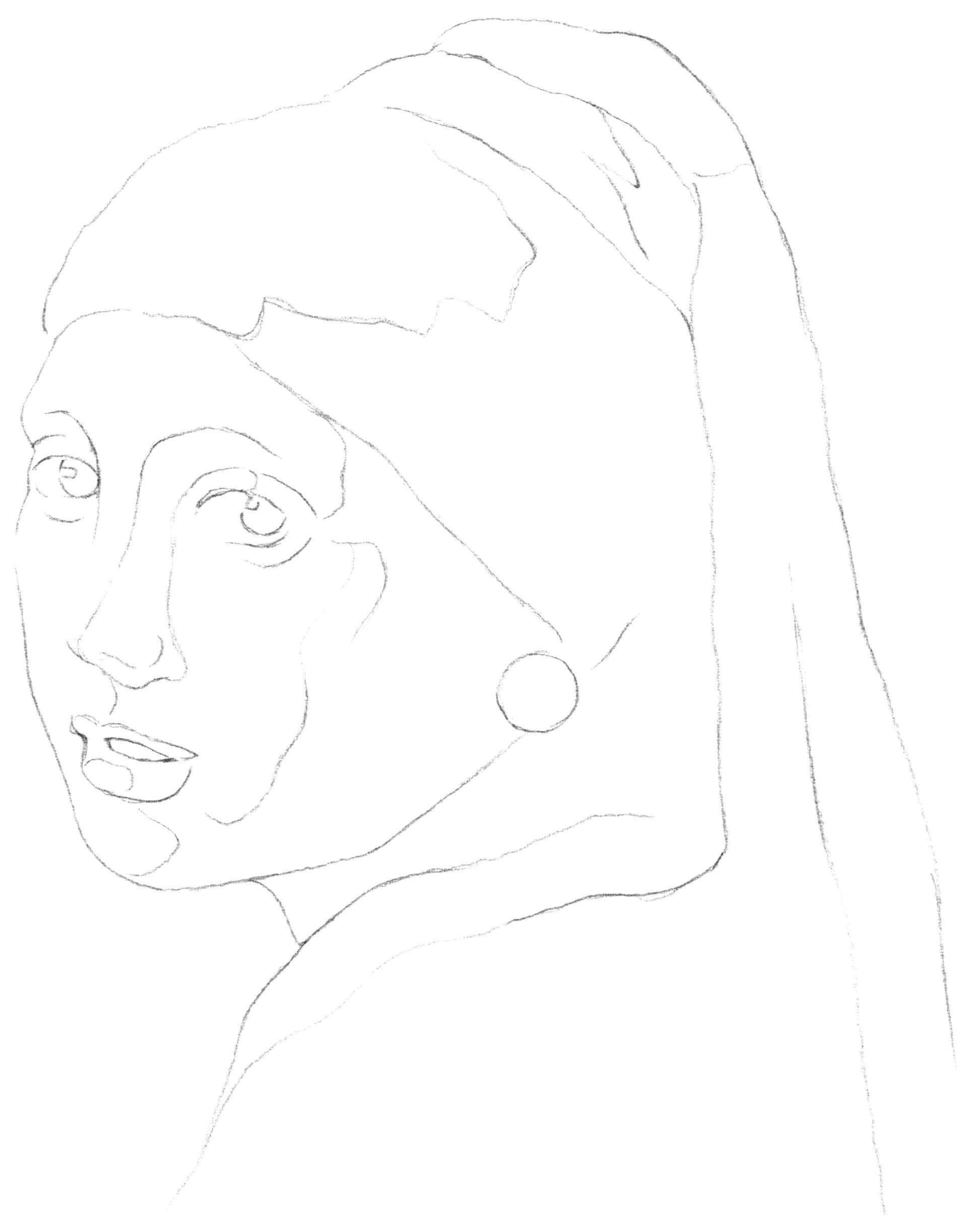

# MARTIN
## *Luther King*

Martin Luther King Jr. was one of the most significant human rights activists of our time. Peacefully and devotedly, he campaigned for a just world, free from racism, oppression and discrimination of black people.

He was the leader and spokesperson of the Civil Rights Movement, which fought – at least on paper – for the abolition of legal racial segregation in the United States. M. L. King ultimately paid for the fight for justice with his life when he was assassinated in 1968.

An incredibly courageous and inspiring personality, he showed the world that peaceful resistance can achieve great things.

**COLOR PALETTE:**

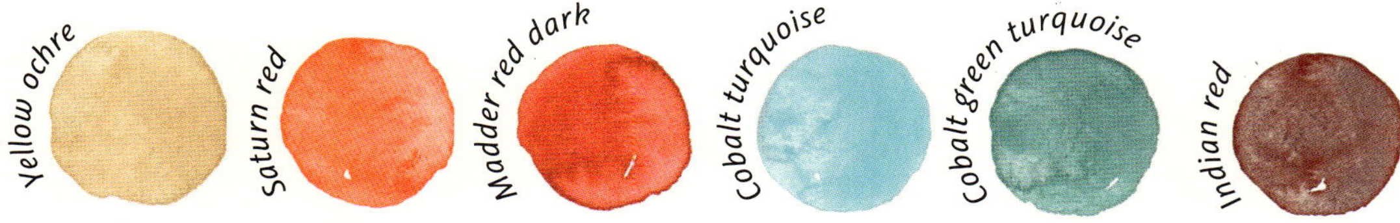

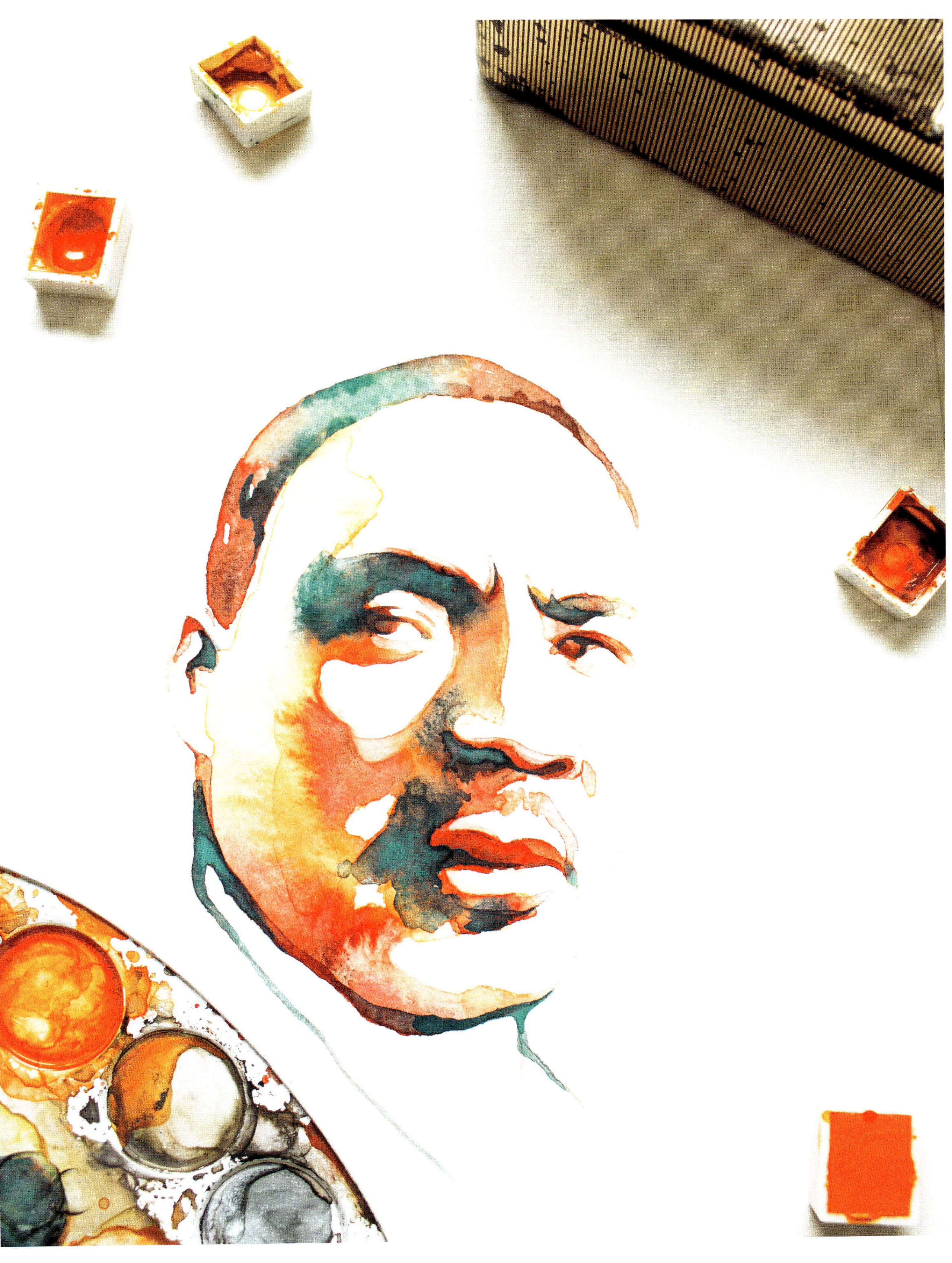

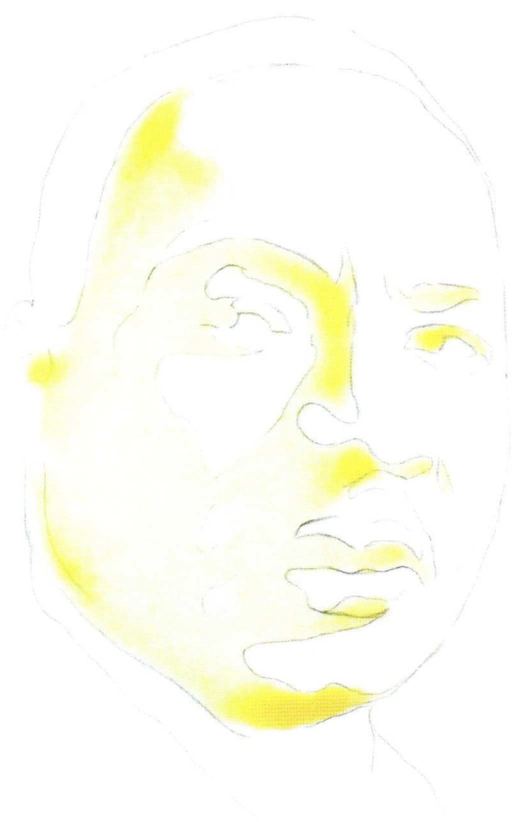

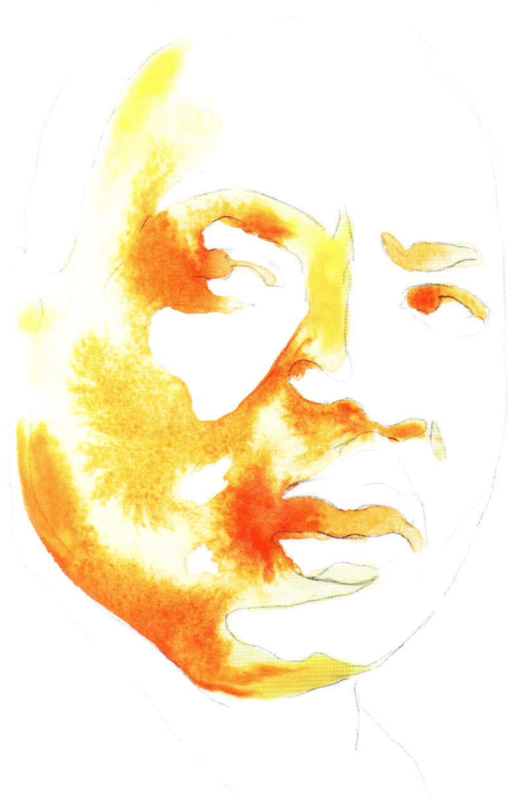

**1.** *Wet-on-dry:* Underpaint all the facial shadows with a warm, well-diluted shade. Start on the cheek space with a thick brush, and work your way to the smaller areas. Once you've reached the mouth, nose and eye areas, switch to a finer brush to paint in with more precision.

**Tip:** *Guide your brush with pressure over the paper surface so that it bends sideways. This will allow you to paint a wash over large spaces quicker.*

**2.** *Wet-on-wet:* Next, wait briefly for the ideal stage of dryness, and then, using a fine brush with lots of orange pigment, start dabbing on the upper lip, corners of the mouth, eyes and chin line.

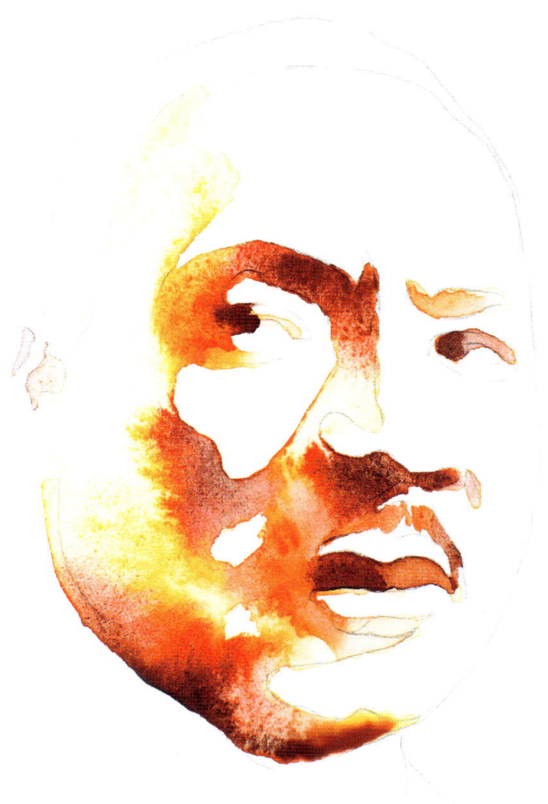

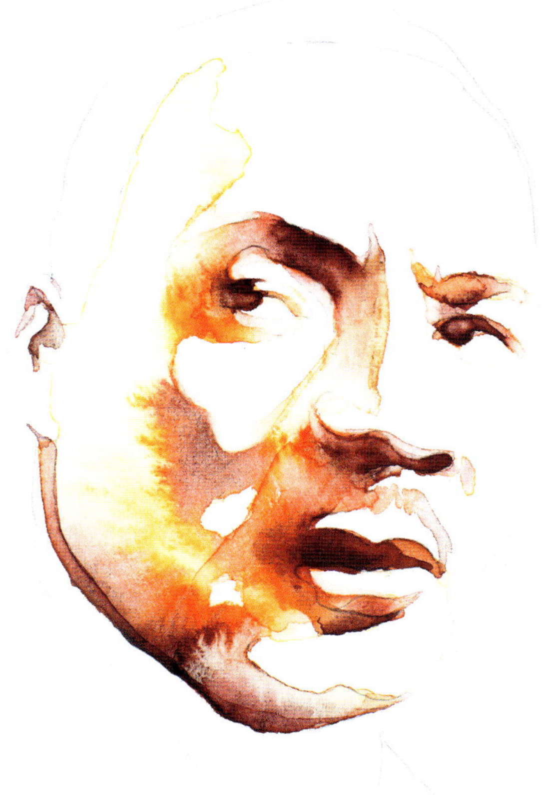

**3. Wet-on-wet:** Repeat the previous step with a deep brown. Always wait briefly for the colors to evolve on the damp surface, then go in again with a bolder color to create a strong light-dark contrast. Do not wash the colors in together, however, but leave them as they are so that the other colors still remain discernible.

**Tip:** *Now and then, switch between the parts of the face. For example, if you notice that the eyes are not dark enough, dab onto the area again before the layer has dried!*

**4. Glaze:** Add some intermediate shadows with a fine brush. To do this, outline the tip of the nose, lower lip, temples and eyelids with a light shade, as well as the delicate outer lines on the right side, which thus frame the face.

**Tip:** *Wipe your brush off beforehand to achieve lighter tonal gradations.*

Intensify the shaded areas of the eyebrows, iris, the nose shadow, the upper lip and the ear, and create a visual separation between the head and the neck by applying the glaze line on the jaw.

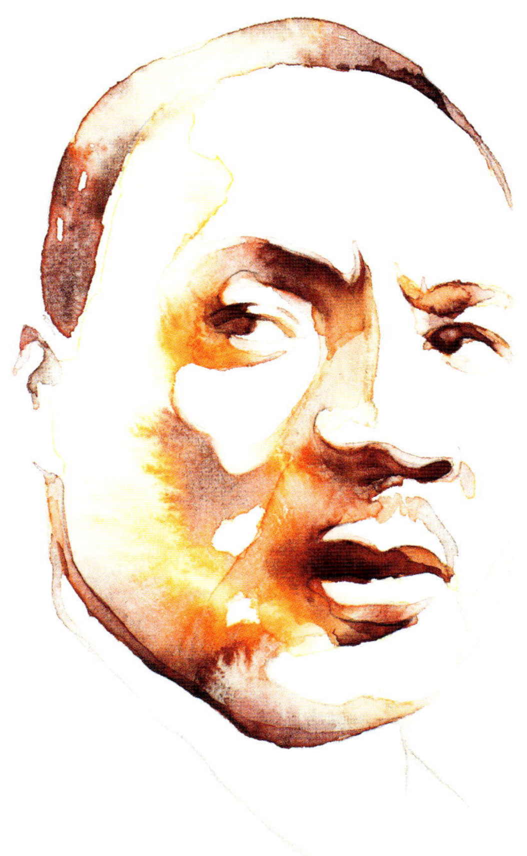

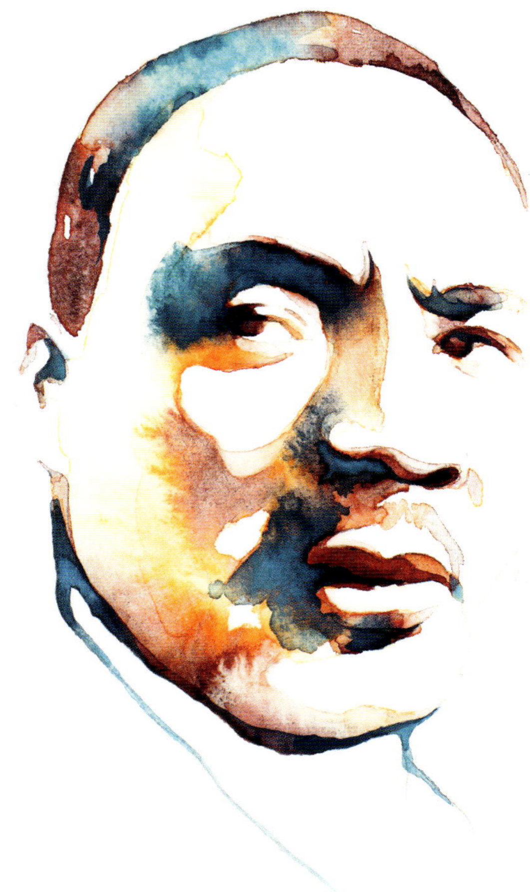

**5. *Glaze & wet-on-wet:*** Add more pale shadows over the eyebrow and upper lip, and trace over the shoulder lines and the outer line of the ear. Now paint a wash of the same ochre as used in the first step onto the hair space. Then, dab a strong brown onto the outer parts of the hair.

**6. *Wet-on-wet & glaze:*** Carefully moisten all of the facial shadows with a clear layer of water, and dab on pure turquoise pigment, mainly at the left, outer corners of the eyes, nose and mouth. Wait for a moment, then add some more pigment. Use the same principle for the hair. Since the space here is quite small, it's worth using a thin brush and guiding it across the paper several times in a dabbing motion. Complete your portrait with the shoulder lines.

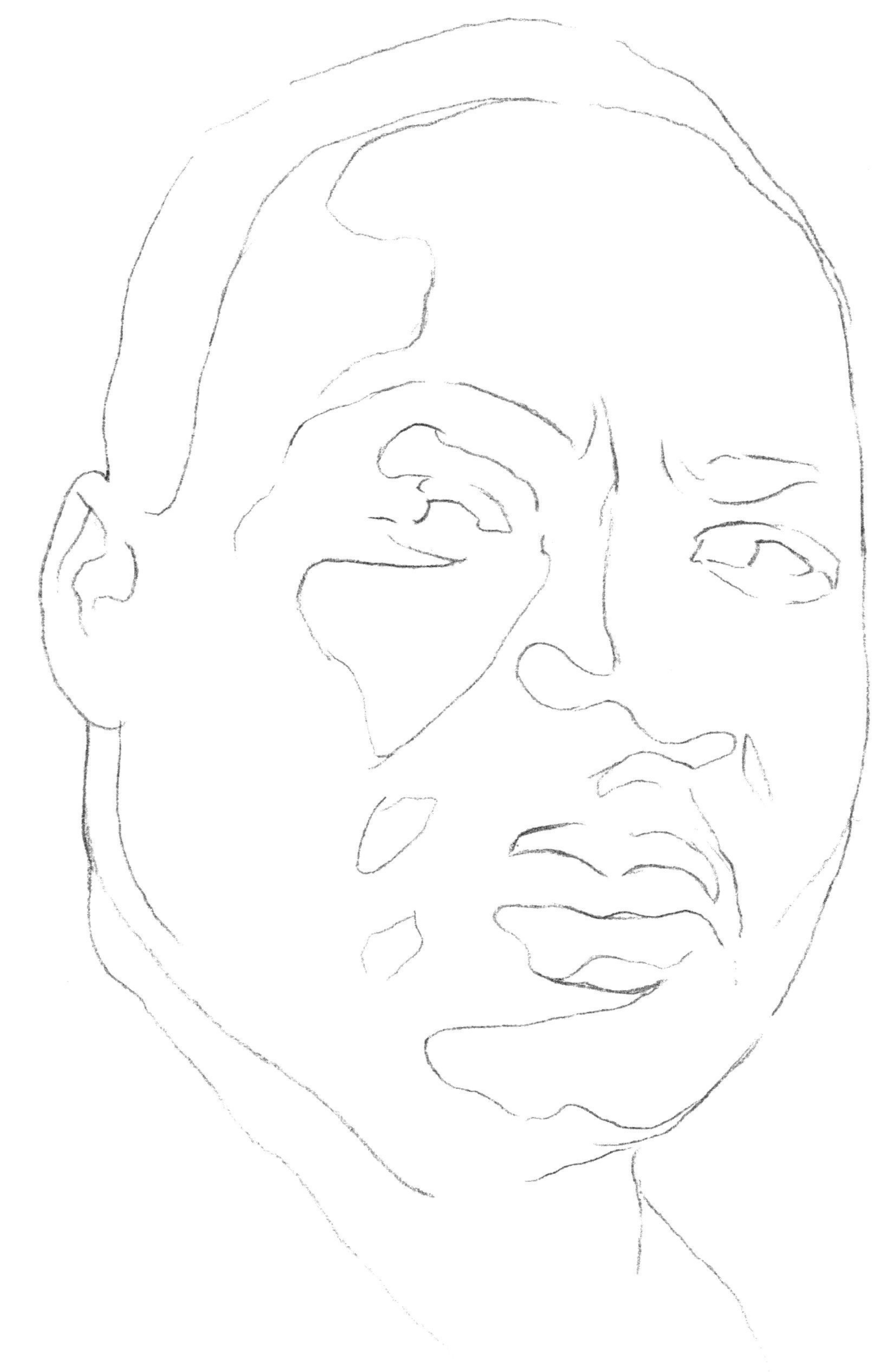

# AUDREY
# *Hepburn*

Audrey Hepburn is one of the most beautiful, successful and down-to-earth Hollywood film icons. She played, arguably, her most famous role in "Breakfast at Tiffany's". On her retirement from acting, she devoted the rest of her life to humanitarian causes, becoming a UNICEF Goodwill Ambassador.

Despite a two-dimensional painting style, her gentle facial features are captured here step-by-step, and rendered in warm colors.

## COLOR PALETTE:

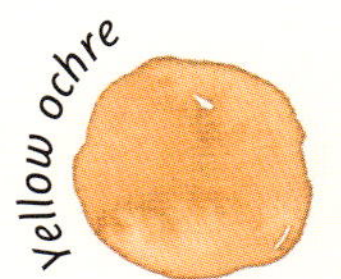


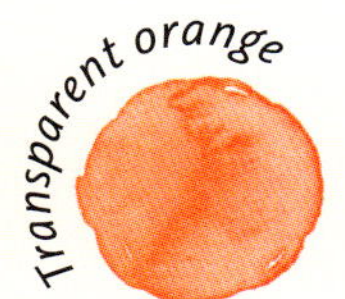


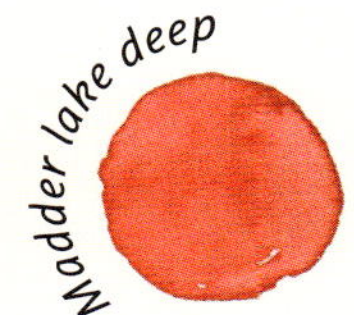


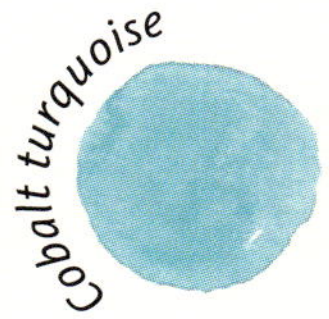


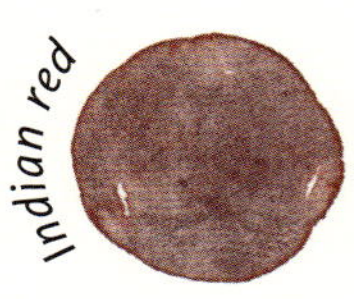

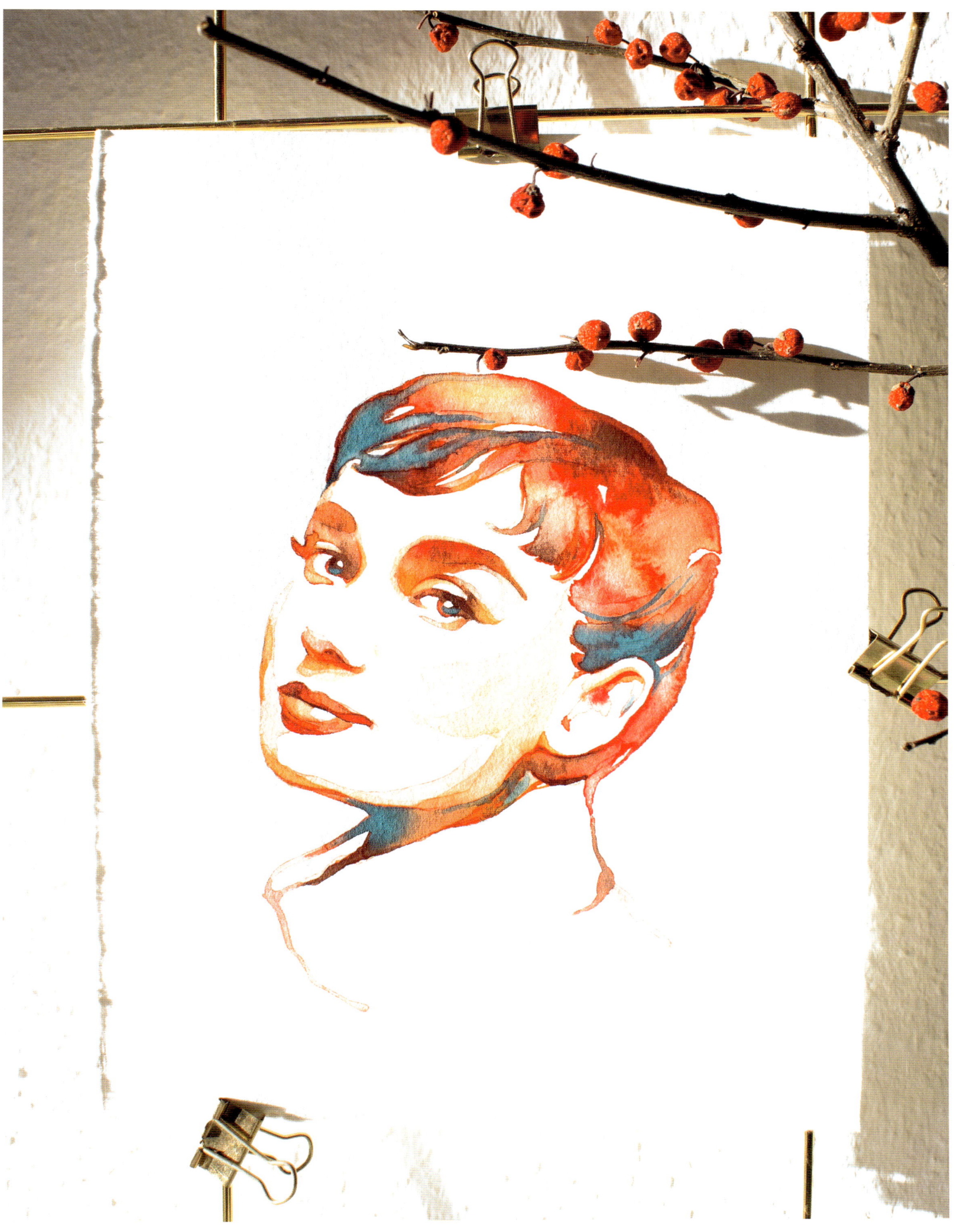

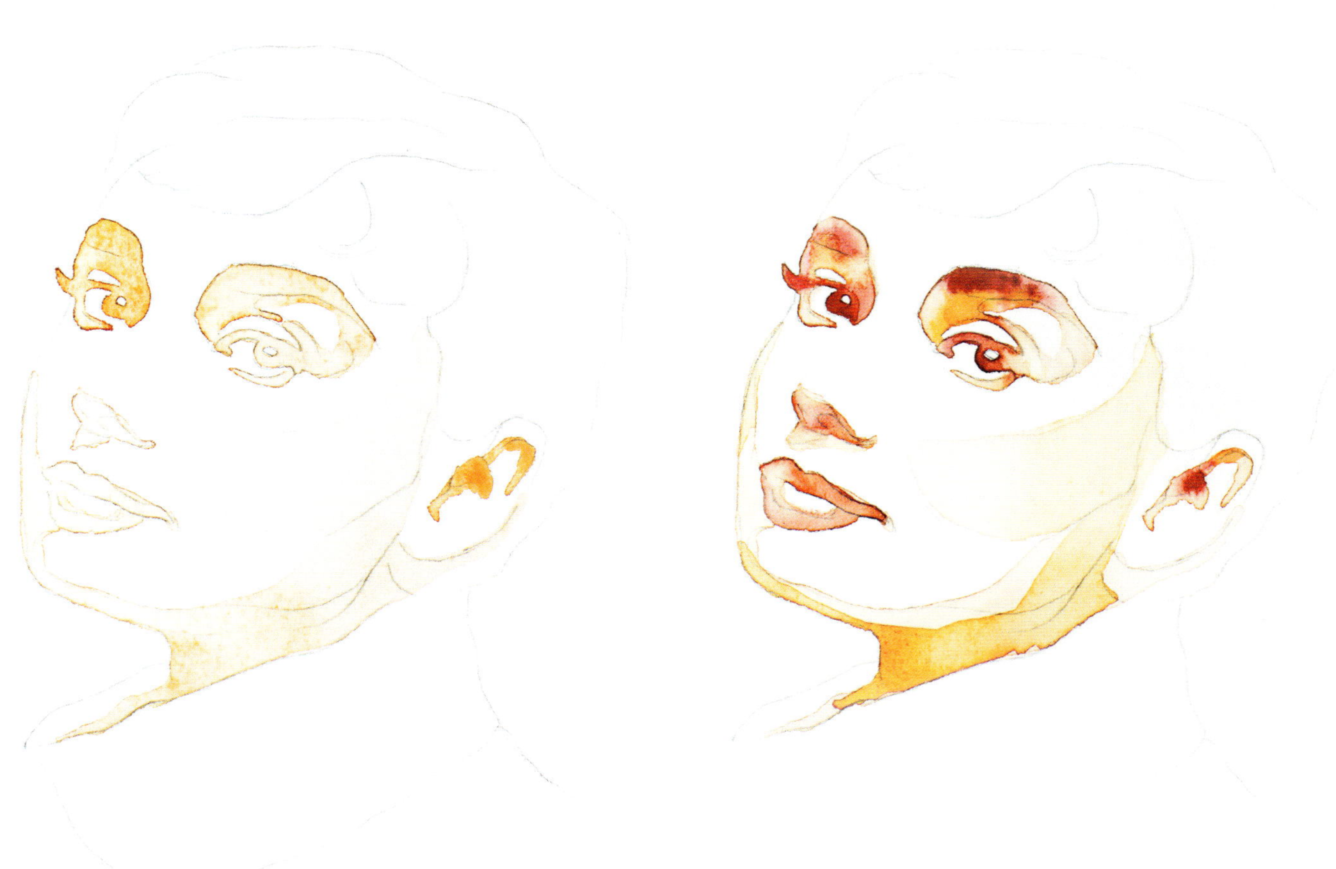



**1.** *Wet-on-dry:* Mix the first shade out of orange, a little pink and plenty of water. Use the tip of your brush, especially for the eyes, to paint very precisely along the lines, leaving out the light reflections, eyelids and the whites of the eyes. Take a thicker brush for the cheek, and starting from the hairline, paint inwards over a wider area. The aim is to paint the shadow as subtly as possible. This works better if you remove the excess paint and blend the edges with a dry brush.

**Tip:** *Wipe your brush several times on a piece of scratch paper to blend the edges more smoothly.*

**2.** *Wet-on-wet:* Take up a large amount of pink pigment with a fine brush, and then dab it into the wet color layer on the eyebrows, ear, upper lip, nose and the corners of the mouth. If there are areas that have already dried, gradually moisten them again, using clear water and a clean brush. Also, paint in the neck shadow with a pale orange and intensify the outline of the jaw.

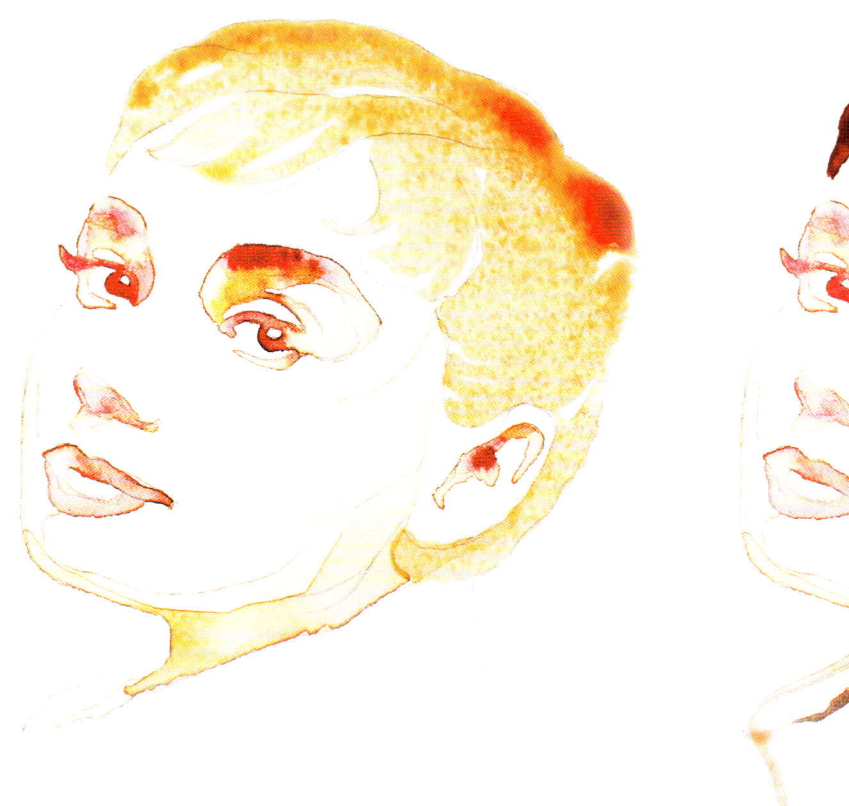

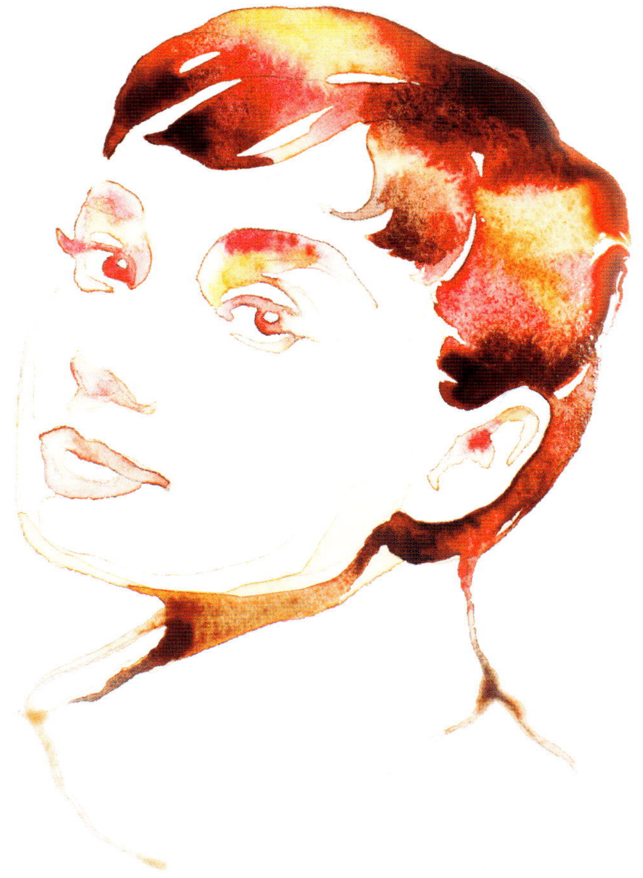

**3.** *Wet-on-dry:* Now use a thick brush again, to apply the diluted paint to the hair space, and paint in the direction of the hair's growth. Start at the crown and draw the paint up to the tips of the fringe, leaving a few gaps in between. Be liberal with the application because you're about to continue painting wet-on-wet.

**4.** *Wet-on-wet & glaze:* Apply an undiluted pink, especially to the outer edge of the hair space. Also emphasize the tips of the fringe in the same way. Then repeat the process with your darkest shade. Wait for a moment and decide if the hair looks bold enough. Then draw several lines of different intensities from the hair space for the collar and neck.

**Tip:** *If the paint runs into areas where it doesn't really belong, remove it with your brush.*

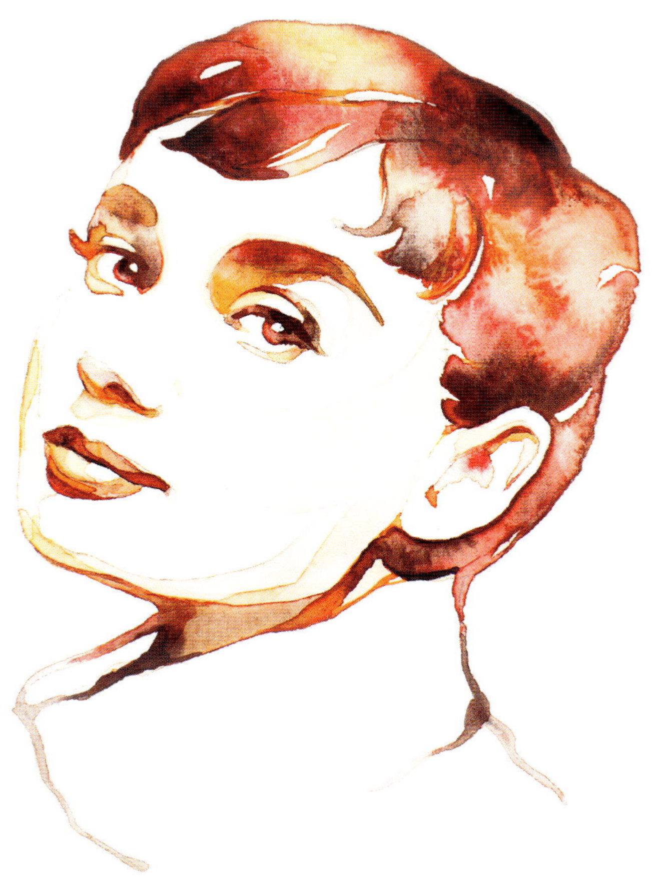
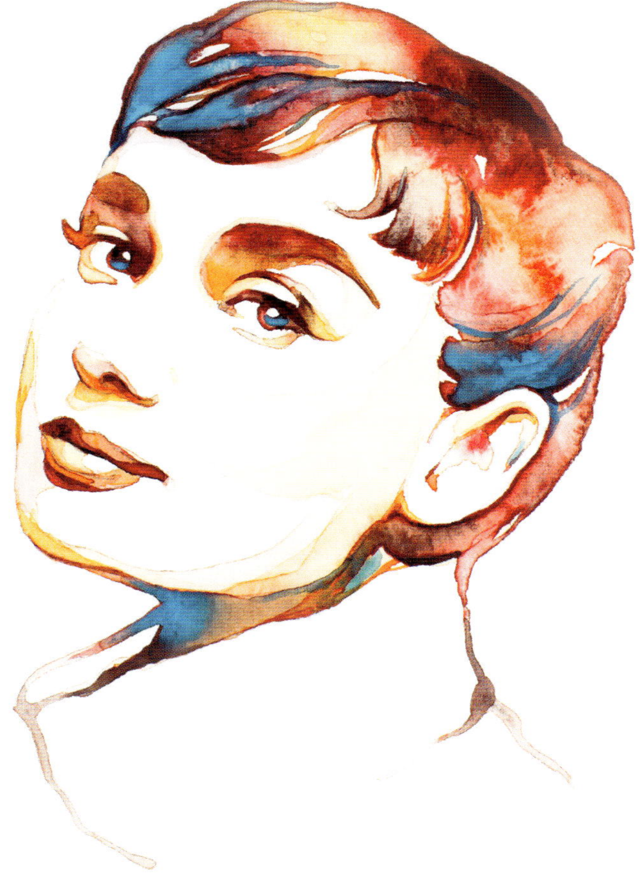

**5.** *Wet-on-wet & glaze:* The facial shadows have dried, but are still too pale. Add some dark spaces to the mouth, eyebrows, iris and eyelash line by moistening successive parts of the face with water, step-by-step. Be sure to paint in the layer as accurately as possible, again leaving out the light spots in the eyes. Start there, and then use a fine brush and brown pigment to dab in the iris and eyebrow. Remember, timing is everything; start on the left side, then repeat on the right side. Enhance the outer lines of the chin and cheek on the left side of the face. Add a small shadow to the nose wing. Partially paint in the gaps of the fringe with sharp lines. Leave a small area light at the upper lip, and partition the lower lip and its shadow with a clear, dark red glaze.

**6.** *Glaze & wet-on-wet:* Mix a pale shade similar to that used in the first step, and use a small brush to blend some of the edges of the face, such as the eyebrows, the tip of the nose, the temples and eyelids. So that your portrait isn't just tone-on-tone, complement it with a contrasting color once it's dry. Using a clean, wet brush and very little pressure, paint over the appropriate areas. Wait a moment, then dab undiluted pigment in, leaving the splodge of color like that so the layers don't mix. I chose a turquoise on the neck and hair sections. Note: Use a glaze for the iris, so paint on the dry background without wetting it first; the brown underneath should still shimmer through.

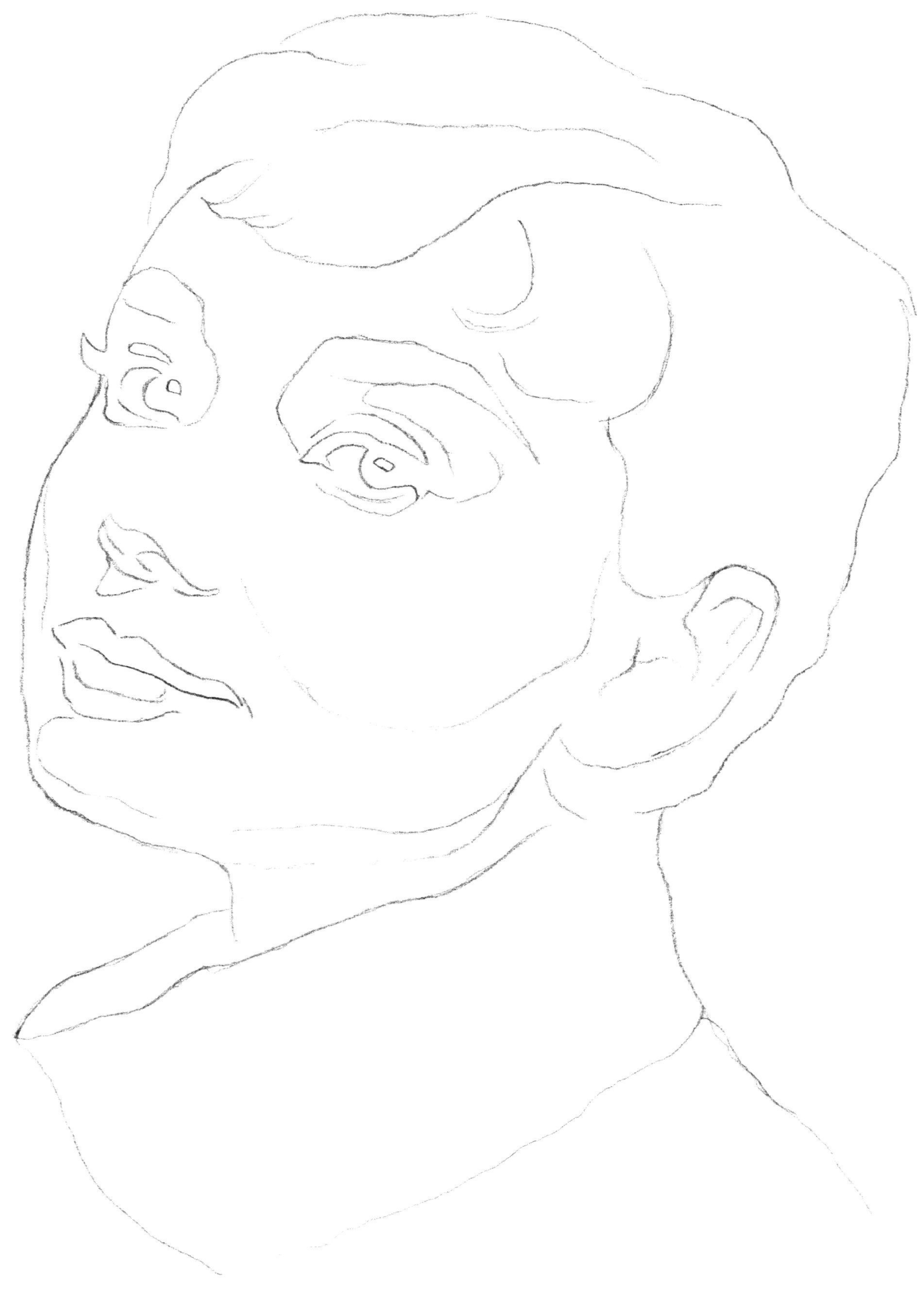

# MONA
## *Lisa*

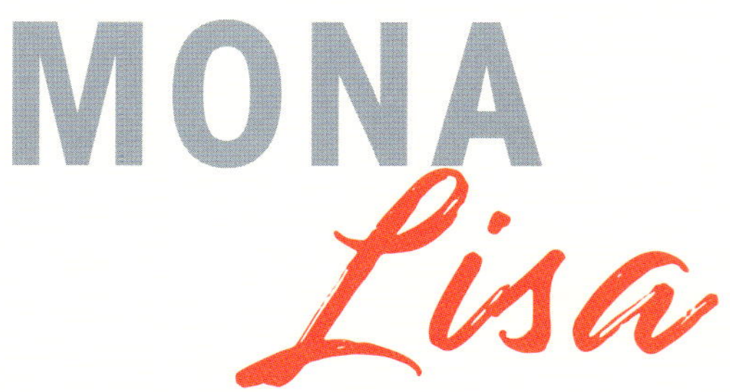

Who doesn't know her – da Vinci's Mona Lisa? Painted more than 500 years
ago, this world-famous oil painting measures just 30 x 21in (77 x 53 cm).

Is she looking content, skeptical or sassy? The interpretation of her look is
a matter for discussion. What can be clearly observed, however, are her soft
facial shadows and a very expressive eye area. The challenge with this
portrait is to reproduce the delicate gradations of shadows in the original
and transform them into a modern watercolor version. The attention
remains on the eyes; added to this are rich colors and a loose brushstroke.

## COLOR PALETTE:

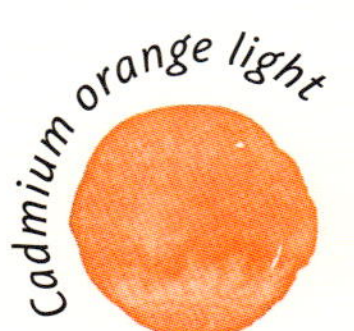

Cadmium orange light

Madder lake deep

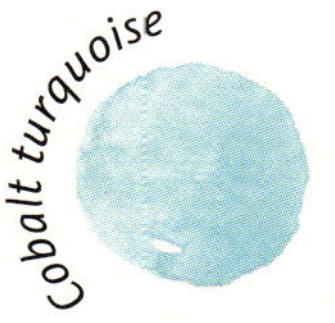

Cobalt turquoise

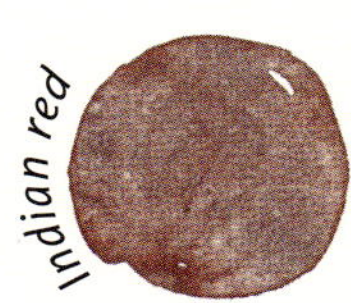

Indian red

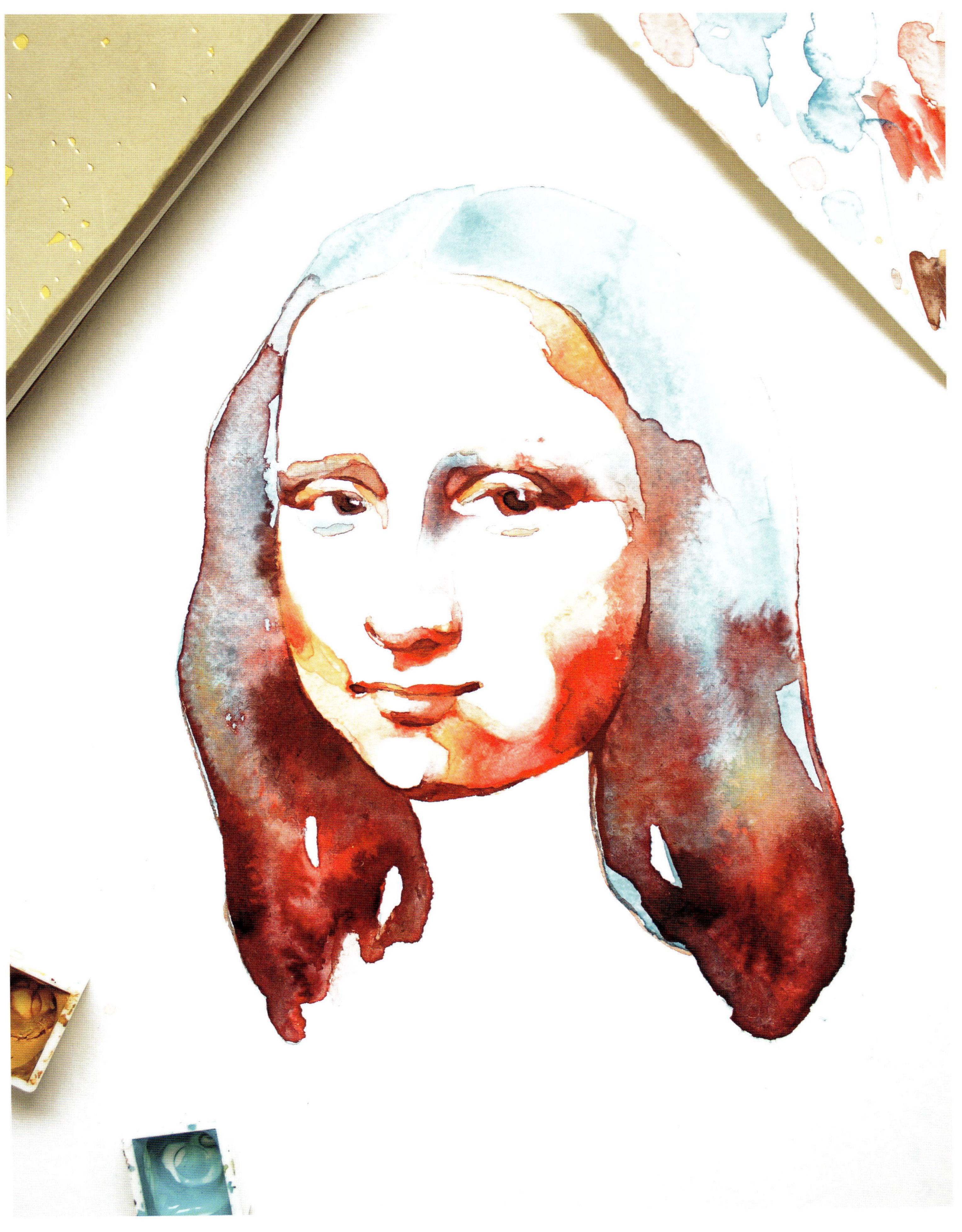

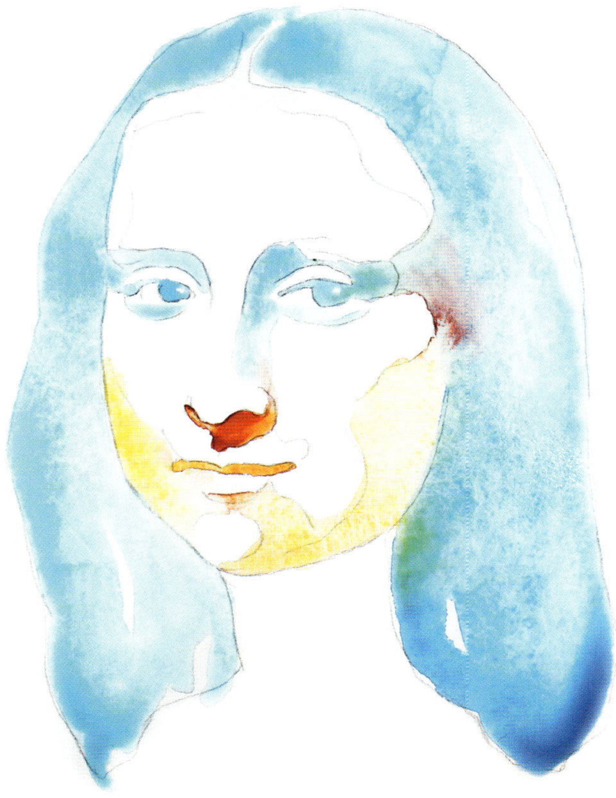

**1.** *Wet-on-dry:* Using a thick brush, paint a diluted turquoise wash over the entire hair space, spontaneously leaving several spots blank.

*Wet-on-wet:* Next comes the underpainting of the facial shadows. Once again, mix your paint with plenty of water, as the wet-on-wet technique will be used immediately afterwards. Start with a thinner brush at the eyes, but pay attention to the eyelids, the whites of the eyes and the light spots — these should remain pale! Connect the temple with the damp hair space, wipe off your brush and with the residual paint, wash the shadow of the nose up to the tip. Wash out your brush, then paint in the shadow under the tip of the nose with a bold red. It is possible that the paint will run into the blue space next to it — but that wouldn't be too bad. Now, dab on the temple as well to see how the red blends with the turquoise. Dilute this shade, and mix in a bit more orange, then paint in the cheek shadows with a coarser brush. The hair space needs to be relatively dry at this stage so that the turquoise doesn't force its way too much into the shadows! Wait for a moment if necessary, and paint in the upper lip with a bolder orange. Also make sure to leave a round white space on the chin.

**Tip:** *Use the tip of your brush for the eye area, and do not take up too much paint, so that you can leave some white space around the pencil lines in particular.*

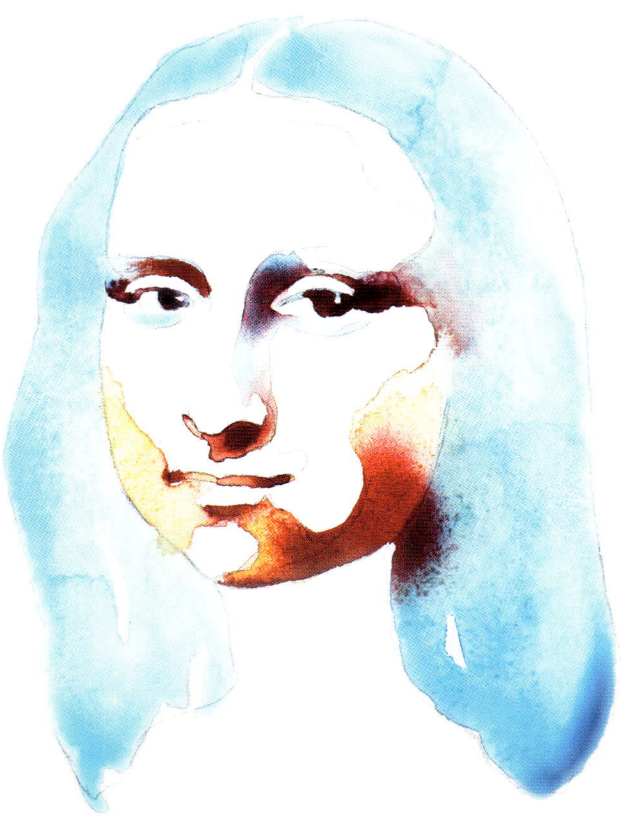

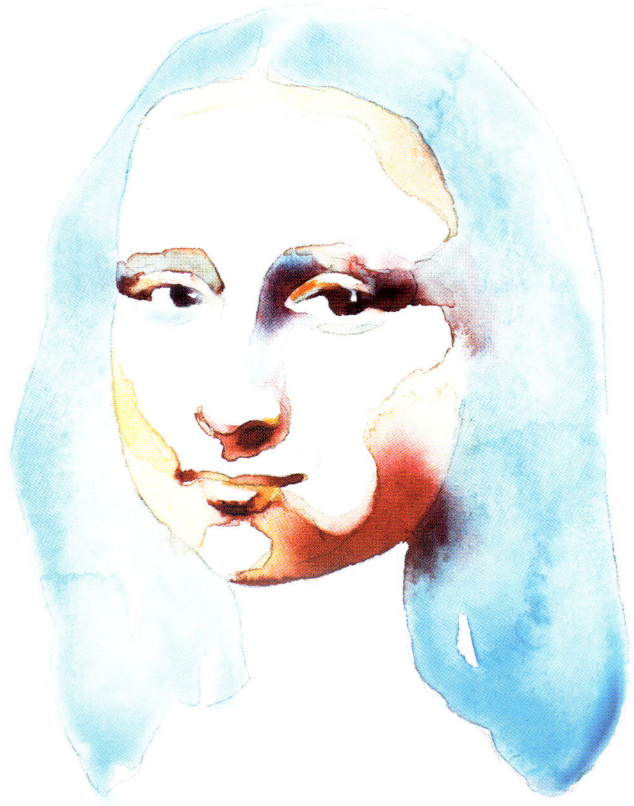

**2. Wet-on-wet:** From now on, paint with less water. The aim is to emphasize strongly the deep shadows of the eyes, nose and mouth. To do this, switch to a fine brush and take up an undiluted red-brown from your tray. Alternatively, mix the paint in advance, with as little water as possible. Then dab into the damp paint layer at the eyelid creases, iris, temple, nostril and the corners of the mouth. Using a larger brush, dab lots of pigment onto the lower right cheek shadow and watch how far the paint runs here. Accentuate the eyes again, because when the color is almost dry, you can create the darkest spaces.

**3. Glaze:** Add the light intermediate shadows to the upper and lower eyelids, forehead, cheek shadows and lower lip. Lighten the left eyebrow by removing the dark color with a bit of paper towel and applying a lighter layer of color over it. Use a well-diluted orange to also paint in the right eyebrow – this should remain very pale.

**Tip:** *If the eyebrow looks too bold, remove the paint with a piece of paper towel.*

Emphasize the eyelid creases, irises, nostrils, the corners of the mouth and the point of the chin using the finest brush and the boldest red-brown.

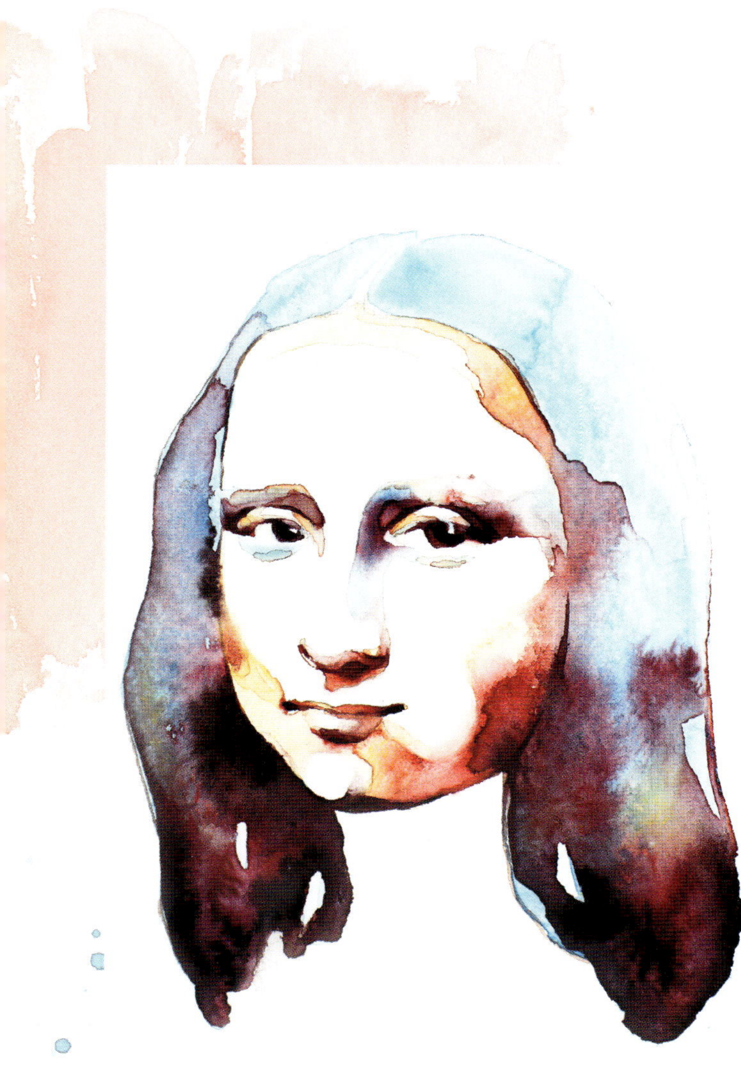

**4. *Glaze & wet-on-wet:*** Take a thick brush and roughly wet the hair space with water – but not entirely, because the top of the head should still gleam in turquoise. Pay particular attention here to the left edge of the face and also leave a few gaps towards the bottom so that the paint is still partially visible there. Immediately afterwards, paint a bold violet wash into the space. Wash and dab, guide the paint where you want it to go, and then let it dry.

The portrait looks very two-dimensional right now. It lacks lines, but also soft edges. Therefore, add some very fine, dark lines to the edges of the face and hair. Finally, blend in the hard edges on the cheeks, chin and nose shadow (see Final Tips: Blending Edges).

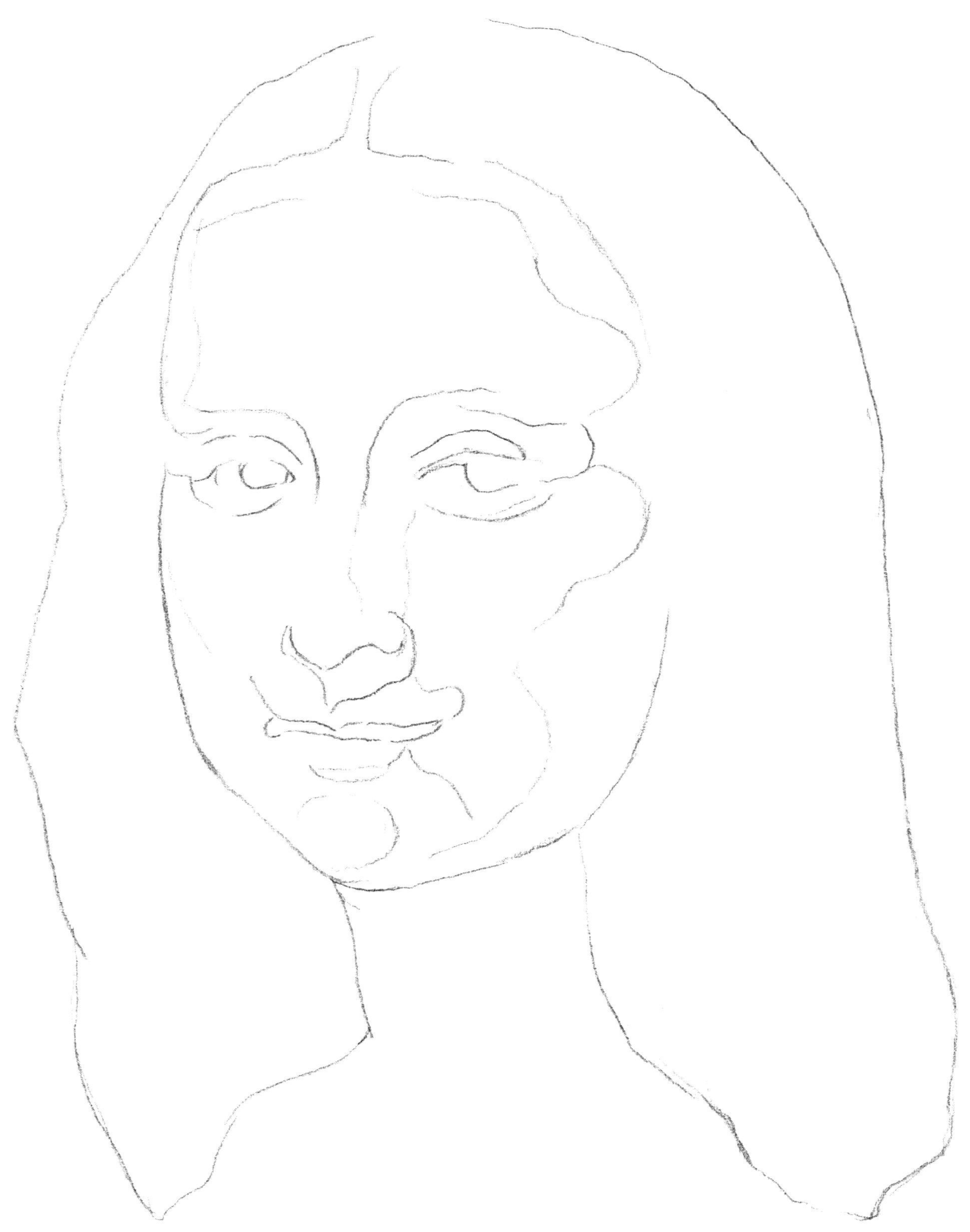

# COCO
## *Chanel*

A tough young woman, Coco Chanel founded her own company in 1910 and began to design clothes that were somewhat scandalous for the time. Skirts up to just above the knee, clean designs and the perfect little black dress – fashion that provoked uproar, change and emancipation!

**COLOR PALETTE:**

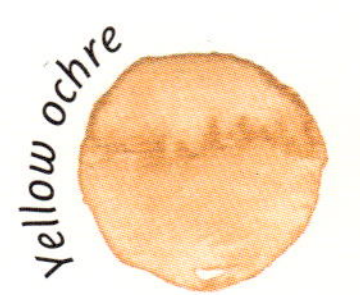


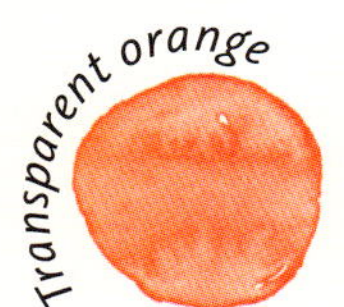


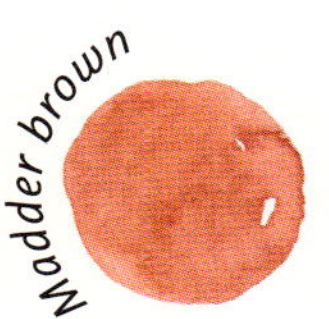


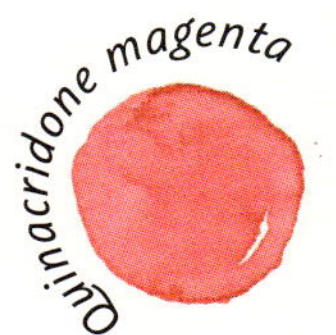


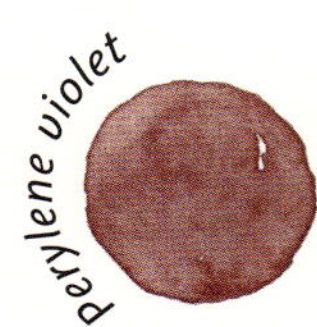

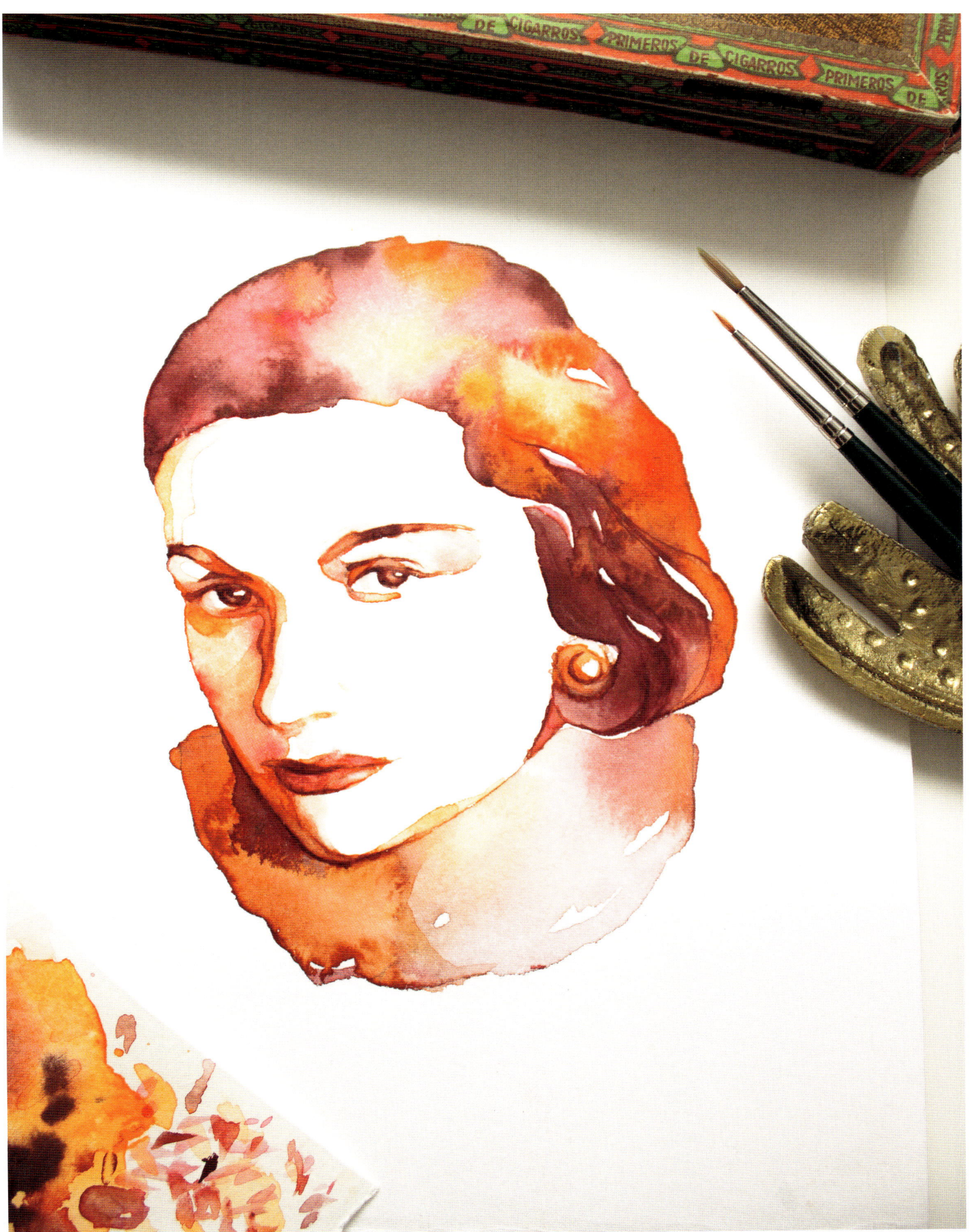

DE CIGARROS   PRIMEROS   DE   CIGARROS   PRIMEROS   DE

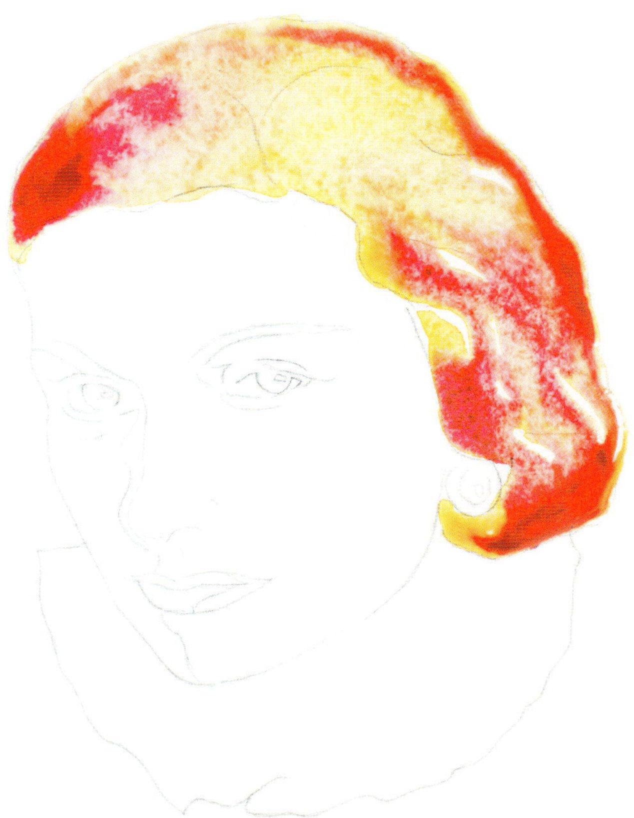

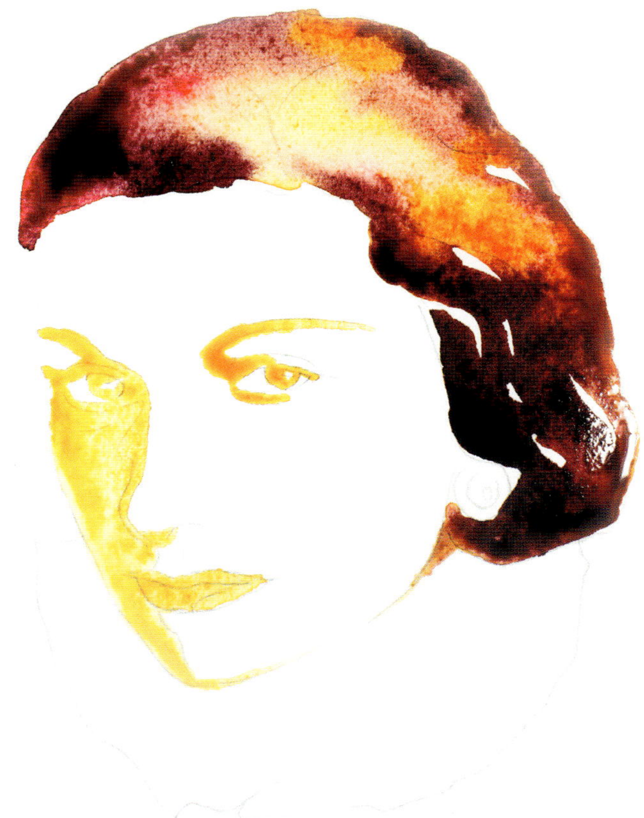

**1. Wet-on-dry:** Mix a radiant orange, and apply a wash, diluted with plenty of water, onto the hair. A large brush is best for this. Start at the left edge of the head and paint in the space in gentle wavy lines. Once on the right side, leave several gaps to give the hair texture.

**Wet-on-wet:** Now take plenty of red pigment (here a magenta) from the tray and place some dark accents to the left and right with your brush. So that the colors run more easily upwards, tilt the sheet forwards.

**2. Wet-on-wet:** Repeat this step on the hair space with a very dark pigment, such as perylene violet. Alternatively, you can mix a cool red with black — but in this case, try to dilute the paints as little as possible to mix them together. Then dab a bold orange in some places to give it more saturation.

**Wet-on-dry:** Use the same orange as in the first step, only more diluted, to underpaint the facial shadows. Start with the large spaces and then switch to a finer brush to paint in the eye area. Leave out the light spots and the whites of the eyes, and draw a narrow line along the jaw.

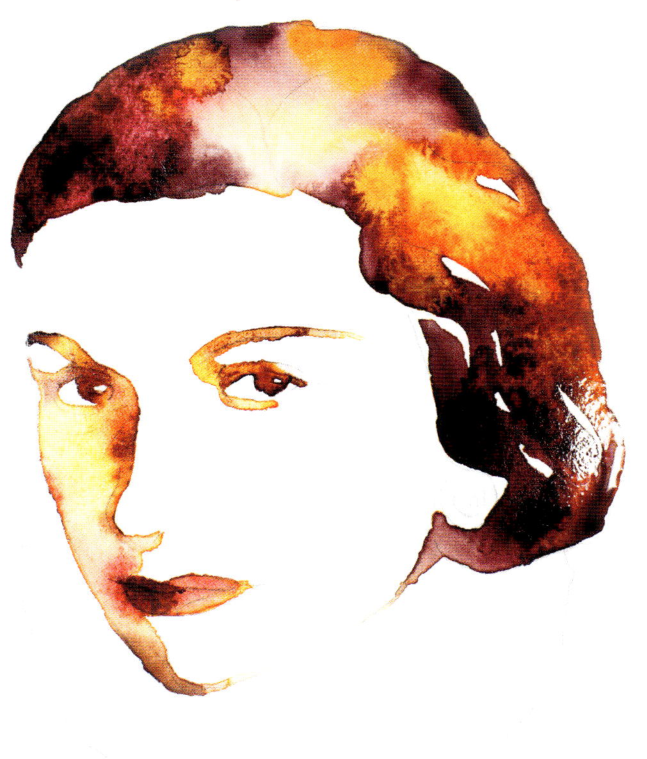

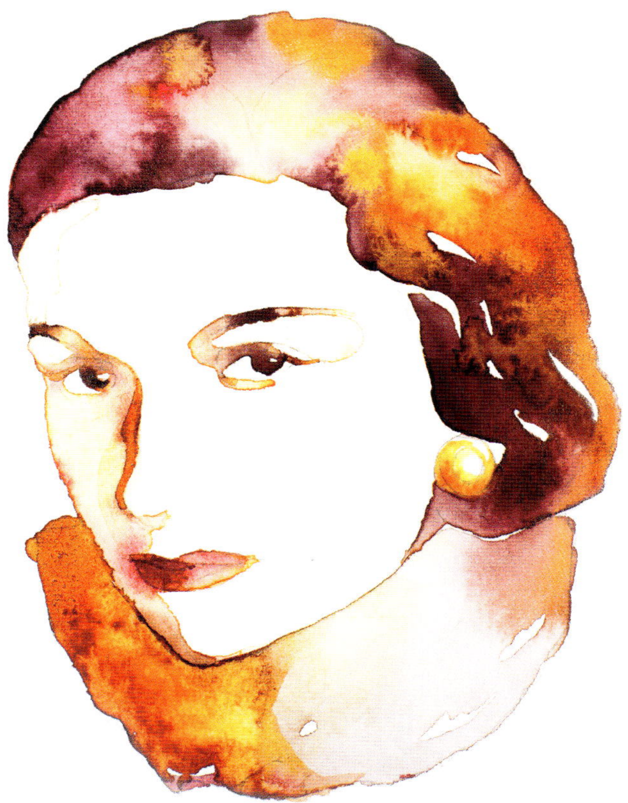

**3. *Wet-on-wet:*** Now build up the shadows on the face. For this you will need the finest brush you own. Wait for the right time to paint in, and using short movements, dab your strong red pigment onto the bridge of the nose, the lips, chin, eyebrows and irises. The mouth area here was almost dry and was worked with an undiluted pigment, so the space looks bold, but still soft due to the feathered edges. Always wait a little in between, and dab briefly on the outer edge of the face as well.

**Tip:** *To give the hair more texture, add some splashes of pure orange – or another color – into the damp space. Alternatively, you could sprinkle some salt over it.*

**4. *Wet-on-wet & glaze:*** Paint an undiluted brown wash on the irises and eyebrows and let it dry. In the meantime, paint in the collar using pale shades. Start with a light orange, add some of the red pigment and paint it into the area, allowing the colors to blend on the paper and conjure up soft color values. Leave a few areas of white. When the space is almost dry, take up a slightly diluted orange and paint it, semi-transparent, onto the left side of the collar. Be careful not to paint over the edge of the face. Add the same color to the earring, adding more pigment to the lower part. Ensuring the facial shadows are thoroughly dry beforehand, dilute the orange and add some intermediate shadows to the bridge of the nose, forehead, whites of the eyes, temples and upper lip crease.

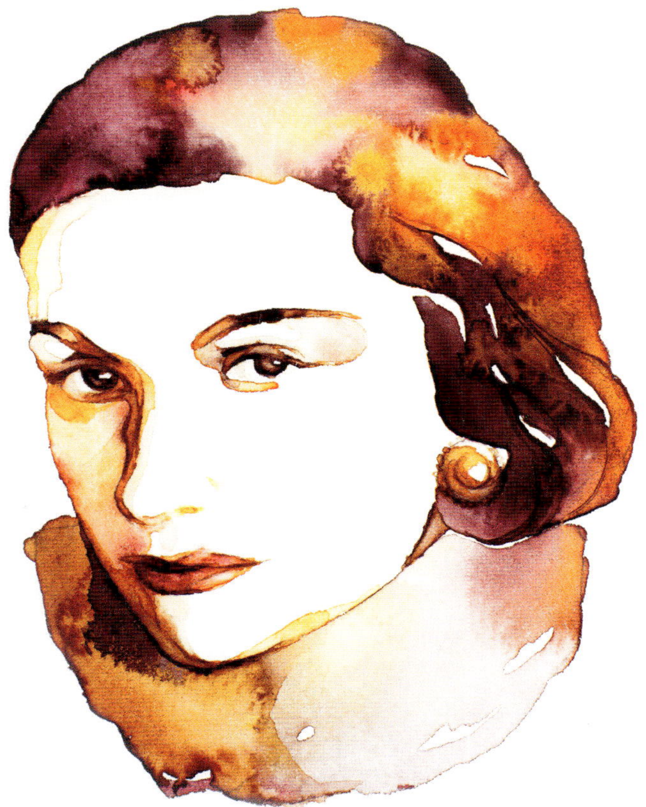



**5.** *Wet-on-wet:* To better distinguish the head from the collar, dab a bold brown into the damp space of the collar.

**Tip:** *If the collar has already dried, you can moisten the area with a little water.*

*Glaze:* Intensify the eyebrows and eyelids with a rich orange-brown. For more definition, draw fine lines for the lower lip line and the creases of the eyelids and mouth.

Using a thicker brush, warm up the cheek shadow with an orange glaze. To do this, start from the chin and paint upwards applying little pressure. Connect the shadow of the bridge of the nose with the lower lid of the left eye, and add a few final dark spaces around the edges of the irises to make the eyes more lively. Also emphasize the forehead shadow and the area under the left eye with another layer of glaze, and finish with delicate shadows on the tip of the nose, the nose wing, jawline and chin.

Define the earring all around to give a sense of the decoration. In addition, activate a small area of the lower lip by using a very small amount of water and remove some of the paint to create a soft light reflection. Blend the edge above the right eyebrow for some soft transitions. Finally, add a layer to give the impression of fine lines of hair that curl wavelike around the white spaces.

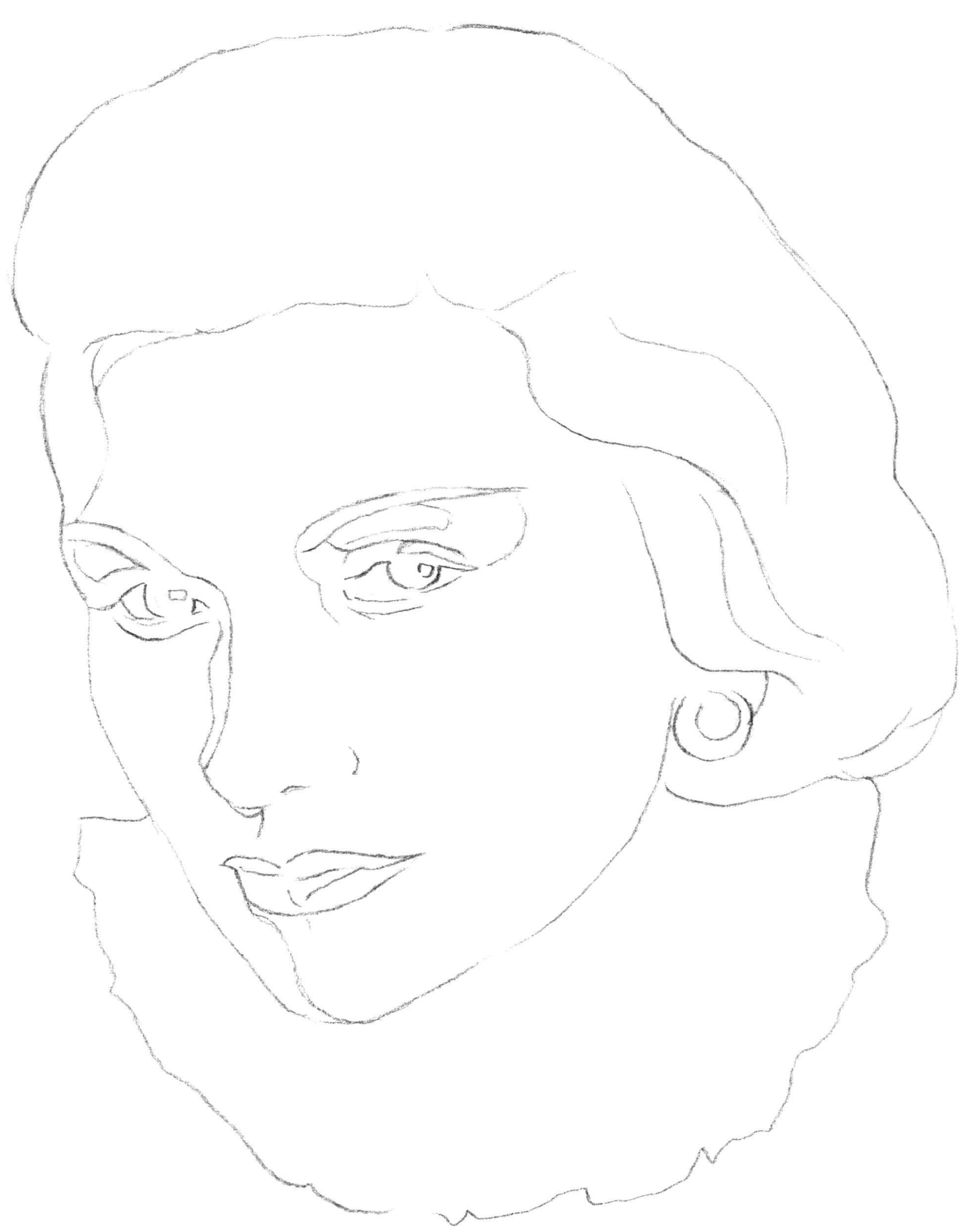

# EMMA
## *Watson*

Emma Watson became world famous through her role as the studious Hermione Granger, one of Hogwarts brightest students. From 2001, she spent a decade playing one of the lead roles in the Harry Potter film series, and over the years, has developed into a self-confident woman. Now in her 30s, in addition to her acting career, she is a passionate activist for women's rights.

**COLOR PALETTE:**

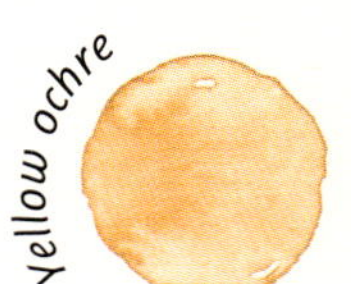


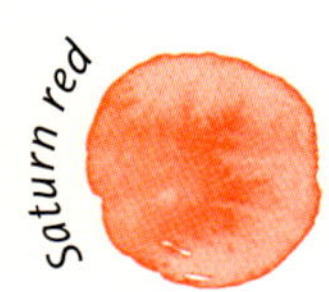


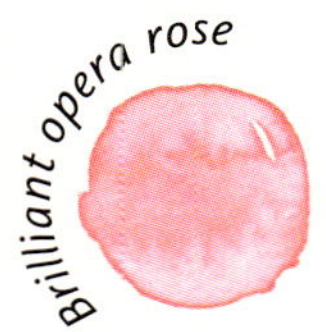


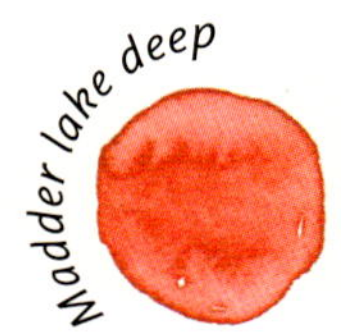


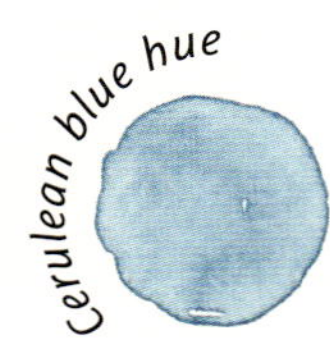

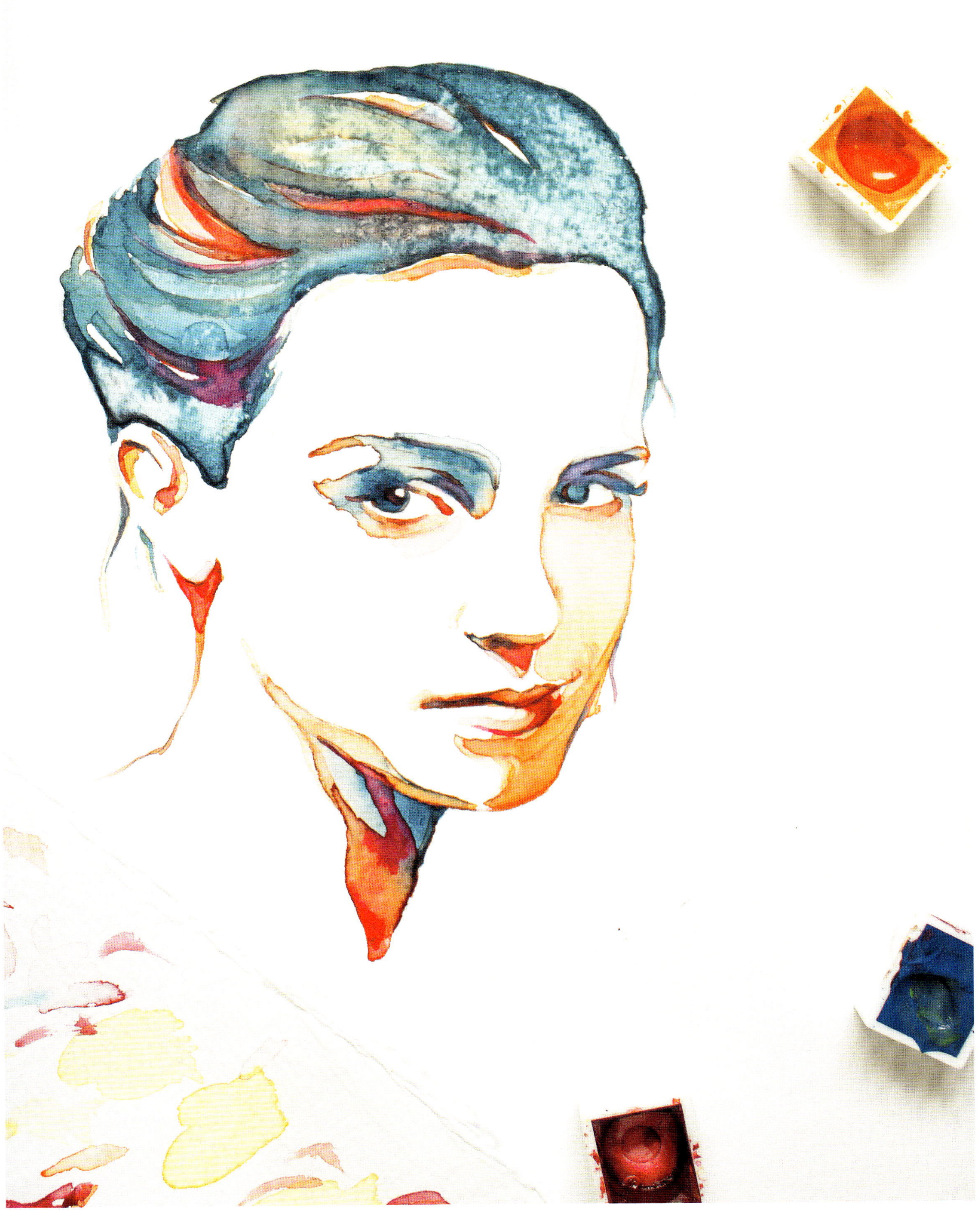

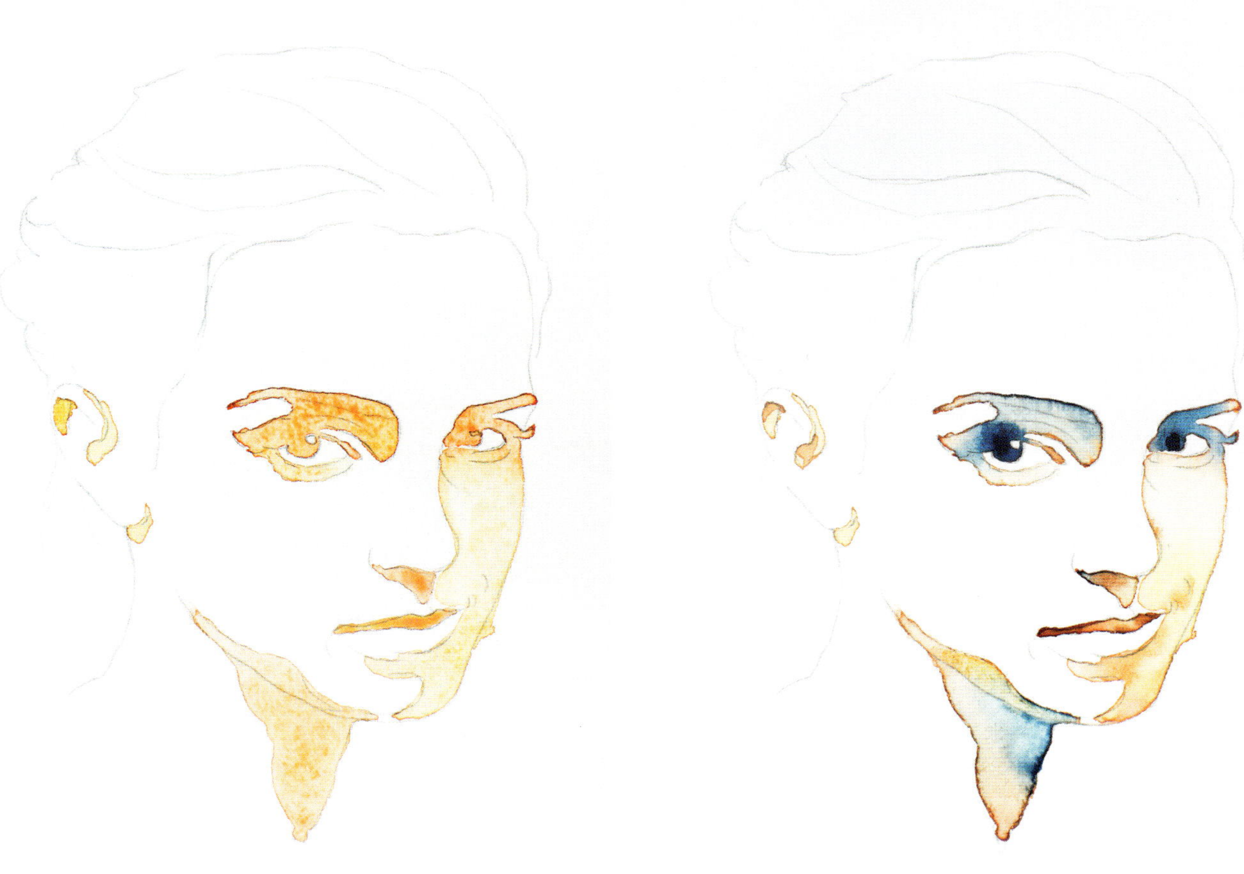

**1. Wet-on-dry:** Begin by diluting a lot of orange pigment with a thick brush. Start at the cheek and paint in the right half of the face. Switch to a finer brush and paint in the eyes, nose and mouth areas as well.

**Tip:** *Pay attention to the white areas of the eyes and paint as precisely as possible along the lines.*

**2. Wet-on-wet:** Once most of the paint has been absorbed by the paper, use a fine brush to dab undiluted blue pigment several times onto the irises, eyebrows and neck. Wash your brush out, and repeat this step with a bold red on the outer corners of the upper lip.

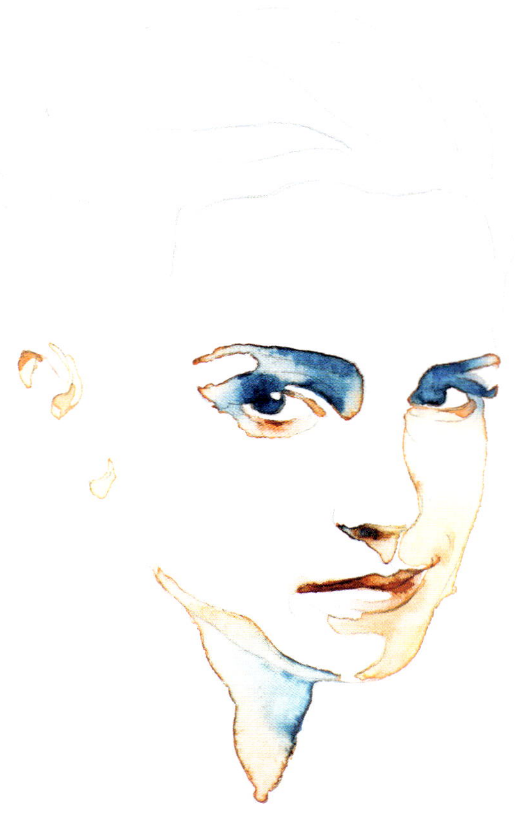

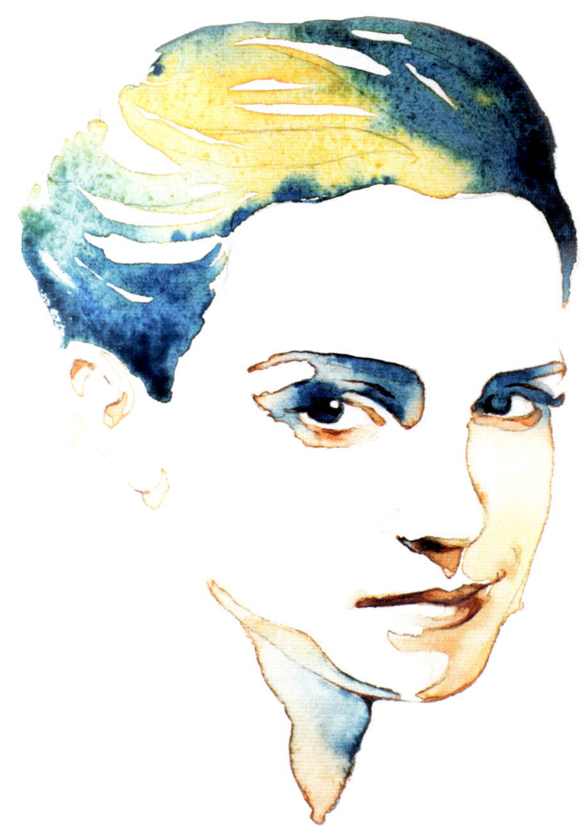

**3.** *Wet-on-wet:* Continue on the lower eyelash line and lower lip, and add a well-diluted shadow to the left corner of the mouth and chin. Emphasize the eyes one last time by painting undiluted blue onto the eyebrows and eyelids, and then define the nostril.

**4.** *Wet-on-wet:* First, underpaint the hair with a dark yellow. Immediately afterwards, use a thick brush to dab a lot of blue pigment into the left and right sides of the colored space to create an impression of shade.

**Tip:** *Start on the right side and follow the strands of hair in a sweeping manner. Leave several gaps of varying sizes.*

*Glaze:* Darken the edges of the irises with red, and define the creases of the eyelids with short brushstrokes. Pale intermediate shadows, such as those on the nostrils and earlobes, provide tenderness and variety next to the bold area around the eyes.

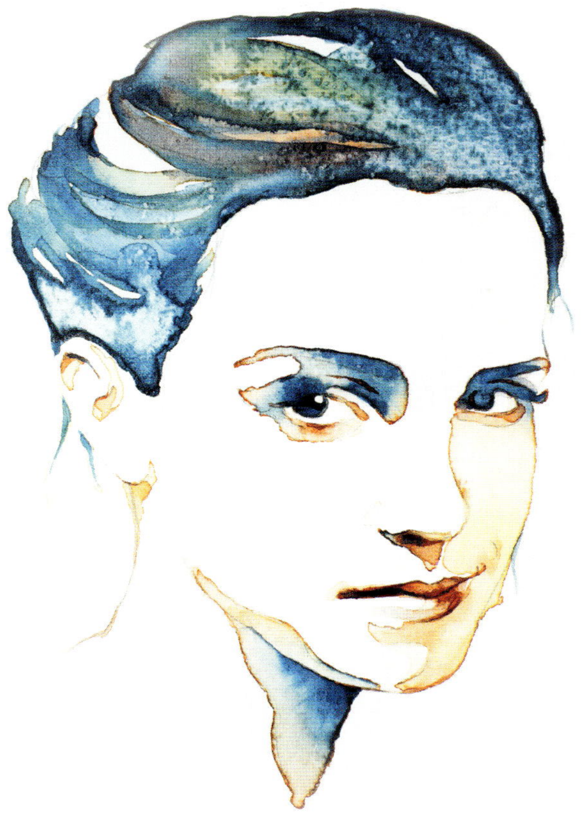 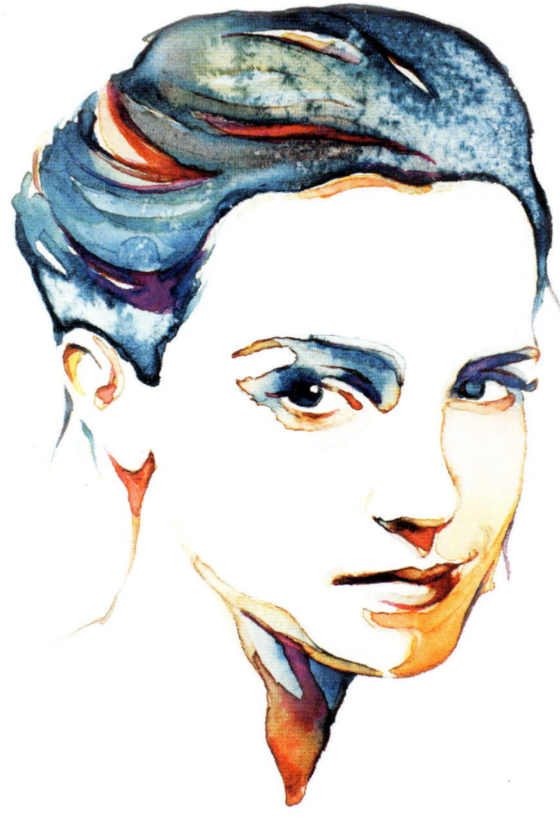

**5.** *Wet-on-wet & glaze:* Wash the colors together in the hair space and close the gaps to have more colored areas. This is important because you will now sprinkle in salt for the texture. While the grains of salt are conjuring up an effect on the surface, warm up the chin and ear with an orange glaze. Starting at the earlobe, draw a line along the neck.

Add a few strands of hair around the face with a thin brush. As soon as the hair is completely dry, remove the grains of salt with a dry brush. Then fill in the white gaps with orange, and draw several thin lines in red.

**6.** *Glaze:* Since I found the colors were still lacking luminosity, I took a radiant pink and painted it on as a glaze, especially on the hair, cheek shadow and neck. I also added it to the forehead shadow and the ear, so harmonizing the tonal value with the hair space. In addition, activate the edges of the eyebrows with a little water and blend them.

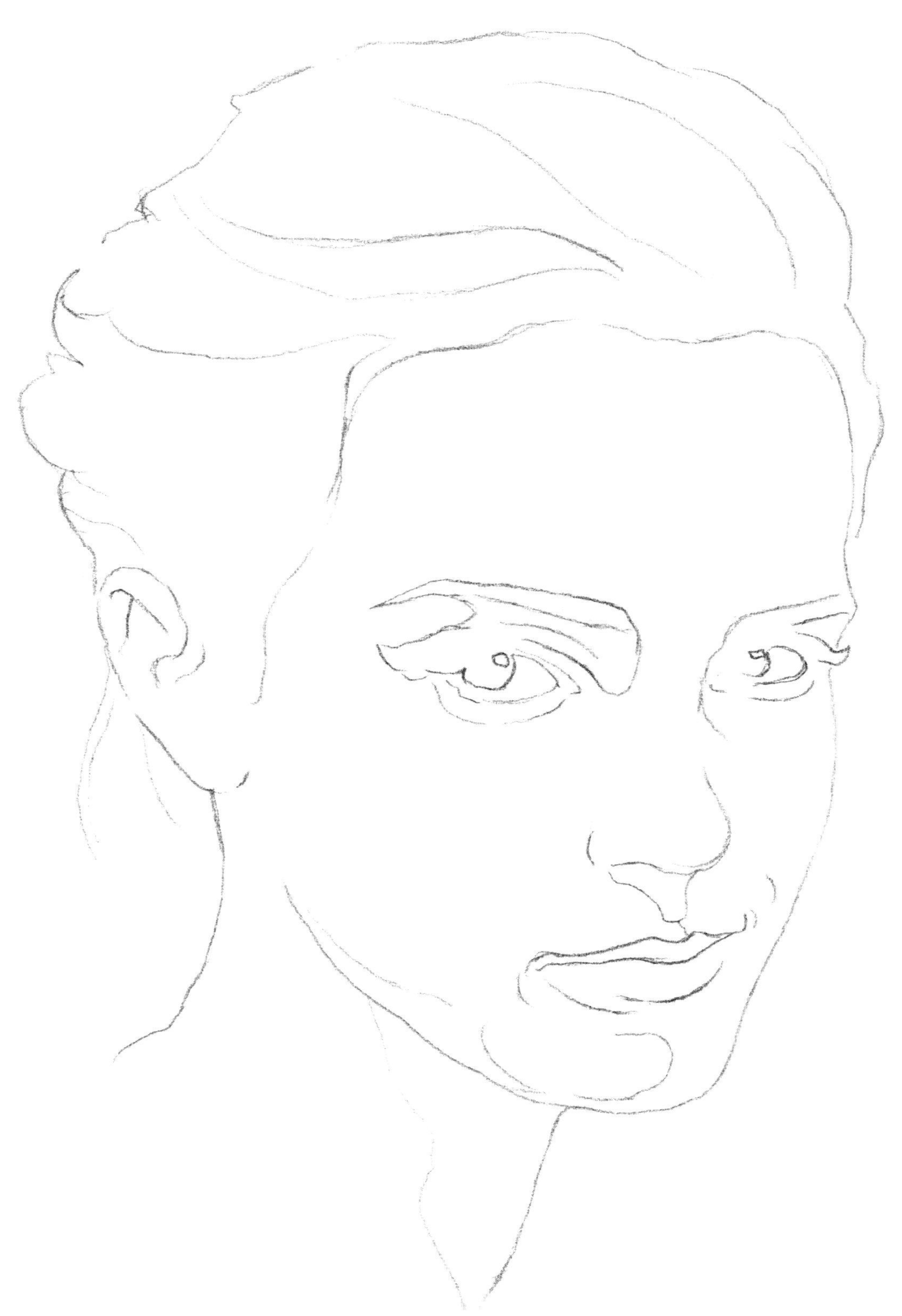

# VINCENT
## *van Gogh*

Vincent van Gogh was a painter who had an incredible amount to give, and yet he struggled in vain for recognition throughout his lifetime. Without really suspecting how influential his art would become, he lived in humble circumstances until his untimely death.

In his paintings, he often used complementary colors and painted impasto, that is, with almost undiluted oil paint. You will imitate his style here, albeit with watercolor instead of oils – layer by layer, and using short but dynamic brushstrokes. The colors are also coordinated and reminiscent of his universally known "Sunflowers" paintings.

**Tip:** *If you want to get an insight into the mind of Vincent van Gogh, I can recommend the letters to his brother, Theo, where he reveals his soul in a very heartfelt way.*

## COLOR PALETTE:

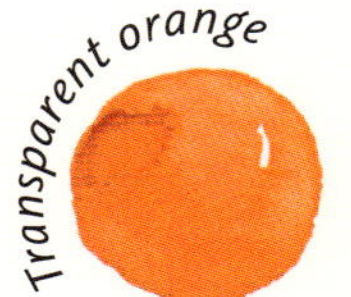


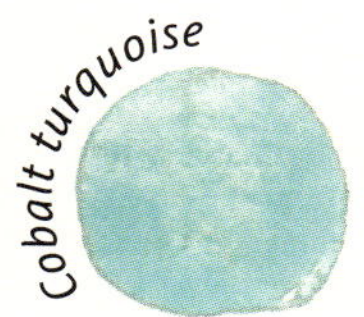


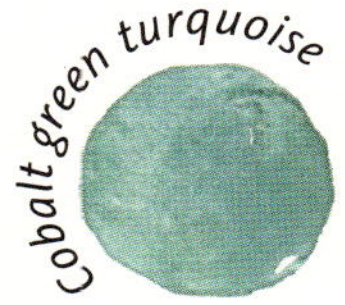


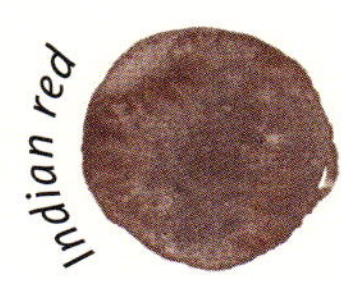

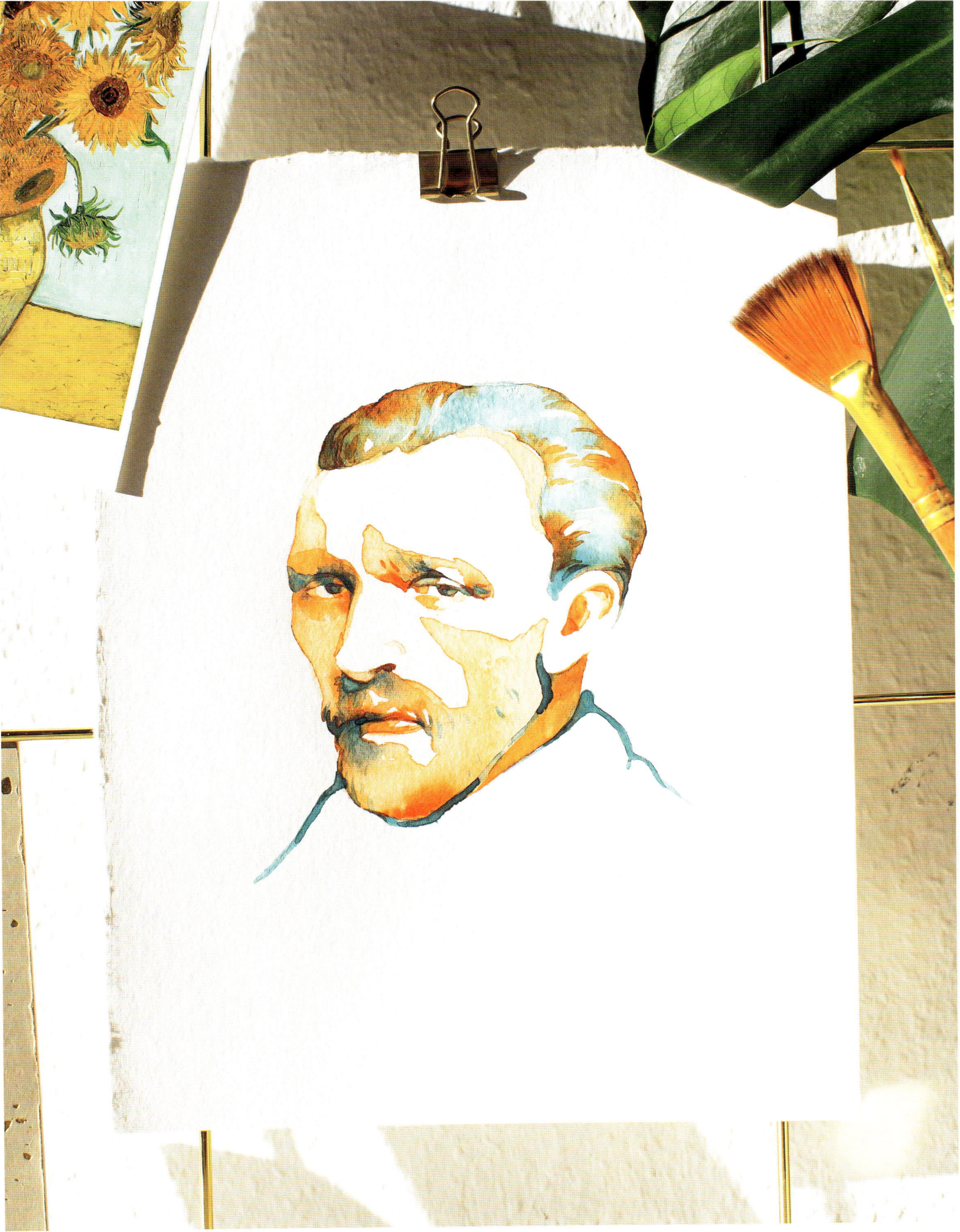

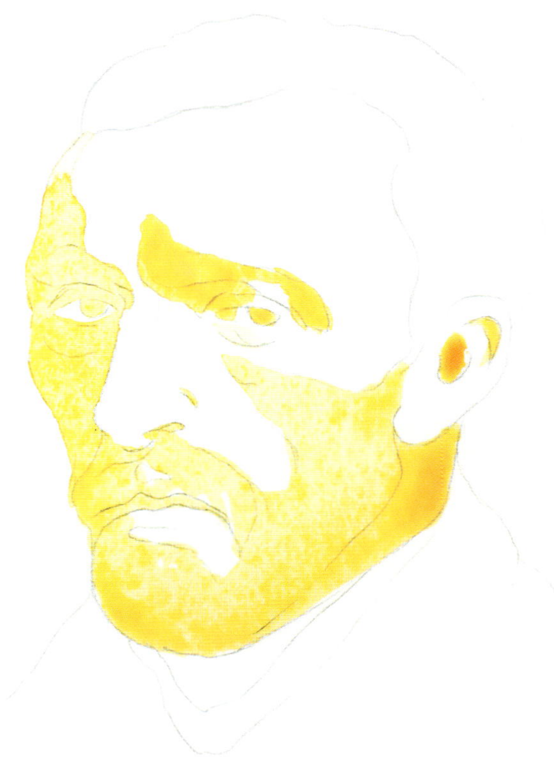

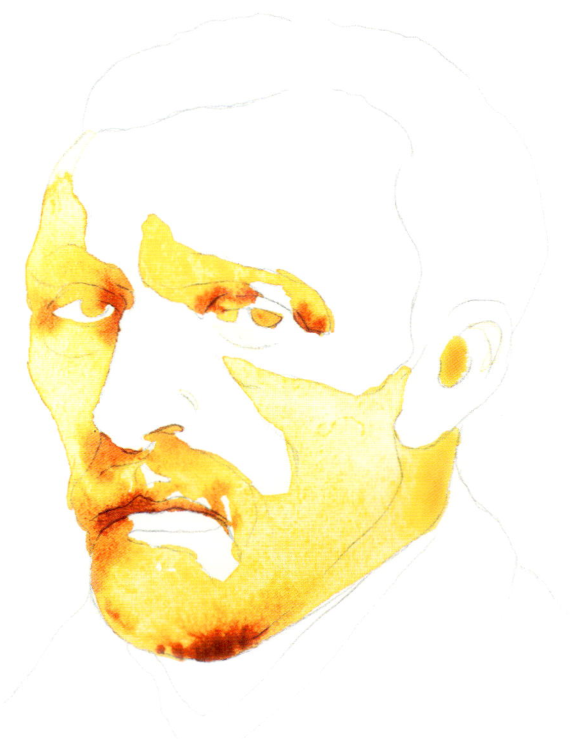

**1.** *Wet-on-dry:* Mix a light shade using plenty of water and a little orange to underpaint the facial shadows first. However, leave out the right eyelid and the lower lip. It is important that you use enough water so that the paint layer remains cor stantly wet. The best way to apply the paint is with a medium to large brush. For the right lower eyelid, wipe off the brush beforehand, and draw a light area with the paint residue at that point.

**Tip:** *Start with the right half of the face and use the tip of your brush to trace precisely around the outer edge. This will make it easier to wash the color inward afterwards.*

**2.** *Wet-on-wet:* As soon as the paint layer shimmers only slightly on the surface, use a fine brush to take up some bold orange pigment. Only use a little water here so that the shadows become more expressive. Dab into the wet spaces of the tip of the nose, the outer corners of the eyes, the upper lip and the chin, one after the other, several times.

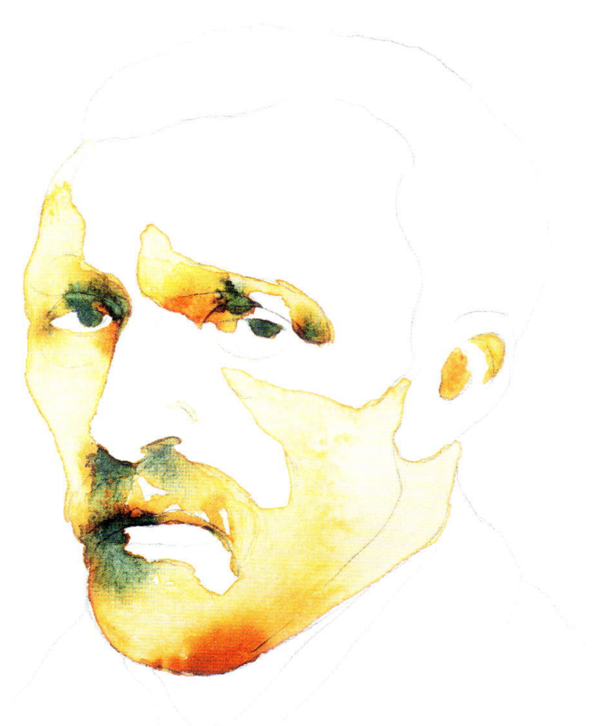 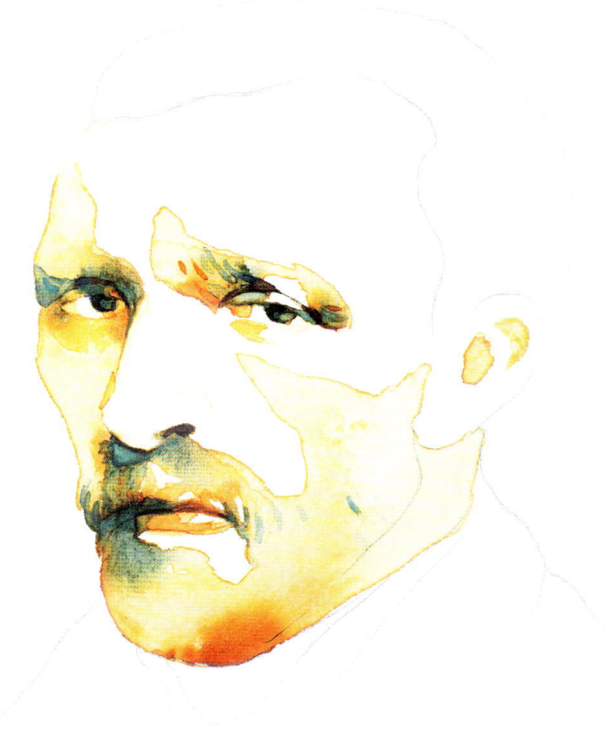

**3.** *Wet-on-wet:* Wash your brush out quickly and then, as in the previous step, go over the same areas with a dark turquoise, also diluted with just a little water. Then wait for your portrait to dry through.

**Tip:** *If the paint runs into areas where it shouldn't, you can easily remove the paint with a clean brush, as described in Final Tips (see Blending Edges).*

**4.** *Glaze:* Now use a narrow brush and a glaze to add all the details in turquoise and orange. Start with orange and emphasize the lower lip and eyelids. Use a slightly lighter shade for the tip and the bridge of the nose. Darken the whites of the eyes on the left side as well. Add turquoise to the outer corners of the eyes. Also make the nose shadow more distinct. Add a few short brushstrokes to indicate the eyebrows and beard. A deep brown also provides more contrast at the eyelid crease and nostril.

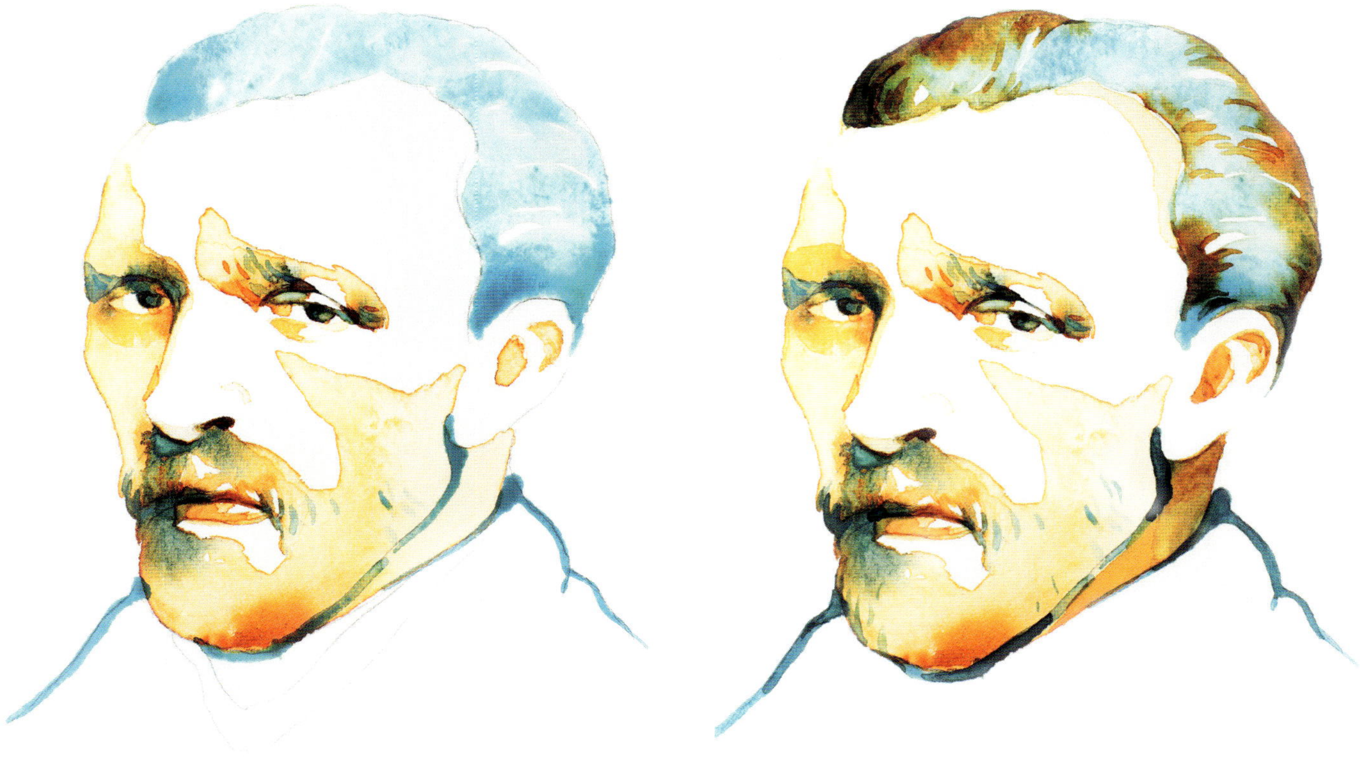

**5. *Wet-on-dry:*** Paint in the hair space with a radiant turquoise. Start at the hairline and work your way across from left to right, with lightly sweeping lines. Leave a few short, narrow gaps for some hair texture. At the same time, bring out the shoulder and jawline more clearly. Paint quickly because you're about to use wet-on-wet for the last time.

**Tip:** *Start from the hairline and paint outwards – it makes it easier to leave gaps.*

**6. *Wet-on-wet:*** Dab some almost undiluted orange pigment into the paint layer on the hair space. Tend to apply more color to the left and right sides, and use quite a lot of paint because the turquoise should not dominate in the final portrait.

***Glaze:*** While the hair is drying, darken the neck and left eyebrow with an orange glaze. I also added a light shadow to the upper right hairline and darkened the jaw and shoulder lines a bit. Once the hair space is dry, you can once again incorporate Van Gogh's characteristic brushstroke style – adapt to the direction of the growth of the hair and, above all, go over the areas that are already underpainted in orange.

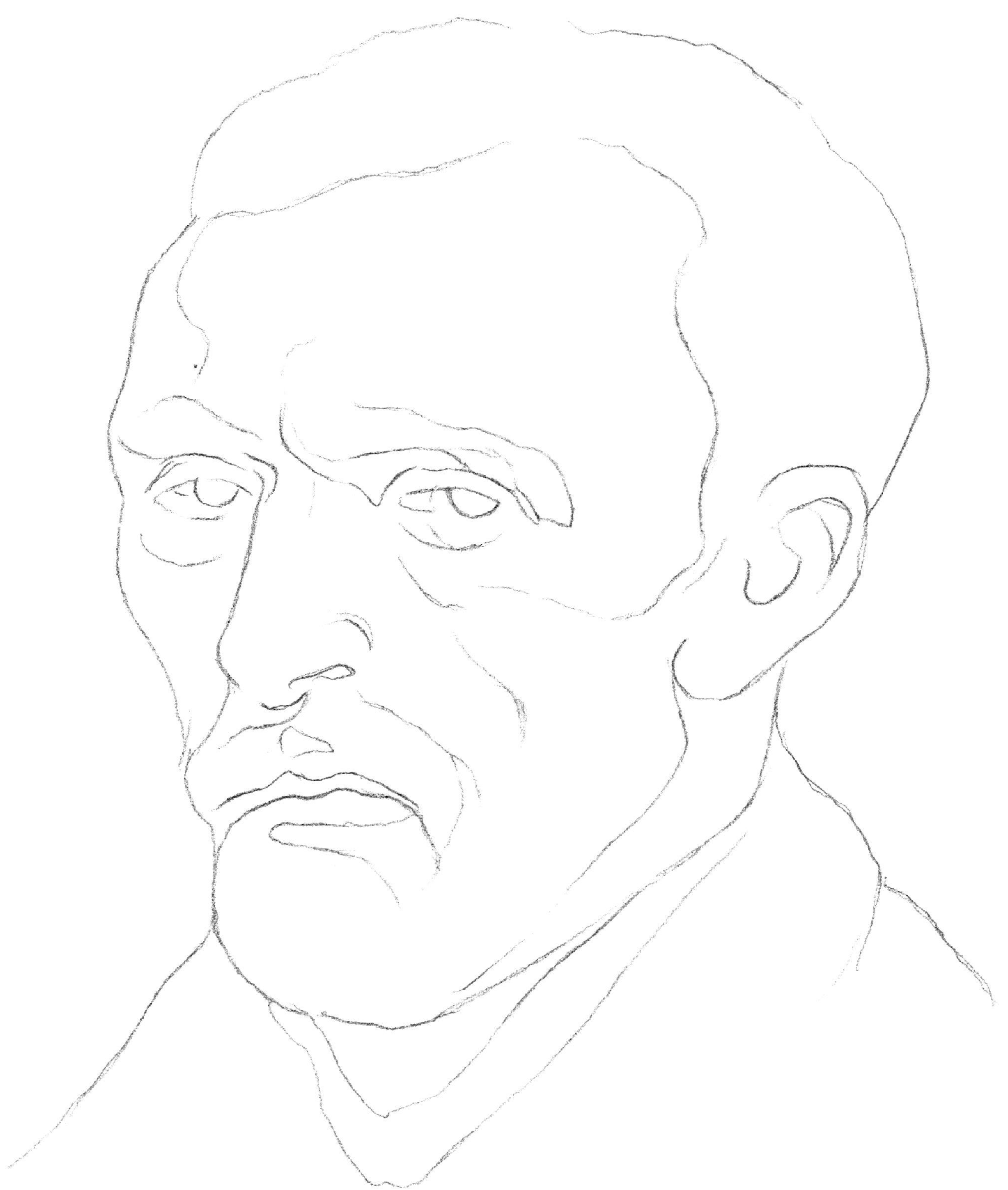

# About the Author

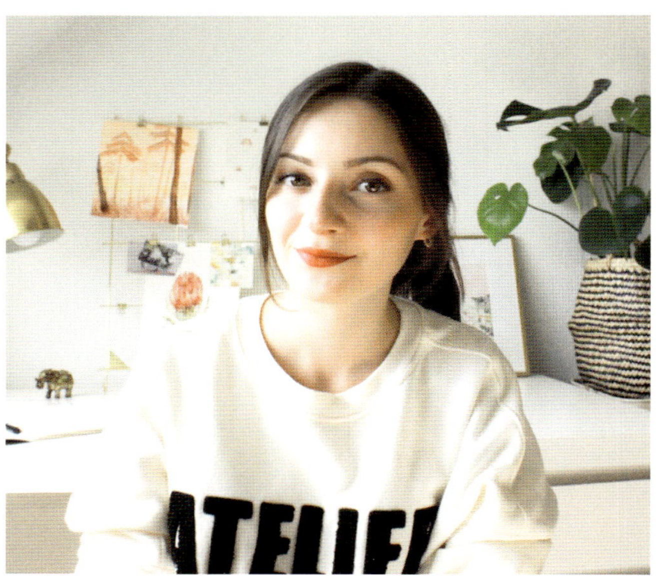

Nelli Andrejew was born in Karaganda, Kazakhstan, in 1995 and was raised for most of her life in Germany. She studied art education, art history and educational science in Giessen. She currently works as an art educator and illustrator in Frankfurt am Main.

During her studies, she discovered her passion for watercolors, and has since specialized in this medium, inspired by nature and her travels.

## THANK YOUS

I would like to thank EMF Publishing for their trust and support – especially my editor Franziska Klorer, who always stood by me with her advice and made our collaboration so wonderful for the second time.

Thank you to all the wonderful people who inspired me with their suggestions and made me take a deeper look at the personalities! Here, also, a huge thank you to all my previous art teachers. You have helped to shape me, and always given me the courage to never lose sight of my passion and goals.

Last but not least, I would like to thank my family and friends, who have supported me while giving me enough space to work on this project. The biggest thanks go to my favorite people: My parents, my grandma, my sister and best friend. You guys are the most amazing souls. Thank you for always believing in me, unconditionally sharing my happiness and letting me have you so close by my side!

Instagram: @nelliadee

Website: www.nelliandrejew.de

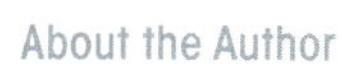

# *Index*

A DAVID AND CHARLES BOOK
© 2021 Edition Michael Fischer GmbH,
Donnersbergstr. 7, 86859 Igling, Germany
www.emf-verlag.de

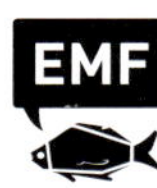

David and Charles is an imprint of David and Charles, Ltd
Suite A, Tourism House, Pynes Hill, Exeter, EX2 5WS

This translation of *WATERCOLOR PORTRÄT*, originally published in
Germany by Edition Michael Fischer GmbH in 2021, is published by
arrangement with Silke Bruenink Agency, Munich, Germany.

First published in the UK and USA in 2022



A catalogue record for this book is available from the British Library.

ISBN-13: 9781446309148 paperback
ISBN-13: 9781446381526 EPUB
ISBN-13: 9781446381519 PDF

This book has been printed on paper from approved suppliers and
made from pulp from sustainable sources.

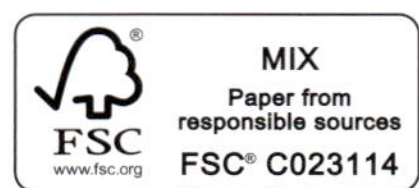


Printed in the UK by Page Bros for:
David and Charles, Ltd
Suite A, Tourism House, Pynes Hill, Exeter, EX2 5WS

10 9 8 7 6 5 4 3 2 1

Cover design: Lena Albert
Editing and proofreading: Dr. Franziska Klorer
Layout and typesetting: Lena Albert

David and Charles publishes high-quality books on a wide range of
subjects. For more information visit www.davidandcharles.com.

Share your makes with us on social media using #dandcbooks and
follow us on Facebook and Instagram by searching for @dandcbooks.

Layout of the digital edition of this book may vary depending on
reader hardware and display settings.